Managing EU–US relations

Actors, institutions and the new transatlantic agenda

Manchester University Press

Managing EU–US relations

Actors, institutions and the new transatlantic agenda

REBECCA STEFFENSON

Manchester University Press
Manchester and New York

distributed exclusively in the USA by Palgrave

Published by Manchester University Press
Oxford Road, Manchester M13 9NR, UK
and Room 400, 175 Fifth Avenue, New York, NY 10010, USA
www.manchesteruniversitypress.co.uk

Distributed exclusively in the USA by
Palgrave, 175 Fifth Avenue, New York, NY 10010, USA

Distributed exclusively in Canada by
UBC Press, University of British Columbia, 2029 West Mall, Vancouver, BC, Canada V6T 1Z2

British Library Cataloguing-in-Publication Data
A catalogue record for this book is available from the British Library

Library of Congress Cataloging-in-Publication Data applied for

ISBN 0 7190 6970 X *hardback*
EAN 978 0 7190 6970 3

First published 2005

14 13 12 11 10 09 08 07 06 05 10 9 8 7 6 5 4 3 2 1

Typeset by Freelance Publishing Services, Brinscall, Lancs
Printed in Great Britain
by Biddles Ltd, King's Lynn

Contents

Figures, boxes and tables

Figures

Boxes

Tables

Preface

A number of people are owed a debt of gratitude for their contribution to this book. I would like to thank John Peterson for his advice, supervision and support. Dave Allen and Patricia Hogwood provided detailed comments on an earlier draft. Brigid Laffan and Patrick Callahan played important roles in the nurturing and early development of many ideas contained in the book. The participants of the UNC Chapel Hill Advanced PhD Workshop (2000), the participants of the *E2K: A New Vision for Europe* conference (Institute on Western Europe, Columbia University, 2000) and the staff and postgraduate students of the Politics Department at the University of Glasgow offered valuable comments and suggestions on the research at various stages. A huge debt is owed to Ricardo Gomez who read many drafts, spent numerous coffee breaks talking about the research and gave magnanimously of his time. The research would not have been possible without the generous support given by the A.L. Macfie Research Scholarship. Chris Berry, in his capacity as Head of the Politics Department (Glasgow) provided much needed funding for field research and conferences on both sides of the Atlantic. Thank you to the many busy people who took time out of their schedules to share their insights on the 'inside' process of transatlantic relations. I am grateful to Mark Pollack, Helen Wallace and the Robert Schuman Center at the European University Institute for the opportunity to spend a year in Florence revising this work; to Elizabeth Meehan, John Barry and the Institute of Governance at Queen's University Belfast where I was given the space to finish; to Adrian Van Den Hoven (UNICE) for his many insightful comments; Roisin McCabe, Claire Finn, Colleen Freeman, Santi Roberts, Kerri Horton and Jill Johnson for providing invaluable 'extra sets of eyes' when it came to proof-reading. My thanks to Tony Mason and his editing team for their hard work. Finally, I am eternally indebted to my family and friends for their support. This book is dedicated to my son Edison Kai who very patiently slept in my office and played under my desk while I finished this manuscript.

Abbreviations

ACP	African, Caribbean and Pacific States
BBC	British Broadcasting Corporation
CABs	Conformity Assessment Body
CEE	Central and Eastern Europe
CEN	Comité Européen de Normalisation
CENELEC	Comité Européen de Normalisation Electrotechnique
CFSP	Common Foreign Security Policy
CI	Consumer International
CIA	Central Intelligence Agency
COG	Chief of Government
DG	Directorate-General
DSB	Dispute Settlement Body
DSU	Dispute Settlement Understanding
EEB	European Environmental Bureau
EETIS	Electronics, Electrical, Information Technology, Telecommunications Sectors
EPA	Environmental Protection Agency
ESDP	European Security and Defence Policy
EUTC	European Trade Confederation
FDA	Food and Drug Administration
FDI	Foreign Direct Investment
FSCs	Foreign Sales Corporations
GATS	General Agreement on Trade and Services
GATT	General Agreement on Tariffs and Trade
GMO	Genetically Modified Organism
IOM	International Organization on Migration
JAP	Joint Action Plan
JHA	Justice and Home Affairs
MEP	Member of the European Parliament
MFN	Most Favoured Nation
MRA	Mutual Recognition Agreement

NIS Newly Independent States
NTA New Transatlantic Agenda
NTM New Transatlantic Marketplace
NTMA New Transatlantic Marketplace Agreement
NWF National Wildlife Federation
OSCE Organization for Security and Co-operation in Europe
OSHA Occupational Safety and Heath Administration
SEM Single European Market
SLG Senior Level Group
SME Small and Medium Sized Enterprises
TABD Transatlantic Business Dialogue
TACD Transatlantic Consumer Dialogue
TACS Transatlantic Advisory Committee on Standards
TAD Transatlantic Declaration
TAED Transatlantic Environmental Dialogue
TAFTA Transatlantic Free Trade Agreement
TALD Transatlantic Labour Dialogue
TEA Trade Expansion Agreement
TEP Transatlantic Economic Partnership
TLD Transatlantic Legislators Dialogue
TPN Transatlantic Policy Network
TPPC Transatlantic Partnership on Political Co-operation
TRIPs Trade-Related Aspects of Intellectual Property Rights
USIA United States Information Agency
USTR United States Trade Representative
WEEE The European Waste Electrical Equipment Directive
WTO World Trade Organisation

1

Understanding the 'New Transatlantic Agenda'

Introduction

The transatlantic relationship is arguably the most significant relationship in the international system. Western Europe and the United States (US) have the largest concentration of individual and combined political and economic power, making the European Union (EU) and the US each other's most important partner world-wide. Common values, culture and history make them obvious political partners, while their economic ties account for one third of global trade in excess of $668bn.[1] More importantly, in economic terms, the EU and the US are the recipients of around one half of each other's Foreign Direct Investment, (FDI) which means that transatlantic investment sustains roughly ten million jobs.[2]

European–American relations were analysed in the 1990s, as they were affected by radical structural changes to the international economic and political orders (see Featherstone and Ginsberg (1996); Gardner (1997); Monar (1998); Peterson (1996); Smith and Woolcock (1993)). The end of the Cold War visibly reduced the security threat on which the transatlantic alliance previously hinged. However, geopolitical and economic shifts in the international system, caused in part by increasing flows of people, capital and goods, created a number of new incentives for EU–US co-operation and conflict. The transatlantic relationship was viewed as a way to promote western ideas of democracy and security in an era of change and uncertainty. Deepening European integration, including the creation of Common Foreign and Security Policy (CFSP) and Justice and Home Affairs (JHA) pillars under the Maastricht Treaty (1992), signalled to the US the growing capacity of the EU to act as a foreign policy actor in its own right. The 1990s marked the first time in the history of the transatlantic relationship that the EU and the US faced the task not only of keeping the 'alliance' together but also of facilitating a partnership of – more or less – equals (Peterson 1996).

This new dynamic to European–American relations raises a number of questions about how the transatlantic partners chose both to 'manage' the relationship in an era of such rapid international change and to exercise governance in response to new transnational challenges. The focus of this book is on three transatlantic agreements: the Transatlantic Declaration (TAD) (1990), the New Transatlantic Agenda (NTA) (1995), and the Transatlantic Economic Partnership (TEP) (1998). These transatlantic agreements warrant examination because they mark, to a considerable point, a break from the pre-1990s past and together they form a new framework for managing the transatlantic relationship. The TAD, the NTA and the TEP are the first bilateral agreements signed between the EU and the US, despite earlier attempts to fortify the EU–US relationship in the 1960s and 1970s.[3] The 1990s mark the development of an institutionalised structure for transatlantic governance because the agreements introduce institutional arrangements for managing the relationship in addition to specific policy commitments.

These transatlantic agreements focus on economic and political ties. They expand the scope for bilateral cooperation to a range of new (largely) non-traditional security and economic policy areas.[4] Specifically, the NTA commits the EU and US to approach jointly, where possible, rising transnational crime, terrorism and environmental degradation. It acknowledges the role that the transatlantic partners can play in promoting peaceful transitions to democracy world-wide. The NTA and the succeeding TEP contain strategies for facilitating increased economic integration and dispute management in direct response to competing forces both to liberalise trade and protect domestic producers. In substantive terms, the agreements explicitly acknowledge the capacity of the transatlantic partners both to promote *and* undermine global economic liberalisation. EU–US trade and investment agreements have the potential not only to open the transatlantic marketplace but also to lead the way for further liberalisation at the multilateral level. On the other hand, transatlantic trade disputes and a lack of solidarity at the World Trade Organisation (WTO) have the potential to undermine the multilateral trading system. In short, EU–US relations are significant because it is this partnership that can make or break the foundations of the western economic and political orders.

This is not the first book to highlight the importance of what can be characterised as the 'new transatlantic dialogue'. Studies of the NTA including Bail *et al.* (1997); Gardner (1997); Krenzler and Schomaker (1996); Monar (1998); Peterson (1996) have all linked policy coordination and cooperation to transatlantic institutions. However, most of these works focused mainly on describing the prospects for such coordination and cooperation under the NTA, in part because they were released before the NTA had produced substantive results. Recent studies of the NTA focus more narrowly on transatlantic policy outputs and the role of the NTA in fostering actual coordination and cooperation. For example, Pollack and Shaffer's (2001) characterisation of intergovernmental, transgovernmental and transnational actors provides a useful actor based explanation for who governs in EU and

US relations. Philippart and Winand's (2001) examination of not only policy-making, but also policy shaping opens the policy process up to a range of actors who have an input into the transatlantic policy process. Their policy-based study tries to measure the success of the NTA by applying numerical values to individual sectors based on the discrepancy between policy goals and policy output.

This book builds on this most recent wave of literature and revisits a number of questions about both the role of institutions in EU–US relations and the capacity of actors to exercise transatlantic governance through them. The emphasis is on the creation of a framework for transatlantic policy-making and on the different levels of decision-making that affect the outcome of transatlantic policies.

This chapter provides an analytical introduction to the new transatlantic dialogue. The first section raises a number of research questions and argues that transatlantic institutions, no matter how loose, matter because they form the basis of a transatlantic governance structure. Transatlantic decisions are determined not only by transatlantic structures but also by how transatlantic actors use them. The second and third sections delve deeper into a theoretical discussion on the role of institutions and on processes of governance. This book examines transatlantic relations at the highest level of interstate negotiation while considering transatlantic policy-making at the most micro level. Therefore, it does not limit itself to the confines of either the international relations or comparative politics literature, but rather uses concepts outlined in both. The final section of the chapter outlines a new transatlantic decision-making model that categorises the input of different actors into transatlantic policy-making. It argues that intergovernmental, transgovernmental and transnational actors have different roles in making, setting and shaping transatlantic policy.

Institutions and the actors that use them

In contrast to Philippart and Winand (2001), this book does not attempt to measure quantitatively the success, or not, of transatlantic policy-making. Transatlantic cooperation, or at least coordination, was being pursued in many policy areas before the creation of specific transatlantic institutions, making it difficult to establish a causal relationship between the NTA framework and policy output. Furthermore, the short-term pressure to produce results out of the NTA reflects the political cycles which govern the behaviour of governments on both sides: 'Quite simply, whilst the development of strategic direction in US–EU relations is a long-term exercise to be judged over a period of years if not decades, political leaders are judged over periods of five years at most' (Smith 2001: 271). Finally, a numerical measure of successes in one area is not necessarily comparable with polices pursued in another. As one senior EU official interviewed for this book argued, 'How do you compare the levels of success? Is it more important that the EU and the US go to Russia with a common position on food aid or that they run joint trafficking programmes in Central and Eastern Europe?'(CEE).[5]

Perhaps above all, this book eschews attempts to measure quantitatively the success, or not, of transatlantic policy-making because it is concerned with *process* as much as policy: it emphasises the importance of not only policy output but also the process of policy-making. Policy agreements are important measures of the capacity to govern in the short term, but so too is the creation of dialogue structures and the ability to foster long-term strategies of co-operation.

This analysis of EU–US relations seeks primarily to make clear the perceptions of actors who participate in the policy process and to gauge the impact that different variables – including the creation of new transatlantic institutions – have had on the policy process. The significance of the new transatlantic dialogues cannot be gauged simply by relying on the public declarations of senior transatlantic policy-makers – specifically contained in so-called 'Senior Level Group reports' – because of a tendency by transatlantic policy makers to 'recycle' and 'repackage' their announcement of policy successes. This study relies on elite interviews to determine the relevance of transatlantic institutional structures, their effect on the actors who participate within them, and the impact on the policies they seek to influence in the overall process of transatlantic governance. The evidence collected supports a number of claims about the nature of institutions and actors in the new transatlantic dialogue.

Institution building

Evidence is sought throughout this volume to verify that the EU–US relationship has been institutionalised by the three transatlantic agreements signed in the 1990s (the Transatlantic Declaration, the New Transatlantic Agenda and the Transatlantic Economic Partnership), and that the institutionalisation of the transatlantic dialogue has had a significant impact on the EU–US relationship. First, however we must define what we mean by institutionalisation.

The term institutionalisation is defined in the work of scholars such as Keohane and Nye (1993), Risse (1995a) and Ruggie (1998) which suggests that by no means should we expect international institutionalisation always to result in supranational organisations. Rather, many international institutions are in effect 'regimes' which can be broadly defined by 'patterned behaviour' (see Puchala and Hopkins 1983) 'specific rules' (Keohane 1989) and even 'principles, norms, rules, and decision-making procedures' (Krasner 1993). The definition of institution used in this book comes from Peters (1999: 18). It assumes that institutions are generally characterised by:

- formal and informal structures, including networks and shared norms;
- patterned and sustainable interaction between actors;
- constraints on the behaviour of its members;
- some sense of shared values.

Thus, institutionalisation is a process whereby a coordination and pattern of behaviour between actors is established and developed (see also Ruggie 1998: 54).

It is not enough to prove that institutions exist. We also need to question the role that institutions play. A rich literature now exists that argues firmly that 'institutions matter' and that they constitute the 'central component of political life' (Peters 1999: 150; see also March and Olsen 1989). This book is not the first to claim that institutional ties could manage the transatlantic relationship and overcome diverging interests (see Keohane and Nye 1993). The effectiveness of transatlantic institutions in place has also been questioned. Peterson (1996) argued that a genuine partnership would require 'better-organised exchanges'. Smith (1997) argued that policy coordination could not take place without a clear allocation of political authority or a clear legal framework, both of which required considerable institution building. The formal dialogue structures and policy framework created by the New Transatlantic Agenda, although not legally binding, have established a new structure of transatlantic governance.

Governance through institutions

'Governance' is a term that is now widely used to characterise the actions of actors in the international arena. What is 'governance' and how do we study it? Eising and Kohler-Koch (1999: 5) argue that, '"governance" is about the structured ways and means in which the divergent preferences of interdependent actors are translated into policy choices "to allocate values", so that the plurality of interests is transformed into co-ordinated action and the compliance of actors is achieved'. For his part, Rosenau (1992: 4) contends that governance, 'embraces governmental institutions, but it also subsumes informal, non-governmental mechanisms whereby persons and organisations within it purview, move ahead, satisfy their needs, and fulfil their wants'. Simply put, governance is 'the imposition of overall direction or control on the allocation of valued resources' (Peterson and Bomberg 1999: 5). It is, in all of these definitions, seen to be a synthetic process in that a variety of actors – not all of them governmental – are involved in decisions that determine who gets what, when and how.

The structure of governance created by the NTA is one that has facilitated a process for policy coordination or joint policy-making. It has produced policy outcomes that would be unimaginable in the absence of such a structure. However, the test for transatlantic governance is not only the existence of transatlantic policy output but also of attempts – both successful and unsuccessful – to accommodate the interests of different actors' input in the policy process in order to facilitate integration and manage disputes. The examination of transatlantic institutions as decision-making forums for transatlantic policy-making ultimately sheds light on the capacity of the EU and the US to manage the transatlantic dialogue and to govern in both the transatlantic marketplace and the international political order.

Actors exercising governance

Once it is established that the EU–US relationship has been institutionalised and that a governance structure now exists, the question remains: Who exercises transatlantic governance? In other words, what space does the formal transatlantic structure leave for agents, both governmental and non-governmental, to influence the coordination, convergence or mutual recognition of transatlantic policy? When and how do actors influence the transatlantic policy process?

This book makes two assumptions about the role of different actors involved in transatlantic policy-making. The decision-making approach discussed below hinges on the idea that different actors influence the policy process in different ways. This analysis of EU–US relations focuses not only on the big decisions that establish the scope for transatlantic policy coordination, but also on the decisions that determine policy details and policy options. It is therefore interested in the actors who make policy *and* those who set and shape it (see Peterson and Bomberg 1999).

Following on this logic it can be argued that the creation of an institutional framework by the transatlantic agreements has led to a decentralisation of decision-taking powers to both mid and low level state actors and also non-state actors. These actors participate in transgovernmental and transnational networks through which they exercise increasing influence over transatlantic policy output.

To summarise, the explanatory power of a number of variables in the process of transatlantic policy-making is discussed throughout this book. Institutions and actors are considered as important factors of policy input, and agreements and declarations serve as final policy outputs. The next section explores what light international relations theory and literature from comparative politics can shed on the institutionalisation of different levels of transatlantic dialogue, and what has essentially surmounted to the creation of a multi-level system of governance.

Institutions in international relations theory

The next two sections examine what the existing literature conveys about why institutions emerge and the scope for cooperation through transatlantic institutions. The starting point for this discussion is international relations theories, where there are many relevant ideas about cooperation, conflict and the role of institutions.

Neoliberal institutionalism

Neoliberal institutionalism provides a good starting point for a discussion on institution building. This wave of international relations literature makes a clear break from the previously dominant neorealist paradigm, which generally dismissed the probability of cooperation through international institutions (see Baldwin 1993: 8).[6] Institutionalists believe that states will choose to cooperate when it is in their interest to do so and that institutions, shared values and norms are one way of facilitating cooperation in order to maintain peace and stability (Keohane and Nye 1977; 1986). Where mutual interest exists, international institutions acting as 'brokers and negotiators' serve state interests by mediating policy coordination among powerful actors. They influence the policy agenda by opening channels of communication, creating value networks between states and providing focal points of coordination (Keohane *et al.*. 1993: 8; Keohane and Nye 1993: 3, 7). International institutions also reduce the likelihood of conflict by creating opportunities for negotiations, reducing uncertainty about others' policies and affecting leaders' expectations of the future (Keohane 1993b: 284).

For these scholars EU–US institution building is seen as a logical response to the ever increasing 'complex independence' experienced by Europe and the US (Hasenclever *et al.* 1996; Keohane 1989; Keohane and Nye 1977; see also Peters 1999).[7] Predictions that international institutions would increase after the Cold War have been validated by NATO enlargement and the creation of the WTO, as well as the Treaty of Maastricht which increased the scope and depth of European institutions, and made way for the institutionalisation of the transatlantic relationship.

Institutionalism effectively tackles the question of why institutions are built, however it is less adept at explaining how states interact within institutions. Part of the problem is that states are treated as unitary actors. By downplaying the impact that domestic actors have on international politics, institutionalists fail to recognise the range of actors and multiple levels of networks which are involved in the process. Therefore, this theoretical discussion needs to go a step further and address assumptions about the rationality of policy actors.

The rationalist–constructivist debate

The idea that domestic and international politics are not separable, and that domestic agents – be they political institutions, domestic groups, state or non-state actors – influence international negotiations, has united a number of emerging international relations theories (see Milner (1997); Putnam (1993; 1998); Risse (1995a). In the 1990s fewer scholars began to question whether or not institutions were important as the focus instead shifted to actors' motivations for pursuing institutions. Two factors contributed to the emerging rationalist–constructivist debate. On the one hand Legro and Moravscik (1999) argued that the divide between realist and liberal camps became less structured as realist, institutionalist and liberal studies 'rallied' around the idea that states are rational actors motivated by self-interest.[8] On the other hand the rise of rationalism was countered by a resurgence of sound constructivist approaches to international relations.[9]

The rationalist–constructivist divide is summarised by the distinction between the logic of consequentialism – associated with rationalists – and the logic of appropriateness – used by constructivists (who themselves have 'borrowed' the concept from institutionalism: see Boekle *et al.* 1999; March and Olsen 1998; Peters 1999). The two logics offer competing explanations for why the EU and the US chose to establish new transatlantic institutions, and why under those institutions dialogue has been encouraged between policy-makers as a means of attaining interest convergence or norm compliance in a number of policy sectors. Both constructivists and rationalists concede that institutions and communication 'matter' between agents but they offer different explanations as to why (Checkel 1998, 1999).

The logic of consequentialism assumes that actors are motivated by self-interest and that they seek to realise preferences and use strategic action to attain utility maximisation. For rationalists, transatlantic agreements can only be viewed as interstate bargains that represent both EU and US attempts to secure gains – be they security assurances or economic welfare. Many game theorists do try and account for domestic politics when explaining interstate bargaining. For example, Putnam (1993: 70–1) describes diplomacy as a 'two level' game where leaders simultaneously try to rationally calculate strategies that successfully appease both levels. Putnam's dual game theory envisions the American position during international negotiations as a product of international and national interest and the European Union's as a reconciliation of the global, the Community and the national levels (Putnam 1993: 80).

Constructivists argue that the logic of consequentialism oversimplifies the decision-making process. While rationalists tend to focus on the behaviour and policy outcomes, social constructivists tend to concentrate on a larger process that is characterised by communicative action and discourse between actors (Risse 1995b: 6–7). Constructivists argue that self-interest is not the sole instigator of international politics, rather they emphasise common values, norms and institutionalised decision-making procedures that determine the way democracies interact in the international system (Lumsdaine 1998: 6).[10] The argument is that actors are guided not by material gain but by a desire to adhere to 'rule-based' systems. The rules are determined by shared norms and ideas, which are not the product of actors' interests but rather precede them. In other words, the logic of appropriateness suggests that states' interests are defined through social communication (see also Boekle *et al.* 1999; Ruggie 1998).

Communication is especially important for constructivists such as Risse (2000) who argues that 'communicative action' extends beyond the logic of appropriateness to encompass a 'logic of truth seeking or arguing'. He argues that, 'international institutions create a normative framework structuring interaction in a given issue area. They often serve as arenas in which international policy deliberation can take place' (Risse 2000: 15). According to constructivists transatlantic institutions, such as the NTA, make up the structured 'normative' framework. In addition, the new transatlantic dialogue fulfils a number of conditions which precede 'truth seeking' behaviour. One is the institutionalisation of issue areas; a conscious effort by actors to construct a 'common lifeworld' through the build up of dialogues. These dialogues seek to compensate for the uncertainty of interests or a lack of knowledge between actors in certain policy sectors and the build up of non-hierarchical relations within dense, informal, network-like settings (Risse 2000: 19).

Separate roles and rationality

The two logics discussed above offer different explanations for why actors make the decisions they do. However, it is worth questioning whether Checkel (1999) was right when he argued that both paradigms capture and explain important but different elements of the norm compliance process.

On the one hand, rationalists offer sound explanations for why co-operation is pursued at high political levels. A rationalist explanation for EU–US institution building assumes that transatlantic leaders worked under the knowledge that common values could not keep the alliance together. Rationalist institutionalists argue that transatlantic institutions were created as a way of fostering shared interest in cooperation and establishing norms. Under this view, the TAD, the NTA, and the TEP are tools used to facilitate goals such as liberalising the transatlantic marketplace, burden sharing in Eastern Europe and combating transnational challenges. Chapter 2 discusses in more detail the establishment of these institutions and the interests that drove them.

On the second point of interest – the conduct of dialogue and production of policies under transatlantic institutions – constructivist arguments are harder to dismiss. The NTA specifically outlines a number of policy sectors where the EU and US have a broad interest in cooperating. It can be argued, however, that this agreement forms the boundaries or establishes the rules, for actor compliance on a number of shared norms.[11] Communication and information sharing are important by-products of daily interaction between different actors.

An important test for constructivism comes from examining the level of importance attached to the transatlantic dialogue. The distinction between rationalist and constructivist explanations for communication between actors is summarised by Checkel's (1999: 10) statement,

> Using different language to make the same point many rational choice scholars emphasise so-called simple learning, where agents acquire new information as a result of interaction. At a later point (that is, after the interaction), this information may be used to alter strategies, but not preferences, which are given. Not surprisingly, all this rationalist theorising reduces communication and language, which are central to any process of social learning, to the 'cheap talk' of agents with fixed identities and interests. The result is to bracket the interaction context through which agents interests and identities may change.

On the other hand,

> Specifically, the constructivist value added should be to explore complex social learning, which involves a process whereby agent interests and identities are shaped through and during interaction. So defined, social learning involves a break with strict forms of methodological individualism.

Has the construction of the NTA resulted in a process where communication between transatlantic actors is 'cheap talk' which may be used to foster a general sense of cooperation but not to change preferences (as rationalists explain)? Or will we, as constructivists contend, uncover a complex social learning process whereby agents' interests and identities are shaped through and during interaction?[12] Do actors have 'fixed' preferences in negotiating agreement under the NTA or is the output of policy agreements under the NTA actually shaped through transatlantic dialogue?

Governance below and beyond the state

This study of EU–US relations focuses not only on institution building, but also on the capacity of actors to exercise governance through institutions. The definition of governance outlined above is indicative of a process that requires policy makers to accommodate a range of actors with different interests. In order to understand collective transatlantic governance, we must examine both the composition of EU and US foreign policy formation and the organisation of transnational interest groups. This section explores three different trends in the governance literature: global governance beyond government, the rise of trasnational policy networks and the 'action capacity' of multi-level systems of governance.

Global governance

The literature on global or transnational governance questions how states balance the goals of economic liberalisation, through the deregulation of markets, without undermining the capacity of the state to deliver public goods such as social welfare and law enforcement. The new challenges that arise from globalisation have led some to argue that the state is 'shrinking' (Sbragia 2000) or being hollowed out (Strange 1996). The reality is that individual states are becoming increasingly unable to govern alone in a world characterised by rising transnational challenges and increasing economic interdependence. Political integration is one way to secure collective action, however, states' reluctance to give up sovereignty means formal integration arrangements – except and especially in the case of the EU – are limited. The New World Order envisioned by President Bush (Senior) has not created a supranational government, nor has rising globalisation and integration coincided with a clear-cut growth in the autonomy of international organisations (see Murphy 2000: 794).[13]

On the other hand, it can be argued that there has been a growing trend away from a centralised authority. Scholars preoccupied with the idea of 'governance without government' presume the absence of an overarching authority and hold that informal governmental mechanisms – as well as international organisations – can exercise governance. The functions of governance may be limited when compared to government's rules because informal mechanisms are not established by law and/or lack sovereign authority (Rosenau 1992: 7, 51). Nonetheless, Finklestein (1995: 357) agrees that global governance can encompass many of the functions that governments perform at home.[14] Governance above the state can be conducted not only through formal rules and regulations (see Cable 1999) but through shared norms, values and ideas (see Haas 1992) even in the absence of formal international organisations.

Given the lack of centralisation of authority at an international level, many scholars have begun to recognise that broader forms of institutionalised networks perform the functions of governance (see Ruggie 1998: 88). The emergence of public networks – made up of state actors – reinforced the idea that the state was not, as the New World Order suggested, due to disappear but rather as Slaughter (1997) argued, likely to disaggregate. That the NTA is an attempt to impose governance through national bureaucrats supports the argument made by Nicolaïdis and Howse (2001: 1) that

> In the long term, the nation-state may prove to be more resilient than many argue, but only if it is able to adapt, evolving or accepting modes of governance that permit both legitimate and effective accommodations with the many entities, both above and below the state which increasingly shape the public world in our century.

Transnational policy networks

The policy networks literature tries to come to grips with the shift from a strong executive to a more segmented mode of governance characterised by bargaining within and between networks (Rhodes 1997: 4). A policy network is a forum where numerous actors, all of whom have the ability to affect policy outcomes, exchange resources and information in order to facilitate reconciliation, settlement or compromise between different interests (Peterson 1995: 77; Rhodes 1997: 11). Policy networks are based on the premise that agents, be they regulatory agencies, interest groups, enterprises, think tanks or academics, participate in the policy process by working as partners on joint problem solving (Jachtenfuchs and Kohler-Koch 1995: 9). A variety of specialised 'communities' of agents may form alliances and collectively try to control or influence decision-making within policy networks. These include epistemic communities, which Haas (1992: 3) describes as networks 'of professionals with recognised expertise and competence in a particular domain and an authoritative claim to policy relevant knowledge within that domain or issue-area'.

A strong case can be made to suggest that policy networks and epistemic communities can effectively become 'institutions', provided they are characterised by substantial stability, patterns of expectations between actors (that is, interest groups expect to be consulted and governmental actors may even rely on them for information and advice in policy-making) and a membership that holds common values (see Peters 1999: 119). The test for the transatlantic networks discussed in Chapter 4 is whether they display these properties.

The literature on policy networks and epistemic communities is consistent with the institutionalist literature insofar as all are fundamentally concerned with norms such as shared knowledge, information and communication. Institutions, policy networks and epistemic communities are all functionally similar in that they are believed to facilitate cooperation by defining problems, identifying compromises between different interests and devising international solutions for government (Haas 1992: 15; Peterson 1996: 29; Keohane *et al.* 1993). Constructivists also depict policy networks and epistemic communities as forums that can, in effect, institutionalise 'policy learning'. For example, Stone (2000: 66) notes that think tanks act as 'policy entrepreneurs' by providing some of the conditions for policy transfer: developing knowledge, assessing policy options and drawing lessons. In essence they try to promote policy learning by 'teaching' governments about preferred policy outcomes.

Policy networks are visible structures of governance at the domestic level,[15] the EU level[16] and, we argue, the transatlantic level. Peterson and O'Toole (2001: 46) note that policy networks are likely to remain and even increase in importance in both Europe and the US as complex issues continue to occupy the policy agenda. A growing interest in resolving technical disputes, for example over biotechnology, and in harmonising and mutually accepting regulatory standards, means that policy networks are also likely to remain as important features in transatlantic governance.

Policy networks are often considered to be a more 'effective' mode of governance than, say, formal international institutions, because they bypass political problems and concentrate instead on bureaucratic and technocratic policy collaboration. They bring different interest groups into the policy-making process and provide a forum for many state and non-state actors. If policy networks have become an important new mode of transatlantic governance, however, one effect is to raise new questions about the 'legitimacy' of EU–US decision-making forums. Peterson and Bomberg (1999: 269) argue that, 'governance by policy networks is not very democratic: the same type of "democratic deficit" which plagues the EU is becoming visible in many of the world's most important international institutions'.

In other words policy networks are criticised for taking important issues out of the political arena, where they are dealt with by elected officials, and shifting them to the technocratic arena, where they are dealt with more quietly by bureaucrats. The technical need to facilitate 'effective' governance has been challenged by demands of legitimacy, and broader influence, particularly from private interest groups (Peterson and O'Toole 2001: 328). In turn, interest groups have been invited to participate in the transatlantic governance process in order to make the process appear more transparent.

Multi-level governance

Multi-level governance theories categorise the input of multiple actors into a system of 'shared governance' where competency for policy-making is distributed between different institutions and different levels of government. This approach challenges rationalist state-centric theories – such as intergovernmentalism (see Moravcsik 1998), which stress the unitary interest of the member states. Multi-level governance offers the alternative view 'that European integration is a polity creating process in which authority and policy-making influence are shared across multiple levels of government – subnational, national and supranational' (see Marks *et al.* 1996: 342).[17]

A revealing barometer of the extent to which competencies are shared between European institutions in foreign policy-making is the number of articles that have the basic objective of determining 'who speaks for Europe'?[18] In external relations competency is shared between the member states and the Community and between the Commission and the Council (and to a lesser extent the European Parliament).[19] In the Common Foreign and Security Policy (CFSP), Europe lacks a clear spokesperson – despite the appointment of a High Representative, Javier Solana – because pillar two is fundamentally intergovernmental (see Allen 1998). The Commission has more authority on trade policy – including exclusive competence to negotiate on behalf of the Community – but even then the EU does not speak with one voice when negotiating with the US (see Table 1.1 and Meunier and Nicolaïdis 1999: 482). The Commission can only negotiate subject to the Council's approval of a negotiating mandate and then finally ratification. In areas of mixed competency the Commission is subject to more intervention by the member states, including in a number of areas where it has agreed to cooperate with the US (for example on services and intellectual property). Smith (1998: 79) has argued that shared competencies in the external trade policy of the Union result in a 'negotiated order' where responsibility is shared and action is the result of a 'negotiated process'.

Table 1.1 Competency in EU decision-making

Article 133	*Authorisation*	*Representation*	*Ratification*
Exclusive competence *Most Trade Policy	133 Committee, Council (QMV)	Commission	Council (QMV) informal veto
Mixed competence *Services and IP	133 Committee Council	Commission	Council, Parliamentary ratification

Source: based on Meunier and Nicolaïdis 1999: 481

Rivalry between the Commission and the Council and between EU institutions and the member states compounds claims that the EU is a semi-formed polity and that it lacks the political authority to conduct a coherent foreign policy (Laffan 1997: 4). Although the Commission is able to exercise strategic authority in some areas of policy-making, it is clear that institutional deficits and the lack of a single EU negotiating authority adds to the EU's 'capabilities–expectations gap' (see Hill 1993, 1996).[20] In addition, the recent growth in the power of the European Parliament has the capacity to increase tension with the EU's trading partners. A good recent example is European legislation, supported strongly in the EP, to regulate airline hush kits, which prompted a bitter EU–US trade dispute.[21] In short, it can be argued that the EU's emergence as a multi-level polity considerably complicates transatlantic governance.

Transatlantic governance appears even more complicated if one also considers the US to be a multi-level system of governance (see Smith 1997; Peterson and O'Toole 2001).[22] While it may be easier to determine who has negotiating authority in the US than it is in the EU, it is certain that EU negotiators are certainly not the only ones with their 'hands tied' in transatlantic negotiations. US foreign policy-making is characterised by power shifts between the executive and legislature and between state and national institutions. Many scholars have claimed that the two-part system exacerbates friction as divided government in the US impedes international cooperation, undermines trade agreements and slows economic liberalisation (see also Lohman and O'Halloran 1994; Milner 1997).[23] US trade policy is affected not only by varied levels of party support for liberalisation, for example, but also by Congressional control of executive powers, such as Fast Track negotiating authority (see Karol 2000: 826).

In addition, the US Congress regularly passes laws that are at the heart of EU–US disputes. For example, it introduced US extraterritorial legislation (see Chapter 3) and the Carousel Retaliation Act (see Chapter 7) which exacerbated the Helms–Burton and banana disputes. Members of Congress also have the power to 'make or break' projects, which require their approval of budget lines. To complicate matters even further, state legislators can also pass laws that undermine the capacity of federal negotiators to reach and deliver on external agreements. In short it can be argued that the US also suffers from the capabilities–expectations gap which is usually applied exclusively to the EU.

A transatlantic decision-making model

A decision-making model tries to account for different levels of actor interaction at different stages of the policy process. It essentially establishes that transatlantic governance is best understood by examining not only the big decisions that mould the contours of the process, but also the day to day decisions which determine the policy output. The transatlantic decision-making model outlined here seeks to explain not only who governs but also how they govern. To distinguish who governs it is useful to draw on Pollack and Shaffer's (2001) model of transatlantic governance, which describes three levels of cooperation created by the NTA (see Table 1.2). At the *intergovernmental* level the high level contacts between chiefs of government (COG) lead to decisions which are constrained by the domestic process. The day to day contact between lower-level officials takes place at the *transgovernmental* level. Here civil servants work with their counterparts to determine ways to coordinate and harmonise policies. Finally, the *transnational* level is occupied by the direct people to people links created by the 'building bridges' chapter of the NTA. This is where private actors work through the civil society process to coordinate strategies through networks such as the transatlantic business, consumer and environment dialogues.

To understand how these different types of actors participate in the transatlantic policy process we draw on Peterson and Bomberg's decision-making model which argues that different types of decisions are made at different levels by different sets of actors exercising different rationale (see Peterson 1995). Peterson and Bomberg (1999: 10) explain in the context of the EU that history-making decisions transcend the day to day policy process, establish the scope for policy-making and address questions of change in governance (see Table 1.3). Policy setting decisions determine *which* policy option will be pursued. Finally, policy shapers determine how to address policy problems. By formulating different policy options they address the problem of 'how do we do it?' (Peterson 1995: 73–4; Peterson and Bomberg 1999: 16). The decision-making model outlined here argues that these

Table 1.2 Types of transatlantic actors

Intergovernmental	*High level contact between Chiefs of Government*
Transgovernmental	Day to day contact between sub-units of Government (civil servants)
Transnational	Contact between private actors – businesses and NGOs

Source: based on Shaffer and Pollack (2001)

intergovernmental, transgovernmental and transnational actors exercise decision 'making', 'setting' and 'shaping' capabilities through transatlantic institutions.

Intergovernmental policy making

In the context of transatlantic dialogue, intergovernmental actors represent the highest level of government (Shaffer and Pollack 2001). The President of the United States, the Commission President and the leader/s of the Council Presidency meet at EU–US summits, and it is here that the most significant transatlantic decisions are made. In the context of the transatlantic relationship these actors are policy makers, because they are responsible for 'history making decisions'. History making decisions in the transatlantic policy process are those which form the pillars of EU–US institutionalisation. They create transatlantic institutions and establish the scope for policy reach by outlining broad intergovernmental commitments to cooperation in certain policy sectors. In other words history making decisions in the context of the transatlantic relationship are decisions that conclude, 'we will cooperate'. The TAD, the NTA and the TEP were all products of such decisions, even if these institutions now in themselves are largely responsible for determining where the transatlantic process will move and at what pace it would do so.

Table 1.3 A categorisation of decision-making

History making decisions	*Policy setting decisions*	*Policy shaping decisions*
• transcend the day to day policy process • alter legislative procedures, rebalance the relative power of institutions • take place at the highest political level • are political decisions	• determine which choice of action should be pursued by policy makers • deal with specific details of policy • are taken at the systemic level • are technocratic decisions	• involve decisions about how policy problems can be addressed • involve day to day communication • take place at the sub-systemic or meso-level of policy-making • can be shaped by state as well as non-state actors

Source: based on Peterson and Bomberg (1999)

Peterson and Bomberg (1999: 9) argue that high level 'history making decisions' are political decisions, which are best explained by rationalist theories.[24] In other words, these decisions are the product of rational decisions made on behalf of the Americans by the US President and on behalf of Europeans by the President in office of the Council and the President of the Commission. History making negotiations tend to highlight the determination of both sides to attain power gains. Chapter 2 discusses, for example, how EU support for the TEP was used as a bargaining tool to get the US to make concessions on the Helms–Burton trade dispute.

Intergovernmentalism sheds light on one part of the transatlantic process, but cannot account for the whole of the transatlantic dialogue. While rationalists offer suitable explanations for big decisions taken at the highest level, they do not necessarily account for interaction between transgovernmental or transnational actors. More emphasis needs to be placed on how decisions taken at the top are constrained by decisions at the bottom. Drawing on Moravcsik's (1993a: 25) intergovernmental logic, Pollack and Shaffer (2001) note that COGs can restrain domestic actors (including member states) by altering the domestic ratification process, or in the case of the NTA and the TEP by avoiding it altogether. They can influence domestic groups through side payments (for example making concessions on US sanctions in order to get member state support for the TEP) and through manipulating information about the agreements. Nonetheless, both sides are constrained by a lack of consensus at the top because EU and US negotiators often find their 'hands tied' in transatlantic negotiations by transgovernmental and transnational actors who exert pressure on leaders' decisions and influence the process directly through policy setting and policy shaping. Intergovernmentalism is less suited for explaining the day to day process which determines policy options and policy details (Peterson 1995; Peterson and Bomberg 1999).

Transgovernmental decision setting

The scope for influencing the transatlantic policy process extends well beyond the intergovernmental level because transgovernmental and transnational actors are able to 'set' some policies – that is, to make choices between policy alternatives – as well as to shape policy, or to determine which options are permissible (or not) and what their detailed content will be. The decisions to agree the TAD, NTA and TEP 'made history' in that they institutionalised a number of transgovernmental and transnational networks. In transgovernmental networks, state actors on either side now work directly with their transatlantic counterparts. Slaughter's (1997: 184) conception of transgovernmentalism explains how states have adapted to new global challenges without transferring authority to non-state actors. She argues that states have disaggregated into separate, functionally distinct parts. These parts

– courts, regulatory agencies, executives, and even legislatures – are networking with their counterparts abroad, creating a dense web of relations that constitutes a new, transgovernmental order.

Table 1.4 Actors in the new transatlantic dialogue

Intergovernmental actors	*Transgovernmental actors*	*Transnational actors*
President of the US	EU Ministers/US Cabinet	TABD
President of the Commission	SLG	TACD
Council Presidency Leader	NTA Task Force	TAED
	Transatlantic working groups	TALD
	Transatlantic legislators dialogue	
	Europol/FBI	

Between the EU and the US, these networks are formed by exchanges between the EU Foreign Ministers, the EU Commissioners, and the US Cabinet. These transgovernmental networks were institutionalised originally in the Transatlantic Declaration and have continued to take place on a regular basis. In addition, exchange has taken place between the Commission and the United States Trade Representative (USTR), the European Parliament and the US Congress, and the FBI and Europol under the NTA framework.

Transgovernmental networks are responsible for policy setting and shaping decisions. The power to set policy typically rests with state actors such as agencies of the state in the US and EU ministries represented in the Council. The US Cabinet, EU Council Presidency and EU Commissioners effectively set policy, through for example (see also Chapter 6) the MRA agreement (signed by the USTR and the then DG I Commissioner) and the Positive Comity Agreement (signed by the US Attorney General, the Federal Trade Commission, the Commissioner for Competition and the President-in-Office of the Industry Council).[25] Certain agency directors can also set policy in some capacities. For example, the National Institute of Standards and Technology Director and the EU Commission's Director-General for Research signed the Implementing Arrangement for Co-operation in the Fields of Metrology and Measurement Standards.

In other cases the role of agency directors and DGs are confined to shaping policy through various EU–US dialogues. The SLG Steering Group shapes policy by setting the agenda for summits, as do the TEP Steering Group and the Troika political directors' dialogue. The 'expert level' dialogues, (i.e. the transatlantic working groups, the NTA Task Force and the TEP working groups) shape the agenda by identifying and working towards specific deliverables and by suggesting possible policy solutions. Other 'building bridges' dialogues also serve a shaping function. For example exchanges between Europol and the FBI have been launched with the intention of finding joint solutions to deal with transnational crime. Networks of aid officials have coordinated EU and US projects in Central and Eastern Europe and Africa.

Table 1.5 Transatlantic decision-making

Type of actor	*Type of decision*
Intergovernmental	History making
Transgovernmental	Policy setting and policy shaping
Transnational	Policy shaping

Transgovernmentalism has been pursued by states because it is a pragmatic approach to international governance. It compartmentalises the state into functional units that then serve as effective problem solving mechanisms (Slaughter 1997: 195). Transgovernmental networks are effective because they bring relevant parties together, and they are more flexible than international institutions. Most importantly, they introduce a bias towards compromise in foreign policy-making by expanding the reach of regulations while keeping loss of sovereignty to a minimum. The logic behind transgovernmental networks represents a new mode of governance, whereby networks of sub-national and supranational counterparts, who perform the functions of a world government, create a genuinely new world order (Slaughter 1997: 195).

Whatever the underlying rationale, the creation of institutions below the intergovernmental level allows states to decentralise some parts of the decision-making process. The decentralisation of decision-making aids the process of transatlantic governance, because as Slaughter (1997: 195–6) argues the disaggregation of the state 'makes it possible to create networks of institutions engaged in a common enterprise even as they represent distinct national interests'. It creates opportunities for domestic institutions to establish common causes with their counterparts, sometimes against the will of fellow branches of government.

Still, these networks often do not reflect the growing scope and depth of the transatlantic policy-making process. Strictly transgovernmental networks alienate important non-state actors from the policy-making process, thereby limiting both their effectiveness and legitimacy (Slaughter 1997: 197). The fact that most important negotiations are now surrounded by a mixture of state and non-state agents, working together as transatlantic policy networks, illustrates another growing trend.

Transnational decision shaping

Whereas transgovernmentalism represents a disaggregation of the state, the rise of transnational networks highlights the increased role played by non-state actors. Non-governmental actors influence transatlantic decisions taken at the top by exerting pressure through the domestic process and participating in institutionalised networks.

The Transatlantic Business Dialogue (TABD), the Transatlantic Consumer Dialogue (TACD), and the Transatlantic Environmental Dialogue (TAED) are all examples of transnational policy networks. The transatlantic dialogues are transnational networks, in that they are composed of non-state actors who have an interest or an expertise in the given area. Their role is to advise EU and US state actors on problems and to provide expertise in respective policy sectors. These dialogues can also be characterised as policy networks because they bring government and interest groups to one table. Epistemic communities are also gaining prominence in transatlantic governance, due to the very technical nature of policies addressed at the transatlantic level, particularly within the regulatory sector. Peterson (1996: 76) recognises as epistemic communities three bilateral working groups formed in 1994 on foreign policy coordination, Eastern Europe, and international crime and identifies joint panels of experts that have been assembled to devise cooperative strategies on issues related to trade, science, technology and environmental protection (Peterson 1994: 418). Expert level meetings and seminars have also been employed to combat cyber-crime, the financing of international terrorism, organised crime in Eastern Europe and the informational society.[26]

Transatlantic policy networks play an important role in 'shaping' transatlantic policy. Their influence is typically exerted in early stages of the transatlantic policy-making process where decisions about the substance of the transatlantic agenda are decided. It is at the sub-systemic or meso level (see Peterson 1995) of policymaking that policy shapers provide the government with specialised knowledge required to negotiate policy agreements. At the transatlantic level, the TABD, the TACD and the TAED each present the EU and US governments with suggested policy routes. The goal of these networks is to find areas where they feel the government can cooperate and provide transgovernmental actors with 'ready made' policy solutions.

Different theoretical explanations explain the role played by transnational networks. Pollack and Shaffer draw on Keohane and Nye (1977) and Risse (1995a) to explain why transnational networks emerge. Risse argues that domestic structures and varying abilities to build coalitions between NGOs and international institutions affect the capacity for society actors to form transnational networks. Peterson and Bomberg (1999: 21) explain policy shaping in the context of policy network literature. They argue that this level of decision-making is technocratic due to the specialised knowledge required to decipher policy details and formulate policy solutions. Both liberal international relations theory and policy network analysis help explain how transnational actors come together, and what benefits are reaped from governance through networks. In order for decision shaping to take place, however, at least some logic of constructivist thinking must be present. If actors jointly shape a decision, their dialogue must extend beyond the realm of cheap talk. Thus, EU–US relations offer an interesting test case for the rationalist–constructivist debate.

Overview

The existence of multiple types of actors and multiple types of decisions points to the difficult task faced by transatlantic actors trying to govern in an increasingly transnational world. Institutions provide a forum for both cooperation and conflict management. In the case of EU–US relations, networks are formed to accommodate different levels of domestic actors, including state and non-state actors. Multi-level governance in the EU and the US highlights the fact that negotiators have to contend not only with their foreign counterparts but also with domestic rivals. One of the aims of the NTA has been to internationalise the attitudes of domestic actors. The result, it is argued, is a complex structure of institutions that allow different actors to 'make', 'set' and 'shape' policies.

Chapters 2, 3 and 4 examine the institutionalisation of the transatlantic relationship at an intergovernmental, transgovernmental and transnational level. We also track the input, and where possible the policy output, of different transatlantic actors. Chapter 2 starts by examining the role of intergovernmental decision 'makers' through three history making decisions – those that created the TAD, the NTA and the TEP – and thus established the institutional and policy reach of the new transatlantic dialogue. Chapter 3 examines the role that transgovernmental actors play in setting and shaping transatlantic decisions. Chapter 4 discusses the participation of formal interest based transnational networks in transatlantic decision shaping. It focuses on the organisation of business, consumer and environment interests groups and the impact of the Transatlantic Business Dialogue (TABD), the Transatlantic Consumer Dialogue (TACD) and the Transatlantic Environmental Dialogue (TAED).

Chapters 5 to 7 discuss three policy sectors, which serve as case studies for EU–US decision-making. The case studies were chosen to show the broad range of the new transatlantic dialogue and to incorporate political and economic issues as well as policy areas characterised by integration, interest diversion or 'system friction'.[27] Chapter 5 looks at the decisions that made, set and shaped transatlantic policy coordination on trafficking in women in CEE. A case study of the EU–US anti-trafficking information campaigns highlights the type of low key, technical decisions that are facilitated by the NTA. Trafficking in women is also examined as a case study for EU external cooperation on JHA issues, an area where the EU has normally been considered to be a less supportive partner because of internal institutional gaps.

Chapter 6 presents a second case study, this time in an economic policy sector. It examines intergovernmental, transgovernmental and transnational actor input into the EU–US Mutual Recognition Agreements (MRAs), according to which the regulatory standards governing the production of goods on one side of the Atlantic is accepted as legitimate on the other side. Like the trafficking in women case, the MRAs point to the existence of multi-level governance in transatlantic policy-making. The MRA negotiations represent a policy sector where the EU has the capacity to act more coherently than the US, thus revealing that the capabilities–expectations gap often ascribed to the EU, and held to be a major deterrent to effective EU–US policy cooperation, is mirrored by a similar gap on the American side.

Chapter 7 examines a trade dispute that raged on for most of the 1990s. It questions how effective NTA institutions have been in managing the banana dispute. In short, it moves us towards an understanding of whether the transatlantic decision-making model applies to areas of dispute as well as agreement. The chapter develops the argument that the banana dispute was an 'outlier', or a case where transatlantic institutions have been criticised for not effectively managing conflict. The banana case draws attention to the complicated task of facilitating 'governance' where interests diverge and where disputes become legal under international trade rules. But, it also demonstrates the capacity of the transatlantic institutions to contain policy friction. The chapter asks what the banana case can tell us more generally about the capacity of the new transatlantic dialogue to overcome competition between domestic actors.

To conclude, Chapter 8 reviews the main findings of this research and 'broadens out' to consider the wider implications concerning the role of the EU–US relationship in international politics and the place of institutions in international relations more generally. It reviews the evidence presented in the book to determine whether the case studies point to an institutionalisation, decentralisation and 'privatisation' of transatlantic decision taking. It also questions what impact, or lack thereof, new decision-making processes have had on the overall cycle of transatlantic governance. In short, it asks not only who governs and how, but also what difference it makes? To what extent has the decision-making structure allowed the EU and US to manage relations characterised by cooperation and competition, and at what price does 'effective' management of the dialogue come? In other words, how does transatlantic decision-making fare in the debate on technocratic governance? The anti-globalisation protests at the WTO ministerial meeting in Seattle (1999), at the EU Summit in Göteborg (2001) and the G-8 Summit in Genoa (2001) demonstrate the general lack of popular support for governance structures which exist above the nation-state. Is the legitimacy of transatlantic governance undermined by the absence of a broad acceptance of transatlantic institutions?

Notes

1 See 'Why the Trans-Atlantic Economic Partnership is so Important', www.tabd.com.
2 European investment in the US is believed to support over seven million American jobs, while American investment in Europe accounts for about three million European jobs (see European Committee of the American Chamber of Commerce's website www.eucommittee.be).
3 Kennedy's 'Grand Design' and Nixon's 'New Atlantic Charter', which both failed to re-enforce the transatlantic relationship, are discussed in Chapter 2.
4 The term political rather than security here indicates the focus on 'soft' rather than 'hard' security issues. The scope for policies studied in this book is largely confined to those incorporated under the NTA. For transatlantic security studies see Bronstone (1998); Geipel and Manning (1996); Haass (1999); van den Broek (1993).
5 Interview, Commission Delegation, Washington DC, October 2000.
6 See Henderson (1998); Mearsheimer (1990b); Waltz (1979).
7 'Complex interdependence' is defined by Keohane and Nye (1989: 249) as 'a situation among a number of countries in which multiple channels of contact connect societies (that is, states do not monopolise these contacts); there is no hierarchy of issues; and military force is not used by governments towards one another'.
8 Moravscik and Legro (2000: 184) argued that, 'The category of "realist" theory has been broadened to the point that it signifies little more than a generic commitment to rational state behaviour in anarchy – that is "minimal realism"'.
9 Pollack (2001) argues that contructivist theories, typically criticised by rationalists for failing to produce rigorous, 'good social science' because they do not focus on empirical work or testable hypotheses, had by the end of the 1990s significantly matured through works such as Hooghe (1999a, 1999b) and Checkel (1998; 1999).
10 Norms are defined by Peterson and Bomberg (1999: 53) as 'principles of "right action" saving to guide, control or regulate proper and acceptable behaviour in a group'.
11 Compliance is defined by Checkel (1999: 3) as the extent to which agents act in accordance with and fulfilment of the prescriptions contained in international rules and norms – and not socialisation. Compliance research focuses centrally on short-term processes, coercion, sanctions etc.
12 This distinction is made by Checkel (1999: 10).
13 Traditionally, global governance was seen to emanate from international institutions. In the early post-Cold War years, the concept of a 'New World Order' was promoted by President George Bush (Senior) who argued that a new form of collective governance would emerge in the 1990s based on cooperation within international organisations. International institutions were championed as a way to deregulate barriers to trade while regulating global markets in labour, money, goods and ideas.
14 The list of such functions is quite a long one. It includes information creation and exchange; formulation and promulgation of principles and promotion of consensual knowledge affecting the general international order, regional orders, particular issues on the international agenda, and efforts to influence the domestic rules and behaviour of states; good offices, conciliation, mediation and compulsory resolution of disputes;

regime formulation, tending and execution; adoption of rules, codes, and regulations; allocation of material and programme resources, provision of technical assistance and development programs; relief, humanitarian, energy, disaster activities; and the maintenance of peace and order.

15 See Marsh and Rhodes (1992); Rhodes (1997).
16 See Peterson (1995); Peterson and Bomberg (1999).
17 See also Blank *et al.* (1994: 3–7, 39–40).
18 See for example Allen (1998); Meunier and Nicolaïdis (1999); Meunier (2000).
19 See for example Piening (1997); Peterson and Sjursen (1998).
20 Two sets of negotiations in particular highlight the incapacity of the Commission to 'deliver' in negotiations with the US in light of member state intervention. For example in 1992 the French forced a watering down of the original Blair House Agreement, on extending international trade rules to agriculture, after US officials leaked its content. Commissioner Brittan was reprimanded by the Council and reminded by the French Prime Minister of his role as a 'servant of the Council' (see also Meunier and Nicolaïdis 1999). Commissioner Brittan again ran into problems with the French when negotiating the New Transatlantic Marketplace Agreement of 1998. After blocking the agreement, the French Prime Minister accused Brittan of 'running off to negotiate a free trade agreement without a mandate'.
21 See also Chapter 3.
22 Multi-level governance is consistent with the 'federal vision' (see Nicolaïdis and Howse 2001), which also stresses a process of governance where powers and competencies are shared between federal and state governments. Peterson and O'Toole (2001: 300) note that, 'federalism usually gives rise to less formal intricate structures within which a large number of actors, each wielding a small slice of power, interact'.
23 For discussions on the role of US politics in transatlantic relations see Smith and Woolcock (1993); Heuser (1996); Peterson (1994, 1996); Smith (1997).
24 In the context of the EU they claim liberal intergovernmentalism and neo-functionalism as 'best' theories for explaining and predicting decision-making at the 'super-systemic' level, where history making decisions are taken.
25 The Commission's 'setting' decisions are still subject to ratification by the Council and the European Parliament under EU decision-making rules (see Peterson and Bomberg 1999).
26 Senior Level Group Reports 1997.
27 This term is used by Smith (2001) to describe clashing structures, for example between regulatory or industrial cultures.

2

The institutionalisation of EU–US relations in the 1990s

Introduction

This chapter traces the institutionalisation of the transatlantic relationship in the 1990s and assesses the extent to which policy issues have been placed in a bilateral forum. It examines the creation of formal EU–US dialogue structures to underpin the 'new' transatlantic dialogue. Thus, the focus is on bilateral agreements between the US and the EU, which are the result of intergovernmental history making decisions and on the build up of inter-state institutions, including formal intergovernmental, transgovernmental and transnational networks.[1] Three questions are crucial to understanding the institutionalisation of the transatlantic relationship. First, how was the relationship institutionalised? Second, why was it institutionalised? And finally, what are the repercussions of the EU–US institution building strategy?

We first consider how EU–US relations were institutionalised. Three transatlantic agreements signed in the 1990s form the pillars of EU–US institutionalisation: the Transatlantic Declaration (1990), the New Transatlantic Agenda (1995), the Transatlantic Economic Partnership and the adjoining Transatlantic Partnership on Political Co-operation (1998). These agreements marked a shift in the focus of European–American relations. While the Cold War was characterised by either multilateral relations within NATO, the UN or the GATT, or by bilateral relations between the US and individual member states, the creation of transatlantic institutions in the 1990s marked the beginning of a formal bilateral dialogue between the US and the EU.

The second question addressed in this chapter concerns the motivation for institutionalisation. Successive agreements expanded the relationship in scope and substance, suggesting that the political will and institutional capacity to pursue agreements increased over time. In that respect each subsequent agreement can be characterised as a step or 'building block' in a long-term process of institutionalisation and transatlantic policy integration.[2] Notably, this strategy reflects the nature of integration within Europe. As Frost (1997:

71) argues, 'Just as Jean Monnet's vision of a united Europe found initial expression in small practical steps, supporters of a building-blocks approach argue that more ambitious steps could be undertaken at a later date'.

Finally, this chapter seeks to establish whether and how much transatlantic institutions matter. Here, it comes to grips with the most basic shortcoming of institutionalist theory (see Peters 1999): the inability to gauge precisely how much the behaviour of social actors is shaped or altered by institutional structures. The evidence presented here is based on policy officials' perceptions about the effect that institutionalisation has had on the transatlantic process. What is important is not only the capacity of the transatlantic dialogue to produce concrete policy output or 'deliverables' but also the capacity of transatlantic institutions to forge the channels of communication which, according to institutionalist theory, act to foster cooperation.

The chapter is divided into four sections. The first describes the 'old' transatlantic relationship before the period of EU–US institutionalisation. The following sections examine the three agreements that established the boundaries of a 'new' transatlantic dialogue. The second section examines the launch of the TAD, and the creation of the first formal, bilateral, transatlantic institutions. The third section discusses the expansion of institutionalisation to the transgovernmental and transnational levels and the establishment of a more comprehensive framework for cooperation under the NTA. The fourth and final section considers the further institutionalisation of EU–US economic relations via the TEP. Each section considers why transatlantic leaders chose to further institutionalise the relationship and how the agreements were designed to meet their preferences.

The Cold War

The US and its European allies set out after the First World War to build a transatlantic partnership that would forge and subsequently reinforce multilateral institutions governed by western ideals and dominated by European and American power. This period is often described as a period of hegemony because American power clearly superseded that of any other state.[3] The dollar dominated the economic system. NATO, although technically an agreement between major powers (Calvocoressi 1991: 175), was practically controlled by American military power. It was not only US leadership that defined the relationship, but also Europe's willingness to cooperate to protect its shared interests (Featherstone and Ginsberg 1996: 6). Thus, Europe was a dependant partner in the foundational period of the current transatlantic relationship (Smith 1990: 104; 1997: 90).

Cooperation between the US and the European member states is well documented throughout the Cold War, yet bilateral initiatives between the US and the European Community as a whole did not materialise despite its establishment of external relations with numerous other partners (see Box 2.1). This section examines two failed attempts to forge a more equal 'partnership' first, through Kennedy's Grand Design and second, with Nixon's New Atlantic Charter.

Kennedy's Grand Design

Western Europe gradually became a stronger partner within the European–American alliance, as it pursued economic and political integration through the Western European Union (1948), European Coal and Steel Community (1952), the European Economic Community (EEC) (1957) and the atomic energy community (Euratom) (1957). The US supported European integration because American policy makers considered European unity crucial to strengthening democracies against communism, resolving Franco-German differences, reintegrating Germany, salvaging US export markets and reinforcing efforts to build a new multilateral trading system (Hogan 1984: 6).[4]

The US first began to take serious notice of the new EEC during the Dillon Round of the GATT when trade negotiators encountered the new Common Agriculture Policy (CAP), which imposed variable levies on certain sectors affecting foreign imports, for example the poultry trade.[5] While the US did retaliate, its negotiators chose to conclude the Dillon Round without securing a suitable compromise over the CAP. At this stage in European-American relations the US commitment to European unity, the Western Alliance and the multilateral trading system took precedence over the domestic interests of American chicken farmers (Curtis and Vastine 1971: 23–5).

Meanwhile, the divergence of European economic interests was coupled with growing divergence on foreign policy issues, including the Berlin Crisis (1961).[6] The French President Charles De Gaulle's open protectionism presented the most notable wedge in the Atlantic Alliance. De Gaulle's opposition to 'American imperialism' directly interfered with the American desire to see Britain become a member of the EEC. In 1963, De Gaulle rejected the UK application, questioned British motives for joining and described the UK as 'America's Trojan horse' (Lundestad 1998: 65–7). The transatlantic security alliance became subject to severe transatlantic tensions when De Gaulle withdrew France from NATO's integrated military command in 1966.

Amidst concern about the weakening alliance, President Kennedy announced the 'Grand Design' in 1962, a two-part plan designed to foster 'a partnership of equals' between Europe and the US. The first component of Kennedy's plan was the Trade Expansion Act (TEA) passed by Congress in 1963. The TEA was designed to rapidly boost the liberalisation of trade in agriculture and industry.[7] The second component of the Grand Design was an envisioned 'declaration of inter-dependence' between the US and a united Europe. Kennedy's Grand Design was symbolic in recognising first, the new role of the EEC in the international economy and second, the need to re-forge the weakening security alliance.

Yet despite its grand design, Kennedy's plan had only marginal effects. The Kennedy Round of the GATT was successful in cutting tariff levels affecting $40bn of world trade by 36–39 per cent (Curtis and Vastine 1971: 230). However, it became increasingly clear that American and European interests diverged over the protectionist nature of the EEC's agricultural policy. Once more the single European voice in negotiations over the CAP marked a shift in the balance of power. Curtis and Vastine (1971: 231) explain that,

> The United States found itself seated across the negotiating table from tough-minded representatives of a strong and truly independent new economic unity. Perhaps the Kennedy Round was the first major post-war economic negotiation in which the United States found itself confronted with a bargaining partner of equal strength.

On the other hand, the lack of overall political unity in Europe contributed to the downfall of Kennedy's political declaration (Peterson 1996: 36). While the President spoke of 'an alliance among equals', it was widely believed that the US had an interest in maintaining its position as world leader by making Western Europe a tightly integrated junior partner (see also Carroll and Herring 1996). De Gaulle, in particular, rejected the notion of an 'equal' partnership and a period of French–American discord followed. During this early period of fragmentation, Smith (1990: 107; 1996: 90) argues that Europe took on the role of a 'putative partner'. The alliance forged in the 1950s remained, but the 1960s marked an era of interest diversification and developing tension in the transatlantic partnership.

The New Atlantic Charter

European–American relations in the 1970s and 1980s faced further challenges that undermined communication and cooperation in transatlantic relations. First, US President Nixon employed new economic policies to compensate for the balance of payments problem caused by US military spending in Vietnam. His unilateral decision to devalue the dollar and end the Bretton Woods system returned international currencies to a fluctuating rather than fixed rate system. The 'Nixon shocks' caused a rift in European–American relations and provoked a fresh attempt to reinvest in the transatlantic relationship. In 1972, the European leaders called for a 'constructive dialogue' between the US and the European Community.[8]

Nixon made another attempt to refocus transatlantic relations and put the partners back on track by declaring 1973 the 'Year of Europe'. In the spirit of the Grand Design he called for a 'structure of peace' and a 'New Atlantic Charter'. The Charter was intended to minimise conflict, reinforce security ties and increase economic cooperation (Landes 1977: 22; Smith 1984: 17). Yet, like the Grand Design, the Year of Europe failed under the pressure of diverging economic and political interests (especially in the Middle East) and the breakdown of the international monetary system. In 1973 the decision to back different sides in the Israeli–Arab war soured US–European political relations, and the resulting oil crisis had adverse affects on economic relations not least because it was followed by deep global recession (Peterson 1996: 39; Smith 1984: 17; Tsoukalis 1986: 14).[9]

Trade relations were also bedevilled by large fluctuations in the value of the dollar. Europe faced high stagflation[10] and grew short-tempered with the US policy of 'benign neglect'.[11] Europe employed emergency protectionist measures to protect its industries, and trade wars broke out over cheese and textiles (Smith 1984: 17; Wallace and Young 1996: 131). Meanwhile, the EC made attempts to consolidate its voice and strengthen its foreign policy position in the early 1970s through the creation of the European Political Community (EPC) and the European Monetary System (EMS).[12]

After the failure of the Atlantic Charter, EC–US relations in the 1970s resembled a 'partnership of rivals' (Mally 1974: xv) or, at best, an 'uneasy partnership' (Dahrendorf 1974: 67). The relationship became more competitive as American hegemony started to decline (Featherstone and Ginsberg 1996)[13] and the roles of Europe and the US in the transatlantic relations shifted again. Smith and Woolcock (1993: 5) argue that the US attitude towards the international system turned from one of guardianship to one of ambivalence.

In the 1980s supply-side economics, the US budget deficit, high interest rates and the over-valued dollar met with opposition on Continental Europe (Smith 1984: 219).[14] Industrial and agricultural trade disputes over steel, Airbus, oilseeds, grain, pasta, citrus fruit and beef caused 'dangerous' levels of trade friction (Tsoukalis 1986: 2). The Uruguay Round got off to a shaky start in 1986 and fear of potential European protectionism heightened when the Single European Act was signed in 1987 (Smith 1984: 219). The single market initiative was commonly suspected to be a device to create a 'Fortress Europe', which restricted market access for US imports. Foreign policy differences also arose over Afghanistan, the Middle East and martial law in Poland. The latter triggered a dispute over the use of extraterritorial legislation when the US, in an attempt to punish the USSR, contemplated extraterritorial sanctions against European companies involved in building the Siberian Pipeline.[15] As a result, the end of the Cold War found the partners growing further apart rather than closer together.

The end of an era

To summarise, European–American relations underwent clear shifts throughout the Cold War. What started as a solid foundation based on European dependency developed into a more balanced partnership as the EC grew in size and strength. As the balance of power shifted, conflicts over trade disputes and foreign policy increased. These problems were exacerbated by the fact that little communication took place between European and American policy makers. The need for dialogue was recognised through the creation of ad hoc structures in conjunction with European Political Co-operation in 1974 (Frellesen 2001: 4). However, both Kennedy's declaration of interdependence and Nixon's New Atlantic Charter failed to create bilateral channels of communication until the 1990s.

Poor communication meant that tension in European–American relations went unmanaged; often policy disputes escalated because there were no mechanisms for containing them. Featherstone and Ginsberg (1996: 28) argue that, 'American policy flip-flopped between ignoring or discounting Europeans and overpowering them with calls for co-operation. The EC for its part cried out for recognition of its interest but failed to develop a coherent policy towards the US.' Nonetheless, the partnership was held together by an interest in upholding common values of democracy and economic liberalisation. Multilateral institutions served as anchors for the western alliance and the international political and economic orders. An equally important source of cohesion was the common security threat and the military alliance built to safeguard western values.

The Transatlantic Declaration

The end of the Cold War raised questions generally about the future of the transatlantic alliance. Transatlantic leaders feared that common ideas, values and culture would not be as adhesive as the common security threat had been in mending the widening gap between Europe and the US.[16] The role of NATO and other multilateral institutions came under scrutiny, as many Europeans feared the possibility of American isolationism on the one hand and imperialism on the other. Plans to create a European Single Market made the EC a more cohesive economic and, to a lesser extent, political force. While some American politicians continued to dismiss the prospects for an equal partnership, others worried about it becoming too competitive as an economic power. In any case, American politicians found it increasingly difficult to justify to the domestic population economic trade losses with Western Europe. The dissipated security threat of the Cold War meant that the US now held less bargaining power over its allies, and that it was less willing to compromise its economic interests for the sake of the political alliance (Devuyst 1995: 15).

Towards institutionalisation

These changes created uncertainties and transposed perceptions about how the transatlantic relationship should be defined. Transatlantic leaders realised that common ideas by themselves could not maintain the transatlantic partnership, but they identified mutual interest in promoting democratic transitions in Central and Eastern Europe (CEE) and the Newly Independent States (NIS) and in protecting the multilateral institutions established to maintain the international political and economic orders. Increased capital flows, global investment and foreign trade sparked greater interdependence, and it was clear that European–American cooperation was needed to maintain trade disputes and to complete the Uruguay Round of trade talks.

Again, and in keeping with institutionalist theory, it was argued that a formal European–American agreement was needed to secure the transatlantic relationship. It was thought that a transatlantic partnership could be built now that the EC was a more capable actor (Frellesen 2001). The EC had extensively engaged in dialogue through bilateral cooperation, commercial and/or free trade relations with a number of third countries (see Box 2.1). The re-unification of Germany was a clear signal to the US that the EU could stand as a 'pole of attraction' for Central and Eastern Europe, thereby promoting democracy and economic liberalisation in the region (TPN 1995: 4). The US also welcomed the prospects of burden sharing due to constraints on its foreign affairs budget, which increasingly made it a 'superpower on the cheap' (Peterson 1996, Heuser 1996). A month after the fall of the Berlin wall in 1989, Bush's Secretary of State, James Baker, made a memorable speech in Berlin outlining plans for a policy of 'New Atlanticism' to compliment Bush's 'New World Order' (see Box 2.2).

The concept of closer transatlantic cooperation was clearly supported by the President of the European Commission, Jacques Delors, who wished to see Europe's political links – and the status of the Commission – upgraded in Washington.[17] The Irish Presidency of the EU's Council of Ministers also displayed great interest in closer transatlantic ties, with the Irish Prime Minister, Charles Haughey, engaging in negotiations with President Bush on a structure for consultation, which was later incorporated into the TAD (Devuyst 1990; Peterson 1996).

To summarise, there was widespread recognition in the early 1990s that better mechanisms were needed to manage a relationship characterised by complex interdependence (see Featherstone and Ginsberg 1996). A number of factors helped create a favourable atmosphere for the launch of a new phase in transatlantic relations in the 1990s: the political will expressed by European and American leaders; the realisation of common interest in securing the multilateral trading system; and the need to tackle the security threat posed by instability in Central and Eastern Europe.

Box 2.1 A history of EC trade agreements 1975–95

1975
The Lomé Convention (including 65 African, Caribbean and Pacific countries), Israel, Mexico, Sri Lanka

1976
China, Algeria, Morocco and Tunisia (the Magherb countries), Pakistan, Canada

1977
Egypt, Jordan and Syria (the Mashreq countries), Lebanon

1980
ASEAN countries (Agreement of South East Asian Nations), Yugoslavia, Australia, Brazil

1981
India

1983
Bolivia, Colombia, Ecuador, Peru and Venezuela (the ADEAN Pact countries)

1984
Yemen

1988
Central and Eastern European countries

1990
The United States*

* In contrast to the other agreements pursued by the Commission, the TAD was not strictly a trade agreement.

The Transatlantic Declaration, and its emphasis on bilateral consultation, marked the beginning of the institutionalisation of the EU–US relationship. Signed on 23 November 1990, the TAD is a short document that identifies common goals and transnational challenges. The partners recognised common interest in pursuing economic liberalisation, educational, scientific and cultural cooperation and in fighting international crime, terrorism and environmental degradation. While it briefly identified goals and 'principles' of this partnership, it failed to provide even a proposed agenda for meeting those goals. Its significance lies not in its content, which has been described as cosmetic (Featherstone and Ginsberg 1996), superficial (TPN 1999), 'minimalist' (Peterson 1996) and lacking in substantive innovations (Devuyst 1990). Rather, the TAD served two important functions. First, it symbolically restored a mutual political commitment to transatlantic partnership. Secondly, it introduced an institutional structure to the transatlantic dialogue.

Box 2.2 Main recommendations of James Baker's 'New Atlanticism' speech (1989)

- foster institutional and consultative links that would keep pace with European integration and institutional reform;
- create regular and intensive bilateral consultations to contain trade disputes;
- initiate consultation between EPC working groups and the US;
- conduct more formal consultation on the environment;
- secure greater US input on the discussion of common European technical standards;
- instigate closer bilateral cooperation on the distribution of aid in East European economies.

An infrastructure of co-operation

The political commitments outlined by the TAD were not 'new' ones. They had long been a part of western diplomatic jargon. However, its institutional framework for consultation was a distinguishing factor. It outlined a bilateral structure of cooperation for transatlantic relations, and gave birth to a number of transatlantic 'institutions'. In effect the TAD formalised three sets of bilateral meetings between different levels of policy makers (see Box 2.3).[18] It was assumed that this framework for consultation would open lines of communication, create networks, result in information sharing and hopefully reduce the impact of disputes in transatlantic relations.

Box 2.3 The institutional framework created by the Transatlantic Declaration

Formal structure
President of the European Council ↔ President of the United States
EC Foreign Ministers ↔ US Secretary of State
EC Commission ↔ US Cabinet (later sub-cabinet)

Ad hoc dialogue
US Under-secretary of State ↔ Presidency Foreign Minister (Troika)

Briefings on European political cooperation
Council Presidency ↔ US Representatives

The TAD was the first step in the creation of a political framework specifically geared for EC–US relations. Many have argued that it set the foundation for closer transatlantic relations and that it symbolised a 'new' era in transatlantic relations (see Gardner 1997; Smith 1997: 20 and Smith and Woolcock 1993: 111). However the shortcomings of this agreement were clearly visible. In addition to lacking substance, the mechanisms it introduced were ineffective. Summits tended to be isolated events that did not build on one another and showed no clear line of progress, not least due to the rotating EU Council Presidency and the changing priorities of different member states.[19] The bilateral cabinet meetings were abandoned in 1991, because they were found to be redundant of multilateral meetings. The consultations that did take place tended to take the form of briefings rather than exchanges of dialogue (Gardner 1997: 11–13).

Limited commitment or capability?

Ultimately it can be argued that the TAD was undermined by the underdevelopment of the Community's first pillar and the member states. Although the concept of a European 'Common Foreign and Security Policy' had been introduced prior to 1990, the mechanisms for CFSP were not negotiated until the Maastricht Treaty was signed in 1991, and even then pillar two's intergovernmental structure did not produce a unified European voice on foreign policy issues. Member states and the European Commission turned their attention towards pillar one issues, most notably the internal negotiations on a draft treaty for EMU and the necessary directives for a unified common market (Featherstone and Ginsberg 1996: 32). The decision to sign the TAD but not to follow up on its pledges increased US perceptions of the EU's 'capabilities–expectation gap'.

Some member states, led by France, showed a blatant lack of interest in a new transatlantic commitment. Given the EC's new status as a foreign policy actor, there was apprehension about being overshadowed by the US (Featherstone and Ginsberg 1996: 32). One Commission official argued that, '[The EC] wanted to make sure that it kept its own identity. There was no interest in looking for partners at the political level and no interest in what was being done by others'.[20]

Despite its shortcomings, the TAD's architects acknowledged its role as a starting point, as they encouraged the addition of further 'building blocks' to its foundation.[21] In 1994 transatlantic leaders on both sides were already discussing propositions to build on the TAD, and three expert working groups were set up at the Berlin EU–US Summit to identify political areas where co-operation could be pursued (see Table 2.1). A group on international crime, which was strongly supported by Germany, the US and the European Commission, considered how EU–US cooperation could combat problems of drug trafficking, nuclear smuggling and money laundering in light of growing black markets in the former USSR.[22] The CFSP group, pushed by the US State Department, sought ways to improve consultation and burden sharing with the EU on potential geopolitical hot spots. Finally, the group on Central and Eastern Europe assessed the capacity of the EU and the US to work together in promoting economic and political reform in CEE (Gardner 1997: 57–8).

Table 2.1 The Berlin working groups

Working group	*Task*
International crime	Study the potential for EU–US cooperation on drug trafficking, nuclear smuggling and money laundering.
Common Foreign and Security Policy	Detect ways that the EU and the US could react to the outbreak of hostilities and coordinate humanitarian assistance to troubled areas, particularly in the Third World.
Central and Eastern Europe	Assess the capacity of the EU and the US to encourage political and economic reform through coordinated foreign aid and technical assistance.

The results were mostly disappointing. The working group on international crime immediately met with suspicion by EU member states that feared it was an attempt by the Commission to exercise control over JHA. The CFSP working group was unable to agree on a mechanism for consultation, thus exposing the weaknesses of the second as well as the third pillar. The working group on Central and Eastern Europe was able to identify areas of potential cooperation but backed down from making substantive proposals due mainly to internal EU divisions over the role to be played by Commission (Gardner 1997: 57–9). Although the working groups were set up as a temporary mechanism, their failure to agree on concrete proposals exposed weaknesses in the dialogue structure and helped leaders recognise the need to tie together loose ends (Frellesen 2001; Gardner 1997: 60). The consensus was that a stronger political commitment to a transatlantic partnership was needed.

The New Transatlantic Agenda

If the TAD was the groundbreaking move to create a structured dialogue, the New Transatlantic Agenda (NTA) can be described as the cornerstone of this transatlantic architecture. The NTA gave new structure, focus and drive to transatlantic relations. It introduced new mechanisms for monitoring progress and implementing change, and produced a dedicated agenda, thereby adding substance to the transatlantic relationship.

A widening gap

The NTA arose amidst calls for the further development of transatlantic relations. It was widely accepted that the TAD had failed to revolutionise the relationship, and that its limited institutional framework was unable to contain new emerging tensions. The widening gap between the EU and the US was inflamed by the obvious lack of transatlantic unity in the Gulf War and Bosnia, both of which resulted in bilateral (involving the US and individual EU member states) but not transatlantic political and military actions (Peterson 1996: 67–73).[23] Old as well as new baggage interfered with attempts to close the Uruguay Round. Disputes over agriculture subsidies, beef, bananas, oilseeds, canned fruit and Airbus meant that there was constant talk in the early 1990's of looming trade wars.[24]

The war in Bosnia was particularly damaging for Europe, because the failure to come to a common position exposed the weakness of the CFSP. The lack of European cohesion also spilled over into monetary and trade policy. The Maastricht Treaty was not ratified on the first attempt in Denmark and was controversial in other European countries. European monetary coordination was stalled by serious recession in European economies. France refused to sign the Blair-House agreement after the Commission negotiated a deal on agriculture subsidies with the US to facilitate closure of the Uruguay Round. One Commission advisor recalled, 'This was not a good time in EU–US relations. [Blair-House] created a very bad atmosphere'.[25]

The 1992 US Presidential election also exposed a shift in the focus of American politics. Clinton's domestically focused campaign,[26] the lack of European experts in the Cabinet and the White House's failure to deal with the EU on an equal basis were seen as discouraging signs for the relationship.[27] The capacity of the US to act decisively on the international stage was diminished further when the 1994 US Congressional election returned a Republican majority in both Houses of Congress, thus introducing institutional rivalry fuelled by party politics into US foreign policy (see also Heuser 1996: 77). Fears arose in Europe once again of a shift to isolationism in US foreign policy (see also Peterson 2001a).

The scope of the NTA

Domestic opposition on both sides to the idea of a comprehensive political or economic agreement discouraged the US Administration and the European Commission from pursuing ambitious proposals, including one for a Transatlantic Free Trade Area (TAFTA), in 1994–95.[28] Still, important actors on both sides acknowledged the need to at least reinvest in a more effective transatlantic relationship. Perhaps surprisingly, given initial doubts about his commitment, Clinton himself emerged as an advocate of a transatlantic partnership. He generally engaged with European issues and was able to develop a personal rapport with Delors that had not existed with Bush (Gardner 1997: 6; Lundestad 1998: 117). Stuart Eizenstat, then Ambassador of the US Mission to the EU in Brussels, pushed both sides relentlessly to sign the NTA. On the EU's side, the Spanish Council Presidency of late 1995 injected new enthusiasm into the process of negotiating the NTA.[29]

The New Transatlantic Agenda was signed at the EU–US Summit in Madrid in December 1995. It was a six-page document that recognised the need to strengthen the transatlantic partnership in light of new challenges. As depicted in figure 2.1, the NTA created a common agenda or framework for cooperation under four chapters. The adjoining Joint Action Plan (JAP) outlined specific areas where the partners could pursue deeper cooperation and identified priorities. The New Transatlantic Agenda had a significant impact on the process of transatlantic institutionalisation because it created new scope for policy coordination and new institutions to administer the policy-making process. The individual chapters of the NTA established policy sectors and issue areas where the EU and US aimed to cooperate and produce 'deliverables', in the form of joint agreements, statements and initiatives.

Figure 2.1 The four chapters of the NTA

Promoting peace, stability, development, democracy around the world	Responding to global challenges	Contributing to the expansion of world trade and promoting closer economic relations	Building bridges across the Atlantic

Since 1995 the EU and the US have issued a number of joint statements on cooperation (see Table 2.2). However, the capacity of the EU and US to act has been more limited. Phillipart and Winand (2001: 452) argue, for example, that projects in Africa were restricted to areas of low politics, such as health care and democracy building, and that at its core the 'global partnership' is really restricted to European regional issues. On the other hand development cooperation and humanitarian assistance are cited as two of the most successful policy sectors of the NTA.

The EU and the US were also able to pursue a number of low key projects under the global challenges chapter of the NTA, which like the first chapter, was pre-empted by the Masstricht Treaty and the creation of the EU Justice and Home Affairs Pillar. The scope for global challenges cooperation under the NTA is broad if not deep. Many initiatives, statements and declarations have arisen out of the chapter, however the concrete rewards of individual projects are often limited. Nonetheless, the partners have cooperated in creating the international law enforcement centre in Budapest, the Italian Judiciary Training Centre, the anti-trafficking in women information campaigns in

CEE (see Chapter 5) and regional environmental and energy projects in Russia, Ukraine and Modlova. Efforts to fight drug trafficking included the Caribbean Drugs Initiative and the Precursor Chemicals Agreement. A major setback, however, was the incapacity to address environmental challenges and to reach an agreement over the Kyoto Protocol.

The economic chapter of the NTA was arguably the most ambitious and where the most concrete results have been produced. Under the NTA the EU and the US signed agreements to remove non-tariff barriers to trade in the form of certification and testing requirements through the Mutual Recognition Agreements (1998) (see also Chapter 6) and the Veterinary Equivalence Agreement (1999), of competition rules through the Positive Comity Agreement (1998), of customs requirements in the Customs and Co-operation Agreement (1996) and on data protection through the Safe Harbour Agreement (2000).[30] They made headway at the multilateral level through the TRIP agreements and the Information Technology Agreements. Economic co-operation was also re-enforced through the Transatlantic Economic Partnership (1998).

Finally, the fourth chapter of the NTA focuses on 'building bridges' across the Atlantic aimed to broaden science and technology cooperation, people to people links across the Atlantic, information exchanges and culture and parliamentary links (NTA 1995; JAP 1995). Under the 'building bridges' chapter the EU and the US have fostered cooperation between scientists (through the Science and Technology Agreement, 1997),[31] and educators (through the Higher Education Agreement, 1998). The main achievement of the chapter however, has been the creation of interest group 'dialogues' such as the TACD, TAED and TALD to rival the Transatlantic Business Dialogue (see Chapter 4) and the strengthening of parliamentary ties through the Transatlantic Legislators Dialogue (TLD) (see Chapter 3).

A qualified success

The underlying purpose of the NTA is to generally fortify the transatlantic partnership and specifically re-enforce commitments to shared interests in promoting economic liberalisation, increased 'soft' security and the spread of democracy. Three factors serve as indicators of the success of the NTA: the proficiency for conflict resolution, the reach of bilateral policy coordination and the build up of institutions.

First, the failure of the EU and the US to resolve or 'manage' transatlantic trade disputes within the NTA framework is widely believed to be its downside. The NTA specifically re-emphasises the need to resolve bilateral trade disputes and to reinforce the WTO dispute settlement mechanism. Despite attempts to create an 'Early Warning System' (see Chapter 3) that could effectively curb differences before they become disputes, coverage of the EU–US relationship in the 1990s was overshadowed by talk of transatlantic trade

Table 2.2 Examples of NTA deliverables

NTA chapter	*Statements, Declarations, Agreements*
I	Joint Statement on South East Europe (2000) Joint Statement on Northern Europe (1999) Joint Statement on Chechnya (1999) Declaration on the Middle East Peace Process (1998) Joint Statement on Co-operation in the Western Balkans (1998)
II	Energy Research Co-operation Agreement (2001) Statement on Communicable Diseases in Africa (2000) EU–US Biotechnology Consultative Forum (2000) Declaration on the Responsibilities of States on Transparency Regarding Arms Exports (2000) Joint Statement on Common Principles on Small Arms and Light Weapons (1999) Statement on EU–US Shared Objectives and Close Co-operation on Counter-Terrorism (1998) Declaration on Common Orientation of Non-Proliferation Policy (1998) Statement on Caspian Energy Issues (1998) Precursors Chemical Agreement (1997) Joint Initiative on Trafficking in Women (1997) Caribbean Drugs Initiative (1996) Regional Environmental Centers, Ukraine, Russia (1995)
III	Safe Harbour Agreement (2000) The Veterinary Equivalency Agreement (1999) The Positive Comity Agreement (1998) Statement on Co-operation in the Global Economy (1998) The Mutual Recognition Agreement (1997) Customs and Co-operation Agreement (1996)
IV	Statement on Building Consumer Confidence in e-Commerce and the Role of Alternative Dispute Resolution (2000) Statement on Transparency and the New Transatlantic Agenda Dialogues (1999) Science and Technology Agreement (1998) Higher Education and Training Agreement (1997) TALD (1998), TAED (1998); TACD (1998); TABD (1995)

wars on bananas (Chapter 7), beef (see Skogstad 2002), GMOs (see Young 2001), Foreign Sales Corporations (FSCs) (see Stehmann 2000) and hush kits (see Peterson 2001a). The EU and the US were accused of failing to manage potential trade wars and of undermining the multilateral trading rules.

On the other hand, one has to question whether these trade disputes really threatened to sever ties between the EU and the US? The general consensus is that while cooperation and conflict in transatlantic relations are inseparable, disputes have not undermined the overall effectiveness of the NTA. One US official even argued that the disputes have had little impact on the NTA.[32] European officials maintain the importance of minding the discrepancy between first, the scope of disputes vis-à-vis cooperation and second, of media coverage for dispute vis-à-vis the NTA agreements.[33] A Commission (2001: 6–7) report states that,

> At most, 1–2% of the trade and investment flow is affected. Such questions, however, tend to attract media attention far beyond their economic importance. As a result, trade irritants are sometimes blamed for casting a shadow over other aspects of the relationship between the European Union and the United States. In reality there is little risk of negative spill-over from individual disputes into the overall political relationship which is broader and deeper than ever before.

It could be argued that the NTA mechanisms provide for useful information exchanges on technical disputes, for example through the Biotechnology Consultative Forum.[34] The NTA process has, however, been less successful in resolving bigger disputes – such as bananas and beef – where EU and US domestic interests directly collide. A Council official argued, 'where there are disputes, our hands are usually tied at a political level'.[35] The key is in the capacity of transatlantic institutions to manage disputes in the 'amicable' fashion outlined by the NTA. President Prodi acknowledged that this was one area where more work was needed when he admitted after the June 2000 EU–US Summit that, 'We decided that megaphone diplomacy would be replaced by telephone diplomacy'.[36]

The second measurement of the NTA's success centres on the substance of the transatlantic dialogue. Philippart and Winand (2001: 50) argue that the NTA creates a global adjustable framework for action and widens the scope of the relationship. As one of the main purposes of the NTA is to seek out issue areas where EU–US cooperation is feasible, policy output is an important measure of the NTA. The result, as noted in Box 2.4, is a mixture of joint agreements, statements and declarations. The quality of 'deliverables' has however been criticised first, because joint action is limited in comparison to joint consultation.[37] Donfried (1996: 8) indicates for example that, 'Even some officials have criticised the plan as a glorified laundry list that is long on rhetoric and short on substance. The two sides agree on many principles and general goals but few specific initiatives are outlined.' Second, an argument can be made that the NTA deliverables are fairly insignificant given that many of them were already being discussed in other policy-making forums. For example, the Positive Comity Agreement builds on a previous competition agreement signed in 1991, and the MRAs were under discussion as early as 1992. One Council official argued that the SLG simply hijacked the success of individual departments.[38] Pollack and Shaffer (2001) describe, 'a repackaging of existing bilateral initiatives'. Thus, it can be argued that the NTA warrants claims that it is both broad and boring.

Policy output is, on its own, an inadequate measure of the scope of the NTA. Officials argue that an overemphasis is placed on deliverables. Some argue that the document was specifically designed to be non-controversial in light of domestic opposition to a more comprehensive treaty.[39] Peterson (1996: 16) argues that, 'it [NTA] reflected a conscious effort by administrations on both sides – particularly the American – to find and exploit as many productive areas of co-operation as possible without attracting wider attention'. The NTA does not replace the need for communication through existing multilateral institutions such as the North Atlantic Treaty Organization (NATO), the Organization for Security and Cooperation in Europe (OSCE), the G–7 (8) and the WTO. On the other hand it sought to establish a common threshold of cooperation between the EU and the US in a range of policy sectors. Negotiating between bureaucrats, rather than legislators, increases the threshold for co-operation particularly on 'technical' policies as it de-politicises the process.

Finally, the institutionalisation of the structure is arguably the most visible and most significant change brought by the NTA (see also Chapter 3). To facilitate policy output under the framework for cooperation, the NTA also introduced new transgovernmental institutions to manage the new transatlantic dialogue and to seek out deliverables. Two main mechanisms – the Senior Level Group (SLG) and the NTA Task Force – were created to help drive, coordinate, organise, monitor and implement the agenda for EU–US summits (see Chapter 3). These mechanisms have a role in 'bringing everyone to the table' and establishing dialogue through regular contacts.

Just how important is transatlantic dialogue through these new institutional arrangements? A US official argued that one benefit of increased information exchanges is that it brings more wisdom to negotiations.[40] A Commission official added that understanding one another's policies and preferences was a pre-requisite to acting on them.[41] Finally, one Commission official conceded that the NTA process served to manage the 'day to day' relations between the EU and the US suggesting that, 'Closer contact and more consultation slowly breeds broader understanding.'[42]

Overall, it can be argued that the NTA symbolised a renewed commitment to the EU–US partnership (see also Philippart and Winand 2001: 50). The new mechanisms in the NTA represented a shift from joint consultation to joint or parallel action. The NTA–JAP framework identifies areas of collaboration and sets an agenda for further increased transatlantic cooperation. The new institutional mechanisms give more direction to the policy process and make the EU–US summits more useful mechanisms. As a whole, the NTA placed a renewed focus on transatlantic relations and increased the prospects for cooperation by creating an ever-increasing drive for deliverables. In short, the NTA gives the relationship more shape and direction.[43]

The Transatlantic Economic Partnership

There was a push to facilitate closer cooperation in the economic chapter of the NTA, after the six-month report card (May 1996) revealed that Madrid's expectations had not been met in a number of areas, particularly in the attempt to build the New Transatlantic Marketplace.[44] The lack of concrete deliverables prompted claims that the NTA had run out of steam. However, those working within the NTA process acknowledged the merit of further institutionalisation. Agreements, particularly in the economic sector, helped build confidence between EU and US negotiators and the corporations participating in the TABD. Finally, the continued disputes over bananas, beef and extraterritorial sanctions reaffirmed the need for further transatlantic commitment as a means of facilitating trade and containing conflict.

Debates raged on throughout 1997 and 1998 over how to deepen the transatlantic economic commitment.[45] On 11 March 1998 the European Commission approved Sir Leon Brittan's proposal for a comprehensive trade treaty, the New Transatlantic Marketplace Agreement (NTMA).[46] The NTMA plan proposed a comprehensive agreement that would remove non-tariff barriers to trade across the Atlantic; commit the EU and the US to eliminate industrial tariffs through multilateral negotiations by the year 2010; establish a free trade area in services; and lead to further bilateral liberalisation in areas such as government procurement investment and intellectual property. Sir Leon argued that the NTMA agreement was an opportunity to adapt and apply the lessons learned from the Single European Market (SEM) to the EU–US process of economic liberalisation. However, while the EU and the US had incentive to pursue further institutionalisation, there was domestic opposition in both the EU and the US to anything that resembled either a free trade area or an attempt by the Commission to take control of external negotiations.

A decision taken by the EU General Affairs Council, one month before the London Summit, ensured that the Commission's NTMA proposal never made it on to the summit agenda. The member states, led mainly by France, argued that:

- strengthening bilateral (rather than multilateral) market opening, particularly through the use of a transatlantic dispute settlement mechanism, undermined the WTO;
- the agreement was not feasible in light of the ongoing extraterritorial Helms–Burton dispute surrounding the US Helms–Burton law;
- the agreement would carry negative implications for EC audio-visual services and agriculture policies;
- the Commission did not have a mandate to negotiate the agreement.

The French rejection of the proposal was troublesome for a Commissioner so intent on equalising the credibility of the EU as a partner for the US. Sir Leon had earlier claimed, 'It is inevitable that we should now face the United States as an increasingly equal partner, sharing world leadership more and more as we develop still our own capacity to act together in a united and effective way'.[49] Instead, the Commissioner's attempts to prove that the EU could take a leading role in transatlantic relations backfired, and his worst fears about the action capacity gap of the Union were brought to the surface by internal bickering.[50]

Figure 2.2 The three prongs of the TEP

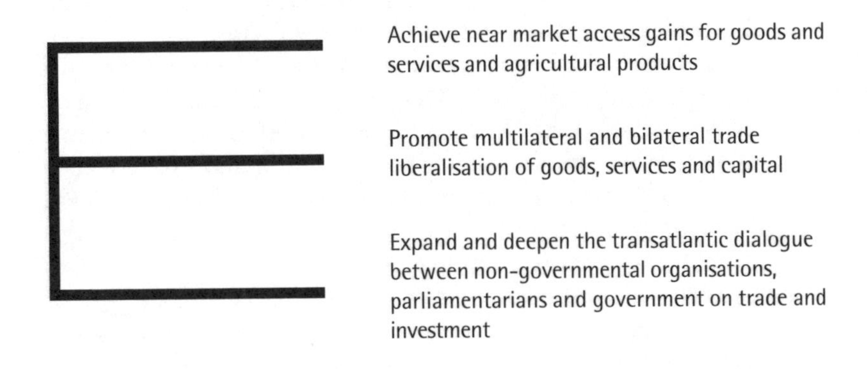

The new economic partnership

The conflicting pressure (mainly from the Americans) to secure some type of economic agreement at the 1998 London Summit, coupled by the lack of domestic support for a comprehensive treaty saw the launch of another compromise, the Transatlantic Economic Partnership (TEP). The TEP ensured that neither party went away empty handed from the summit, and it maintained many of the goals of the New Transatlantic Marketplace while avoiding the political controversy associated with Sir Brittan's proposal.

The TEP aimed to tackle bilateral regulatory barriers to trade and to find common positions for the Seattle Round of the WTO. It set the goal of reducing barriers to billions of dollars of trade through a three-pronged market opening approach (see Figure 2.2). The year 2000 was set, somewhat over-ambitiously, for substantive developments in a number of specific sectors (see Box 2.4). Finally, the TEP looked to the expansion and deepening of the transatlantic dialogue between non-governmental organisations, parliamentarians and government officials on trade and investment issues (US Mission 1998). In this sense the agreement complimented the market-opening objective with a 'commitment to the highest labour, health and environmental standards' (Pickering 1998: 4).

The TEP was followed in September 1998 by the TEP Action Plan, which like the NTA Joint Action Plan sets a more specific agenda but also includes target dates for actionable goals. Building on the success of MRA's, the TEP Action Plan highlighted the need for mutual recognition agreements in services, particularly in intellectual property, food safety and biotechnology. It also contained sections on regulatory cooperation and harmonisation of standards to facilitate the removal of technical barriers to trade.

In addition, the TEP Action Plan added to the transatlantic institutional structure by creating the TEP Steering Group, a construct which is similar to the NTA Task Force but which deals only with economic issues. The TEP Steering Group was charged with monitoring, implementing and reviewing TEP objectives, providing a 'horizontal' forum for transatlantic civil society and a mechanism for early warning on potential trade disputes. It also established specialised TEP working groups at the expert level (see Chapter 3).

The TEP represented another compromise in the transatlantic partnership building. It was announced parallel to the Transatlantic Partnership on Political Co-operation (TPPC) agreement, which represented a commitment to intensify consultations for more effective political cooperation and established a new set of principles for applying economic sanctions. Specifically the TPPC secured a US commitment to end extra-territorial sanctions against EU companies. In an act of 'creative conflict management', EU–US leaders managed to put aside their long-standing disputes over the US extraterritorial legislation and secondary boycott provisions of the Iran–Libya Sanctions Act (ILSA) and the Helms–Burton Act in order to gain the member states' approval for the TEP (Krenzler and Wiegand 1999: 14).[51] Under the TPPC the US maintained the right to use sanctions when diplomatic and political options failed and the EU agreed that maximum effort be taken to ensure that economic sanctions remained multilateral rather than unilateral. Consultation at senior levels was stressed as a prerequisite to imposing sanctions and a number of guidelines were set out to govern situations warranting action by the EU and the US.

In return for the US compromise on Helms–Burton, the EU also made further political commitments on JHA cooperation, an area that the US was eager to pursue further. Statements on non-proliferation and counter-terrorism led to some joint efforts in Iran, but the majority of the language used only uttered vague commitments to pursue cooperation in other regions. There are still glaring foreign policy gaps in transatlantic relations, which surfaced most obviously during the crisis in Kosovo.

What good is the TEP?

The troubled TEP negotiations revealed something about its content and its implementation. The TEP was criticised for its substance, particularly by Europeans who had favoured a more comprehensive agreement. It was argued that the TEP was 'not overly ambitious',[52] that the agreement was the 'result of bad political thinking'[53] and that 'it would never work properly'.[54]

First, the TEP was scrutinised for failing to manage trade disputes, in particular the banana and beef disputes which overshadowed the December 1998 EU–US Summit (see also Chapter 7). Unlike the NTMA, however, the TEP did not contain a dispute settlement mechanism, rather it committed both parties to jointly approach the WTO Dispute Settlement review in order to increase the transparency and functioning of the panel (TEP Action Plan 1998). Second, the TEP was perceived as a forum for reaching EU–US consensus before the Seattle Round. Frost (1998: 3) argued that, 'The failure of the Brittan initiative may have cleared the way for more focused thinking about global trade liberalisation in the WTO', but here too the TEP failed as the lack of EU–US consensus in Seattle contributed to the demise of the Round. Finally, the TEP was opposed by NGOs who feared the lack of transparency in the decision-making process. The controversy surrounding the content of the TEP led the transatlantic decision makers to promote two new 'civil society' dialogues – the TAED and the TACD – in conjunction with the trade agreement under both the NTA's fourth chapter and the TEP's third prong.

Faith in the TEP was undermined further in the first years of its implementation. In 1999 it appeared that the TEP had either stalled or died.[55] The TEP demonstrated that the EU and the US were still grappling with different visions of the transatlantic partnership. Americans argued that the Europeans were ambivalent to the TEP because they thought the agenda should be more ambitious. One USTR official argued, 'It is hard to succeed when they load it with topics that are not going anywhere!'

On the other hand Europeans argued that the Americans were unable to deliver particularly in the services sector.[56] MRAs negotiations were held up by the US because individual states, rather than any centralised body, had control over services certification and the US Administration was unable or unwilling to seek legislation from Congress to uphold the TEP (see also Chapter 7).[57] EU officials also argued that US officials were stalling in working groups.[58] A British MEP complained, 'The US cannot guarantee that every state will be on board. The reality is the opposite of the usual perception that the process is upheld by Community decision-making.'[59]

The limited scope of the TEP and the initial problems implementing it also pointed to a lack of political will in EU–US relations. At the time, it was argued that there was little interest in Brussels or Washington for new transatlantic initiatives (Frost 1998). The EU was preoccupied with enlargement and the launch of the euro. American politics were divided between the Republican Congress and Democrat Administration over the Clinton scandal, and both sides were preoccupied by the US election.

By the time President Bush took office in January 2001, it seemed the TEP was back on track. The TEP Steering Group was making regular reports to

Box 2.4 Sectors covered by the TEP

- improving science and regulatory cooperation
- reducing regulatory barriers
- lowering red tape costs to benefit consumers
- working to keep electronic commerce duty free
- advancing core labour standards
- developing common approaches to trade related environmental areas
- recognising the central role of intellectual property rights as a basis for economic, scientific and artistic creativity
- opening transatlantic economies to include a wider variety of interests

Source: TEP 1998.

the EU–US summits, and the progress on science and regulatory cooperation overshadowed the fact that no progress had been made on agriculture or audio-visual services. Negotiations for new MRAs in goods and in services were underway in 2001 (see also Chapter 6). The TEP process produced EU–US Guidelines/Principles on Co-operation and Transparency in Establishing Technical Regulations (2000), aimed at improving the transparency and effectiveness of planning and developing regulatory proposals. In addition, the EU–US Biotechnology Consultative Forum was established to head off an upcoming dispute over Genetically Modified Organisms (GMOs).

Conclusion

The underlying thesis of this chapter was that EU–US relations have changed in the 1990s as a result of three agreements; the TAD, the NTA and the TEP. These agreements ensured the institutionalisation of the transatlantic relationship on a more equal basis outside the confines of NATO. Each agreement added a 'block' to the transatlantic 'framework' by outlining principles and goals for cooperation and by establishing institutions to manage policy coordination.

Domestic opposition to an overarching transatlantic treaty ensured that the EU and the US strategy for cooperation focused on relatively 'safe' or 'soft' policy objectives. As a result the NTA process is often criticised on the basis that its deliverables are non-controversial.[60] However, the real weight behind the TAD, the NTA and the TEP is not only its 'deliverables'- which are an important part of 'focusing' the dialogue – but rather in its capacity to forge a formal dialogue structure. The agreements ensured the creation of networks which foster communication between political leaders, officials and business and civil society on both sides of the Atlantic. In theory, it is these 'institutions' that increase the threshold for cooperation. One Commission official argued, 'The logic of the NTA is similar to the thinking behind the EU. If we are constantly talking, it is less likely that we will be fighting.'[61]

The reality is that the institutionalisation of the relationship in the 1990s created a new forum for transatlantic policy-making. However, the TAD, the NTA and the TEP, as 'history making' agreements, only indicate a general direction for policy coordination rather than specific agreements. It is the transgovernmental and transnational institutions that are charged with 'setting' and 'shaping' transatlantic polices. The following chapters note that even where the political will exists at the top, the policy process is influenced from the bottom up.

Notes

1 The emphasis is on formal established decision-making networks rather than ad hoc contact between actors.
2 The term 'building-blocks' is embedded in jargon taken from a European Commission (1995) strategy paper (see also *Euracom* September 1995). It refers to the transatlantic strategy to secure closer relations and increase the scope for cooperation gradually through the incremental removal of specific obstacles to economic liberalisation and modest committal to political projects.
3 The international economic system, according to hegemonic stability theory, was able to develop into a liberal order because of the presence of American supremacy. See Ruggie (1998: 64); (Keohane 1984, 1989).
4 The US promoted European integration through the Marshall Plan, an aid package worth $12.4bn. The US supplied financial aid for recovery and redevelopment in Europe on the condition that decisions about allocating the funds be made jointly by European states (see Calvocoressi 1991; Duigan and Gann 1994: 34–60; Eichengreen 1995; Frellell 1996: 25–44; Hoffman and Maier 1984; Hogan 1984).
5 Variable levies continuously adjust prices to an equal level. These levies indirectly formed a trade barrier by creating uncertainty for US exporters who can never be sure of their costs of entry into the EEC market (Curtis and Vastine 1971: 21; see also Piening 1997: 106).
6 While the latter strongly favoured German unification, the American position recognised that a division between East and West Germany was crucial to maintaining stability in US–USSR relations. Henry Kissinger (1994: 577) reports in his memoirs that encounters with the West German Chancellor Konrad Adenauer, 'painfully served to bring home to me the extent of the distrust which the Berlin crisis had engendered between heretofore close allies'.
7 The TEA aimed to facilitate a more comprehensive agreement on the reduction of tariff barriers to trade. It created the position of Special Representative for Trade Negotiations, a cabinet level position designed to deal with US trade interests and it established the office of the USTR. The position gave US trade negotiators standing equal to that of their European equivalent and gave the President new tariff-cutting powers which Kennedy hoped to use in the GATT Round (Curtis and Vastine 1971: 9–14).
8 In 1966 the EEC signed a treaty merging the executives of the European communities, the result being one Commission and one Council but different rules governing both.

The name of the EEC also changed to the European Community (EC).

9 The US supported the Israeli government in the Israeli–Arab war, while European states chose not to follow suit in order to protect economic interests in the Middle East.

10 Stagflation is used to describe a combination of high inflation and high unemployment in an economy.

11 Tsoukalis (1986: 9) describes 'benign neglect' as the American failure to entertain European calls for international economic cooperation in light of the adverse reaction of European economies to US unilateral policies.

12 The EMS was a system of linked currencies often referred to as the 'snake'. This was an attempt to combat the disorder in European currencies brought on by the end of the fixed exchange rate system.

13 As discussed in Chapter 2, the concept of US hegemonic decline is controversial. Some observers downplay the fall of American power. In response to claims of America's declining hegemony Susan Strange (1982: 119) argued that, 'The US authorities make decisions that rock the markets and dislodge foreign governments, but none of these can deflect the dollar from its course.'

14 Some monetary cooperation did occur through the Plaza Agreement of 1985, whereby the G5 agreed to devalue the dollar, and the Louvre Accord of 1987, when the G7 which attempted to stabilise exchange rates (Smith 1984: 219).

15 The EC protested over the American ban on trade with the Soviet Union, and as a result the embargo was lifted after a few months (see Demaret 1986: 133–4; Tsoukalis 1986: 12–14).

16 One of the most widely quoted persons on this point is the former US Speaker of the House, Newt Gingrich. He claimed in 1995 that, 'we will drift apart unless we have projects large enough to hold us together ... We're not going to stay together out of nostalgia ...' (quoted in Gardner 1997: 62).

17 In contrast to its predecessors, Bush granted Delors head of state treatment when he visited Washington in June 1989 (Gardner 1997: 6).

18 Prior to the 1990s, ad hoc meetings were conducted between Troika political directors and US Under-secretaries and annual meetings between Troika political directors and the Assistant Secretary of State for European Affairs (Gardner 1997: 9).

19 Gardner (1997: 12) notes that although Presidencies such as the Dutch, Luxembourg and Spanish were positive for transatlantic relations, the French delayed or blocked every concrete initiative to improve US–EU consultations, 'because of a Gaullist hyper-sensitivity about Washington's *droit de regard* over European affairs'.

20 Interview with Commission official, Brussels, September 1999.

21 In particular the Declaration states, 'Both sides are resolved to develop and deepen these procedures for consultation so as to reflect the evolution of the European Community and its relationship with the United States' (Transatlantic Declaration 1990).

22 Germany favoured cooperation on international crime due to its close proximity to CEE and the Commission saw it as a means of getting JHA policy in through the back door (Gardner 1997: 56). US State Department and Commission officials argued that the push for JHA cooperation came from the US side since its introduction into the EU through Maastricht. (Interviews with US Embassy Official, Dublin July 1998; the European Commission, Brussels, September 1999, and the US Mission, Brussels, September 1999.)

23 This point is disputed by Piening (1997: 45) who claims that Gulf War was a truly international action due to the fact that EC backing was an essential precondition for

US-led military action. He notes, however, that a weak security dimension in European integration meant the EC's contribution was up to individual states rather than the Community.

24 Interview, Embassy official, US Embassy London, January 2000.

25 Interview, Commission official, Commission Secretariat, Brussels, September 1999.

26 Clinton's campaign slogan, 'It's the economy stupid!', seemed to emphasise the shift in focus from foreign policy to trade policy.

27 For example, when President Delors asked for a meeting with President Clinton to resolve the Blair-House dispute he was initially granted only 15 minutes (Smith and Woolcock 1993: 470).

28 Although the TAFTA was the subject of a Commission feasibility study and supported by the US Speaker of the House Newt Gingrich, German Foreign Minister Klaus Kinkel, and Commissioner Leon Brittan it was not pursued because it was feared that the TAFTA would not comply with international or domestic commitments. It was argued that the TAFTA ran the risk of alienating Asian economies and creating an exclusive 'rich men's club'; that it would have to have included difficult sectors such as agriculture and audio-visual services in order to comply with GATT rules; and that domestic opposition to a comprehensive treaty curbed the debate on the TAFTA. EU member states, most notably the French, feared 'Washington's insinuation into EU policy-making' (Gardner 1997: 55), while Congress opposed infringements on American sovereignty. Peterson (1996: 115) notes that during the Uruguay Round, 'Congressional Republicans, led by Senator Dole, voiced alarm about the threat posed to US sovereignty by the WTO, and initiated a debate which in some respects resembled Europe's struggle to ratify Maastricht'. For more on TAFTA see Frost (1997); Gardner (1997: 76–8); Heuser (1996: 82, 105–7), Hindley (1999).

29 The Spanish are credited with being very supportive of the NTA, in part perhaps because it was seen as 'deliverable' and a merit to their Presidency. Interview, Commission official, Brussels, September 1999.

30 Each of these agreements seek to increase trade through the removal of NTBs to trade. The Customs and Co-operation Agreement simplifies customs procedures making it easier to import and export products with the transatlantic marketplace (EU Press Office 1996: 1). The bilateral Positive Comity Agreement (1998) enhances cooperation between EU and US competition agencies. The Veterinary Equivalency Agreement (1999) applies the principle of mutual recognition to veterinary standards and increases exchange between the US Department of Agriculture and the EU Commission for Agriculture and Rural Development in order to increase the trade in animals through mutual recognition of standards. The Mutual Recognition agreements seek to eliminate duplicate testing standards to goods and services.

31 The Science and Technology Agreement (1997) draws on a number of actors as it seeks a means of cooperation (be that joint task forces, studies, conferences, training or information exchanges) in a number of areas where scientific standards form barriers to trade, for example in agriculture, fisheries, communication, intellectual property, and biotechnology policies.

32 Interview, USTR, by telephone, April 2001.

33 Interview, European Commission, DG Trade, Brussels, September 1999; Council Presidency Official, Brussels, September 1999, Commission Delegation to the US, Washington DC, October 2000.

34 Interview, US Congress Staff Member, Washington DC, October 2000.

35 Interview, Finnish Council Presidency, Brussels, September 1999.

36 *Financial Times* 'New Tact but EU–US Disputes Remain', 1 June 2000.
37 Interview, Commission Official, DG External Relations, Brussels, October 1999.
38 One Commission official notes in the case of competition policy, that many within the department preferred to remain separate from the NTA, fearing its broad agenda would undermine the department's specific agenda.
39 Interview, EU Commission Delegation, Washington DC, October 2000; US State Department, Washington DC, October 2000.
40 Interviews, Finnish Council Secretariat, US Mission and European Commission, September 1999.
41 Interview, European Commission Delegation to the US, Washington, DC, October 2000.
42 Interview, DG External Relations, Brussels, September 1999.
43 Argued by US Mission official, Brussels, September 1999.
44 Gardner (1997: 89) notes that while these reports were premature given the scale of commitments and timely process, they exposed shortcomings in the following areas; the testing and certification on telecommunications equipment, telecommunications terminal equipment, information technology, electrical safety, electro-magnetic compatibility, pleasure boats and veterinary biologicals, pharmaceuticals, telecommunications and international maritime transport.
45 Assistant Secretary of Economic Affairs, A. Larson, demanded a New Transatlantic Marketplace initiative that would secure open and honest markets and specifically liberalise the telecommunications, aviation and capital sectors (Larson 1997). US Secretary of Commerce, William Daley, spoke of joint efforts between the political and business communities to define the meaning of a barrier-free 'transatlantic marketplace', to establish realistic targets and to designate further steps in the process (Daley 1997). Grossman (1998) pragmatically identified the need for consultations with Congress, the private sector and non-governmental organisations in order to clarify an American position on the NTM initiative.
46 The initiative sights the advantages in a single comprehensive agreement, '... designed to use an economic instrument to give a much broader impetus to the overall political relationship; to produce important economic benefits and to provide a new mechanism and stronger incentives to prevent and resolve disputes' (European Commission 1998: 3–4). The aggressive nature of Brittan's proposal represented his longing to see the EU display leadership in the international system. Brittan himself cited the unanimous approval of the proposal in the Commission as evidence, 'that the European tiger is beginning to roar' (Brittan 1998).
47 Germany, the Netherlands, Italy and Spain also opposed the NTMA.
48 French President Chirac commented at a press conference shortly before the General Affairs Council's discussion that the NTMA represented 'a personal initiative by Sir Leon Brittan who all alone went off to negotiate a free trade area between the United States and Europe, without a mandate', adding, 'It is unacceptable for a Commissioner to negotiate without a specific mandate from the Council. This must be clearly stated so it does not happen again' (quoted in Sheil 1998: 4). One government source adds, 'The French felt like the whole thing was thrown in their face.' (Taken from an interview with a US official, July 1998. See also 'That Awkward Relationship' (1998: 1); Buckley (1998: 1).)
49 Quoted in *Eurocom*, May 1997, www.eurunion.org/news/eurecom/1997/ecom0597.htm.
50 Had the dispute made it onto the May 1998 Summit agenda, it would have been unlikely to pass US approval either. The initially positive American response to the

NTMA proposal soon turned lukewarm because Brittan's proposal failed to address agriculture. Interview, US Embassy, Dublin, July 1998.

51 The use of the word managed, not resolved, should be stressed here because the Helms–Burton Act was not actually repealed. That would have required an act of Congress. Krenzler and Wiegand (1999: 16) note, 'Of course nothing guarantees that Congress will refrain from passing such sanctions, thus ignoring the Administration's wishes in conducting US foreign policy'.

52 Interview, British MEP, September 1999 .

53 Interview, Commission official, September 1999.

54 Interview, Commission official, Washington, October 2000.

55 Interviews at the European Commission, Brussels, September 1999 and the Commission Delegation, Washington, October 2000.

56 Interviews, European Commission and European Parliament, Brussels, September 1999.

57 Interviews, European Commission, Brussels, September 1999; TABD, Brussels, October 1999.

58 Interviews at the Council Secretariat, the Commission and TABD officials, Brussels, September 1999.

59 Interview, MEP, September 1999.

60 The term 'NTA process' is used throughout the text to generalise about the transatlantic process, as it is the most comprehensive of the three agreements.

61 Interview, Commission Official, Brussels, May 2000.

3

The transatlantic policy process

The transatlantic mechanisms that accompanied the TAD, the NTA and the TEP were designed to foster cooperation and curb conflict in the transatlantic relationship. These institutions have altered the way the EU and the US interact. In contrast to the traditional style of international diplomacy that characterised the Cold War, there is now a 'political process' that surrounds EU–US decision-making. This process is designed to increase dialogue and information exchange, produce policy 'deliverables' and provide a forum for dispute settlement.

This chapter examines both the policy-making process and the actors who operate within it. It seeks to determine the extent to which the new institutions provide a forum for decentralised policy setting and shaping and questions what role transgovernmental actors, in particular, play in transatlantic policy-making. In other words, what room has the institutionalised EU–US structure, which was established through three intergovernmental decisions, allowed for other governmental actors to influence transatlantic policy formation? It argues that the scope for actor access is vast, given the complex nature of transatlantic decision-making structures.

This chapter begins by examining the intergovernmental EU–US summits, where transatlantic agreements are announced. The later sections evaluate earlier stages of the decision-making process. The second section explores both the political and economic policy processes. The third section evaluates the trade dispute settlement process established in part by the 'Early Warning System' (1999). The final section evaluates the impact of the transgovernmental policy process. It questions why the decentralisation of transgovernmental decision setting and shaping 'matters' in the context of transatlantic governance.

The EU–US summit

The EU–US summit, where the Presidents of the US, the Commission and the Council Presidency meet, is the primary forum for intergovernmental exchange in the NTA process.[1] As established under the TAD, these intergovernmental meetings were originally designed as stand alone events. However as the NTA process emerged, a number of ministerial level meetings held in conjunction with or in close proximity to the summits were also formalised. The preparation for summits became more complex with the creation of economic, as well as political institutions under the TEP. As a result EU–US summits developed into an event rather than a meeting whereby economic and foreign policy ministers, US Cabinet officials and EU Commissioners held separate, parallel talks, followed by a joint plenary session and finally, the actual summit meeting.[2]

The EU–US summit has two important functions. First, it is a forum for intergovernmental consultation. It brings together top 'political' officials and places topical or timely issues, including disputes, on the table for discussion. The summits are used to discuss means of coordinating diplomatic cooperation in hotspots such as Kosovo and the Middle East and for discussing strategic issues such as the European Security and Defence Policy (ESDP) and its relationship with NATO. The summit is also used to discuss pending disputes such as those over bananas, beef, steel and EU Airbus subsidies. The London Summit (1998) was, for instance, crucial to the settlement of the Helms–Burton dispute over US extraterritorial legislation.[3]

The second function of EU–US summits is to both initiate and assess policy output in issue areas incorporated under the NTA framework. The transatlantic policy process is a cycle of decision-making that begins and ends with the summit. It is where decisions are 'made' about the general scope for cooperation and where policy achievements or 'deliverables' are announced (see Figure 3.1). Deliverables are an important part of the process and a major goal of summit leaders, because they legitimise the process by producing concrete results.[4] The summits encourage foreign policy and economic policy co-ordination, because they create deadlines for progress reports and exert pressure on lower level officials to produce results.[5] EU and US officials use the summit to flag important issues for further development.[6] In short, as one Council official observed, 'The summits are a good way to see where we are.'[7]

EU and US officials generally describe the summit as a useful mechanism, at least rhetorically.[8] However, the enthusiasm for the event varies depending on domestic political arenas, the quality of potential deliverables and the enthusiasm of the EU Presidency. For example, Clinton was accused of being distracted during the December 1998 Summit when Congress was simultaneously voting on whether to impeach him over the Lewinsky affair.[9] Similarly the EU's attention to the summit waned during the Santer Commission scandal and there was no real interest on the US side in meeting Commissioners before the handover to Prodi.[10] The December 2000 Summit also served as more pleasantry than purpose, while the EU awaited the arrival of the new US Administration.

EU–US summits are one way to keep the EU Presidencies, and thus the European Council, engaged in the transatlantic dialogue because the host state actively prepares the summit.[11] EU Presidencies do tend to attach varied importance to the EU–US summit. For example the Irish, Dutch and British Presidencies were credited with successful summits because they had good channels of communication with the US. Small states also tend to use the summit to assert their role as international actors. For example the Finnish Presidency was able to put 'Northern' issues on the agenda of the December 1999 Summit.[12] Another US official argued that, 'Generally small member states have better presidencies. They recognise their limitations with resources, and prepare years in advance. The Finns are a great example. They are very good at organisation and set realistic agendas.'[13] Many critics downplay the importance of EU–US summits, claiming that they have become mere 'photo opportunities' rather than decision-making forums. Reporting on the May 1998 Summit in London, the *Economist* claimed that EU–US summits 'might normally be expected to produce a batch of dreary photo-calls and a heap of pointless platitudes'. EU foreign ministers have been accused of participating in the summits because, 'it is fun to be in a picture with the US President'.[14] Further scrutiny has come from NGOs who claim that EU–US summits are a place for 'PR statements' and 'parade shows'.[15] Many NGOs would agree that the EU–US summit is not a serious lobbying forum. One TAED official commented that, 'The summit is not a vehicle for getting things done, the agenda is too broad'.[16]

EU–US summits are also criticised for not producing substantial joint action. A limited number of themes are usually highlighted at the summits, and these issues receive only superficial attention at the intergovernmental level due to time constraints. Meetings usually end up being only two to three hours long, which is not enough time to work through the technical details of policies. Furthermore the frequency of summits is blamed for creating a 'treadmill' process whereby deliverables are recycled and resold.[17] One Commission Report of 2001 argued that, 'to make co-operation more action-orientated, EU–US summits need to become more focused and to define clear priorities. Efforts should concentrate on the most important challenges – strategic themes – facing the EU and the US today.' The point is, however, that EU–US summits alone cannot facilitate the number of goals established by the NTA. Many heads of state, and even those in ministerial positions, do not hold the expertise required to formulate technical policies, especially in the area of regulatory cooperation. While the summit is a focal point of the policy process, most contact takes place below the intergovernmental level.[18] One Commission official argued that the summit merely 'launches the practical arrangements' for seeking out specific policies.[19] In other words a decision by summit leaders to cooperate on an issue creates a sort of mandate for further collaboration.

EU–US decision-making must be considered in the broader context of the policy-making process. This process begins at a much lower level where junior officials play an important role. The remainder of this chapter will therefore examine different types of exchange where policy proposals are scrutinised and debated by different transgovernmental actors.

Figure 3.1 The NTA policy cycle

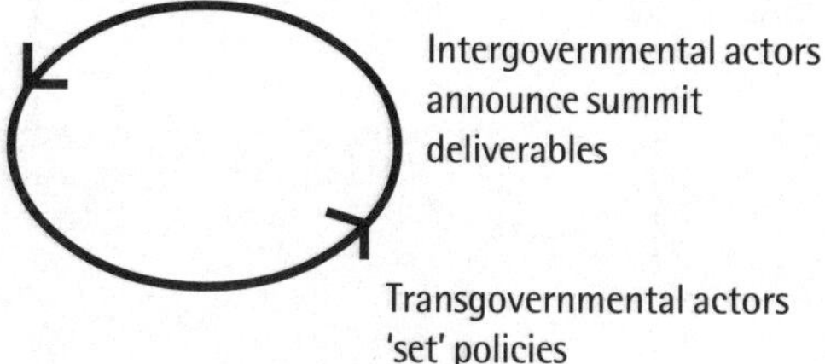

Political and economic decision 'taking'

While intergovernmental actors make decisions that indicate where transatlantic cooperation will be pursued, it is transgovernmental actors who decide how the EU and the US can cooperate through the decision-making processes. The 'plurality' of processes is stressed because the transatlantic decision-making process mirrors EU decision-making structures. The TAD, the NTA and the TEP have established three branches of governmental dialogue to accommodate the different competencies of EU external negotiators.

Generally, the idea is that specific policies for coordination within the reach of the NTA/TEP framework are 'fetched' from the bottom ranks of the transatlantic dialogue and are passed up through lower levels of consultation, finally making their way onto the agendas of EU–US summits. The economic ministerial dialogue, the foreign policy ministerial dialogue and the Senior Level Group form the head of three separate branches of dialogue (see Figure 3.2). This section explains these three transgovernmental processes and discusses how the TAD, NTA and TEP mechanisms have created a formal process for decision setting and shaping.

Figure 3.2 The structure of the Transatlantic Dialogue

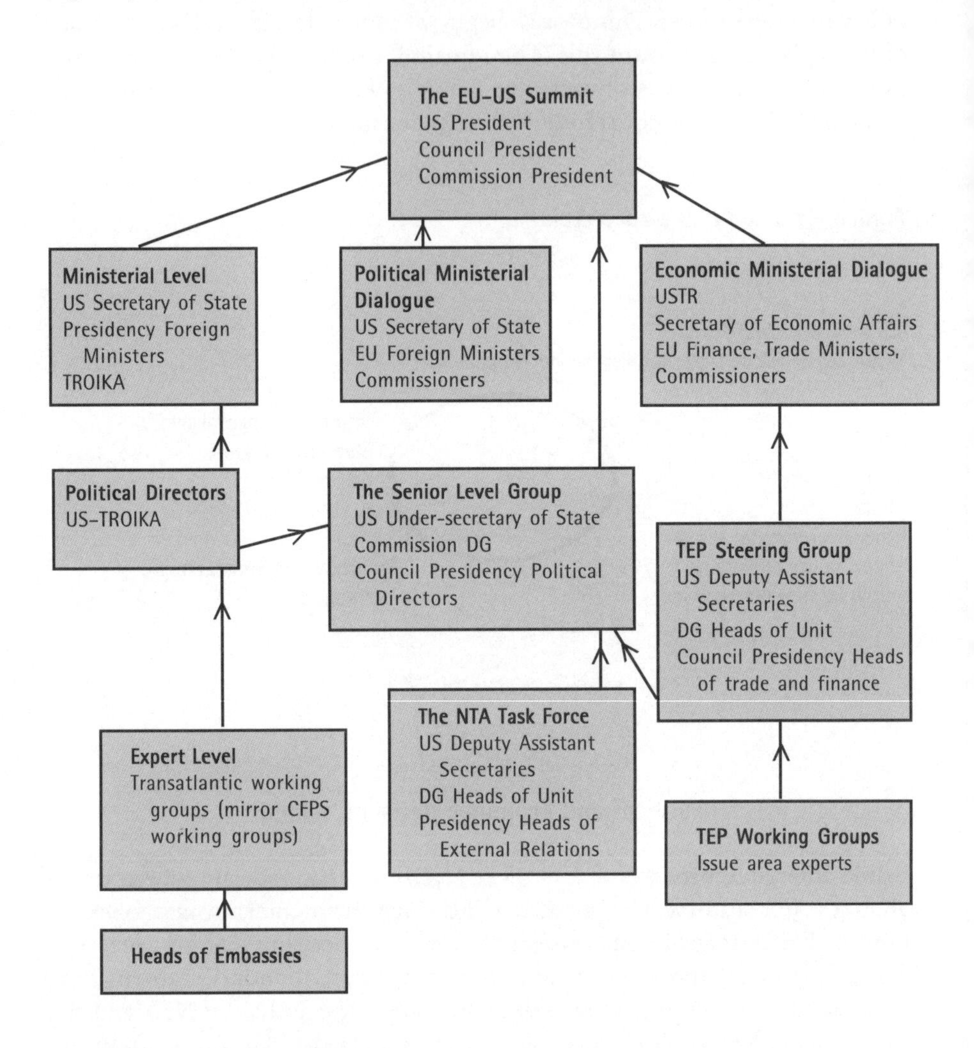

The political process

The political process refers to the process of dialogue built upon TAD mechanisms. It begins when the new Council Presidency assumes its role in the Council of Ministers, shortly after the previous EU summit and EU–US summit have concluded. Once the handover takes place the political dialogue is initiated in a meeting between EU and US foreign ministers and the EU Commissioner for External Relations. Events and circumstances may dictate further contact at the ministerial level (prior to the summit) either under this framework or through ad hoc Troika dialogues.[20]

A number of US–Troika dialogues were established after 1990 to support the foreign policy dialogue. In addition to the ministerial Troika dialogue, there is now interaction at the political director level and at working group level. These transatlantic working groups mirror the CFSP working groups in the Council and are significant because they are the only cross-pillar working groups.[21] These groups were established in 1995 as an extra level of expert exchange, and they deal with a range of issues outlined in Box 3.1.[22] Finally, the Troika dialogue is anchored by regular exchange between Heads of Mission and US Ambassadors.

Combined, these dialogues form the 'traditional' political dialogue (see also Frellesen 2001) and the first branch of EU–US cooperation. The traditional political dialogue is a unique process. The Troika dialogue reflects the complex structure of EU decision-making, and the foreign policy dialogue is particularly important because it covers issues that remain under the member states' control.

Box 3.1 The transatlantic working groups

- Law Enforcement Co-operation
- Middle East Experts
- United Nations
- Security
- OSCE
- Iran Trilateral
- Human Rights
- Turkey, Cyprus and Malta
- Consular Affairs
- Soviet/Newly Independent States
- Latin America
- Non-proliferation
- East and South Asia
- Conventional Arms Exports
- Terrorism
- Central Europe
- Western Balkans
- Africa
- Drugs
- Disarmament

The economic process

According to Article 133 of the EU treaties, the Commission has the competence to act on behalf of the Union in trade negotiations providing it works within the Council's mandate. However, the TEP addresses new areas of trade that fall into 'grey' areas, or areas of mixed competence in EU decision-making. There was thus the need to add new mechanisms to the transatlantic economic dialogue. The TEP Steering Group (SG) and the TEP working groups were established by the TEP Action Plan to study sectors for further liberalisation. These mechanisms form the economic branch of the transatlantic dialogue under the ministerial level dialogue.

The members of the TEP Steering Group hold a similar rank to participants in the NTA Task Force. The Steering Group consists of the US Deputy Assistant Secretary, the DG Heads of Unit for Trade and a Council Presidency Representative, usually the head of external relations for trade. It meets two or three times during the course of a Presidency and reports directly to the SLG. It can also filter into the economic ministerial dialogue through the structure of the independent agencies.

The TEP Steering Group deals with economic points in detail, and its purpose is to fulfil the goals of the TEP by fostering multilateral as well as bilateral trade. In that respect, the TEP Steering Group was originally designed to find compatible strategies for the WTO round, to identify areas where transatlantic services could be liberalised and to act as an 'early warning' system (see the third section) by identifying possible areas of conflict. It also fulfils the task of fostering EU–US economic cooperation and preventing conflict more generally. The Steering Group Report takes stock of EU–US economic relations and the progress in achieving TEP goals. The Steering Group is assisted by the TEP working groups which are sector specific and thus mirror the sectors laid out by TEP including agriculture, trade, services, global electronic commerce etc. These groups, like the transatlantic working groups, meet prior to the summits and their contacts increase as the cycle nears completion. Their main task is to find areas where the EU and the US can work together under the TEP framework and to report any progress or problems to the Steering Group.

The Senior Level Group

The NTA added new filter mechanisms to the transatlantic policy process. The level of exchange and the capacity to produce 'deliverables' was stepped up by these new mechanisms. The Senior Level Group (SLG) and the Task Force serve as the contacts between the economic and the political or Troika dialogues and as focal points of the process. They form the supporting branch of the transatlantic dialogue.

It is the job of the SLG to 'shop for deliverables', determine what should be on EU–US summit agendas and monitor the implementation of the NTA. Its purpose is therefore to help correct the problems that incurred under the TAD. In other words it is a force of focus and continuity in between EU–US summits, which aims to ensure that the summits do not become separate unrelated meetings.

The Senior Level Group has roughly six members. US representatives include Under-Secretaries for political and economic affairs in the State

Department, and the Commission delegates are drawn from the Directorates General for external relations and trade.[23] The Council Presidency has political and economic delegates that represent the member states, meaning SLG membership varies depending on the country holding office. Additionally representatives of the Article 133 committee, which deals with detailed trade issues, and foreign ministers may be present depending on the topics on the agenda.

The SLG meets twice before every summit. The first meeting sets the agenda and 'gets things moving'. The second is held closer to the summit date to finalise the agenda and confirm the contents of the SLG Report. The SLG report is a report card of EU–US progress that is compiled before the EU–US summit. In addition to scrutinising NTA progress, the report card has been employed as a means of drawing positive public attention to the NTA process in order to combat negative media coverage of trade disputes.[24] The SLG serves an administrative function by taking a broader number of issues, thirty or forty points, and slimming down the agenda prior to the summit. It identifies issue areas that are most likely to produce deliverables and slots these into the summit agenda.

The TEP Steering Group and the NTA Task Force aid the SLG in its quest for economic and political deliverables. The Task Force passes potential deliverables up through the NTA structure to the attention of the SLG. While the SLG is the link between both the political dialogue and the economic dialogue, the NTA Task Force is a fusion point between the traditional political dialogue and the NTA process. The NTA Task Force works closely with the transatlantic working groups in its search for possible deliverables. It may instruct the working groups to pursue cooperation in a particular sector or be alerted to progress by the working groups in advance. The Task Force then investigates and passes on details to the SLG.

In addition to seeking out deliverables, the Task Force deals with the day-to-day monitoring of transatlantic relations. It meets four or five times per presidency and communicates via additional videoconferences. Other expert meetings are also conducted, usually on an ad hoc basis depending on events, and individual working groups have been set up by the Task Force to investigate potential coordination of specific policies. For example there is a high level consultation on humanitarian aid and a Task Force on communicable diseases.[25]

Task Force meetings are much larger meetings than those conducted at SLG level, and the membership for these meetings is not formalised. Regular attendees include US Deputy Assistant Secretaries in the State Department, DG Heads of Unit and various Council Presidency representatives.[26] A number of aids, interpreters and departmental officials also tend to sit in on Task Force meetings. Thus, a system of rotating chairs is usually adopted to accommodate different participants depending on the nature of the topics being covered.

Prior to the institutionalisation of transatlantic relations both the political and the economic processes were confined to the hierarchy of government structures meaning lower level civil servants influenced the summit agenda only through their own ministers. Now direct access has been designated to 'sub summit' level contacts through the Senior Level Group, which sets the agenda for the EU–US summit. The TEP Steering Group and the Troika dialogues influence the summit by filtering into both the ministerial level and the SLG. The TEP Steering Group reports directly to the SLG as does the Troika political dialogue, and the Transatlantic Working Groups funnel into both the NTA Task Force and the SLG. The result is that the three branches of governmental dialogue work both separately and in sync and that a dense layer of networks has been created to support and assist transatlantic policy-makers in seeking out new areas of cooperation. The NTA institutions, including the SLG and the NTA Task Force, are cross-pillar institutions (see also Frellesen 2001). They assist the SLG in 'monitoring' or 'managing' the process in order to facilitate increased cooperation.

The Early Warning System

A number of EU–US trade disputes have highlighted the need for transatlantic institutions to play a larger role in settling disputes. The concept of an 'Early Warning System' had been an underlying theme in the institutionalisation process since the Transatlantic Declaration. In the past this simply meant that items on the agenda were earmarked for consideration at sub-cabinet level meetings. After the SLG, NTA Task Force and TEP Steering Group were created these meetings were used to set aside time for raising 'friction points' before they become major disputes (Devuyst 2001: 296). The Bonn Summit (1999) tried to make the Early Warning System more pragmatic by institutionalising new rules and procedures.

It was agreed that existing institutions, the TEP Steering Group and the NTA Task Force, would serve as the primary mechanisms for early warning, with the Steering Group covering trade and investment issues and the Task Force covering political issues. The Senior Level Group would review early-warning items in its preparation for the EU–US summit. The TEP Steering Group and NTA Task Force were then charged with assigning contact points, facilitating consultations and agreeing on timelines for reporting back on items highlighted as potential transatlantic policy frictions (see Figure 3.3; Early Warning Statement 1999).

The logic behind the Early Warning System fits into the larger institutionalist thesis identified in Chapter 1. First, it is argued that by identifying conflict, exchanging information and creating awareness at an early stage, possibly contentious legislation may be avoided in order to prevent conflict in EU–US relations. One US mission official argues that, 'We need to tell people in advance that the problem is coming, then we will be ready when the regulation comes into effect.'[27]

The case most cited by EU and US officials that highlights the need for the Early Warning System was the dispute over 'hush kits'. The hush kit dispute revolved around EU legislation banning planes from being fitted with devices that reduced the noise levels emitted by older aircraft. By the time US industry and Washington woke up to the fact that this legislation hampered US trade (US companies exclusively manufacture hush kits), it was already in its second reading in the European Parliament (see Peterson 2001). Many officials contend that had the EWS system been in place, early dialogue could have prevented the dispute. One US official even claims to have been told by MEPs, 'that had they known they would have written the legislation differently'.[28] The hush kits case highlights two important features of transatlantic dispute resolution; first, the role of the legislators in the transatlantic process and second, the power of domestic economic interests.

Another underlying feature behind the early warning concept is the desire to get both EU and US domestic policy makers to consider the external implications of internal policies.[29] Legislators are central players in the Early Warning System, because decisions made by them go far towards determining the capacity that international negotiators have to negotiate agreements, particularly in the US. Thus, the Early Warning System emphasises the need to 'beef up' the Transatlantic Legislators Dialogue (TLD), another product of the NTA's 'building bridges' chapter. The TLD brings legislators together at the committee level and creates awareness in Congress and the European Parliament of the impact of decisions made in either House.[30] EU and US officials argue that the TLD has a crucial role to play in the Early Warning System.[31]

Figure 3.3 The Early Warning mechanisms

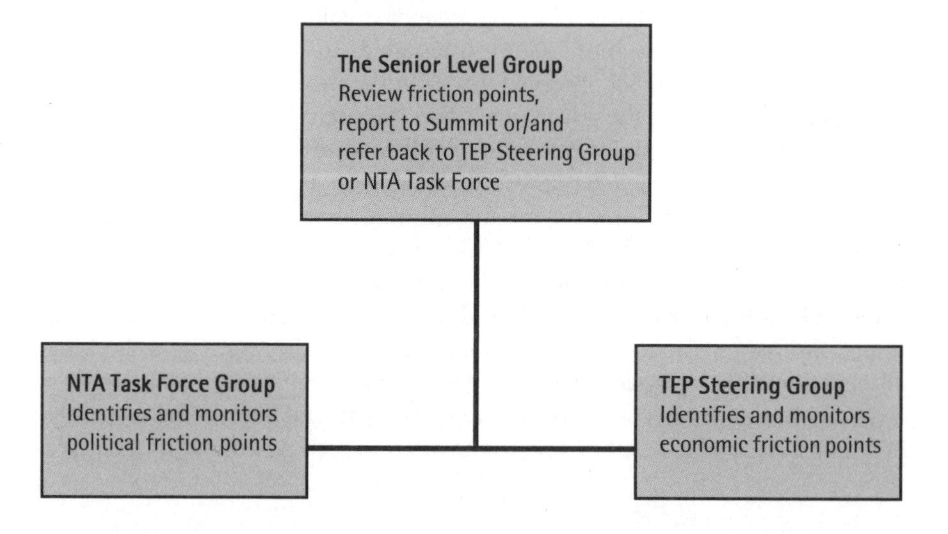

The implementation of the early warning process was slow moving following the Bonn Summit statement in June 1999. Initially, the strategy was to get people talking and to assess ways in which the early warning mechanisms might operate. The Commission discussed the possibility of employing a strategy of 'impact assessment'.[32] Derived from Article 133 committee discussions, impact assessment would mean having proposed policies stamped with a trade impact 'clean bill of health'. The idea was to increase communication between internal DGs and for US policy makers to ensure that national US interests were considered in the EU's internal policy processes.[33] US officials stressed the importance of transparency in the Early Warning System, suggesting that the Transatlantic Regulatory Guidelines (2000) were a means of furthering early dispute resolution. As one official stressed, 'We are interested in more regulatory to regulatory discussion of eventual trade disputes. It works into the early warning mechanisms by ensuring we catch things early on.'[34]

The Early Warning System is also designed to keep both sides informed of potential threats posed by Congress and the European Parliament.[35] The system sparks an inter-agency process that identifies the domestic issues that should be raised for the Task Force, the TEP Steering Group, the SLG and the summit. Officials on both sides stressed the importance of the Early Warning System as a means of developing contacts, comparing notes, exchanging information, pulling together a vast array of contacts, elevating issues from the bottom up and highlighting potential problems.

However, the Early Warning System is criticised as an ineffective conflict resolution mechanism. Although the Commission (2001) report states that the early warning mechanism for trade and investment under the TEP/NTA mechanisms works 'satisfactorily', the need for a more structured process of conflict resolution has been highlighted by EU and US officials. One US official argued that, 'The SLG gets contentious issues on table, but neither side follows up on the Early Warning System to take things off the agenda. The system needs to be more action orientated, to concentrate on finding solutions.' A TABD official observed that, 'On the practical application of the Early Warning System, the government had this great idea. It basically made a commitment to principles but has not followed through on it.'[36] The lack of concrete action has led a number of officials to argue that the system is 'hot air', 'blown up to look big for the summit', and 'a publicity stunt'.[37]

Doubts surrounding the Early Warning System are rooted in a number of technical and political obstacles to the application of transatlantic dispute resolution mechanisms. On a technical level, it is questionable whether an impact assessment process would be either feasible or effective. Cross checking all new domestic legislation poses impossible time constraints and entails a large amount of paperwork. As one Commission official notes, 'The real Early Warning System, if it were to work, would develop such close links, for example that the guys who make chimney regulations would know each other and sit down together before hand to work out regulations. This is unrealistic.'[38] In addition US officials have noted resistance from the Commission and member states to increased transparency in the early stages of domestic decision-making.[39] A European Parliament official pointed out that the European environmental committee does not like the idea of catering to the US.[40] A Commission official, by contrast, notes that, 'no one wants to mark legislation WTO incompatible'.[41]

A more fundamental problem for transatlantic dispute resolution is the view that no amount of dialogue will eliminate conflict rooted in deep political interest. Specifically, the Early Warning System will not work in areas where disputes are interest driven because transatlantic dialogue will not change the domestic opinions of actors, particularly actors who do not participate in the transatlantic dialogue. The *Financial Times* reported that,

> The EU knew its ban on hormones-treated beef and its bananas regime would infuriate Washington – but imposed them all the same. Bill Clinton signed sanctions laws penalising investors in Cuba, Iran and Libya, even though the EU had repeatedly warned that doing so would strain relations.[42]

Likewise a Commission official notes, 'We are quite convinced that if we look at audio visual policy, problems with fundamental ethical issues, or consumer policy, that the Early Warning System will not take away conflict.'[43] The consensus among officials is summarised by the statement of one UK official who argued that, 'The Early Warning System is only strong as the political will behind it'.[44]

The US Congress, as a staunch protector of US domestic interest, has been identified as a major obstacle to the Early Warning System. The potential to resolve conflict through early contact was disregarded by a Commission official who stated that:

> [The Early Warning System] won't control Congress. Early Warning works between Administrations but not Congress. Congress is unpredictable. One or two Senators can wreck the system and Congress does not care about Europe – for example, they knew Helms Burton would upset Europeans but in Congress international relations do not change constitutional make up and domestic political habits are hard to overcome.[45]

A US official agreed that the Early Warning System was not tied to Congress 'but to the desire for the Administration to get in early and deal with things cooked up in the Commission'.[46]

Nonetheless, many EU and US officials have argued that the TLD should be directly linked to the Early Warning System. It is argued that the short-comings of the system are tied to the limited scope and weak institutionalisation of the TLD. As the TLD is mostly an extension of the permanent US and EU delegations in Congress and the European Parliament, membership is limited to members with a transatlantic interest. There is no contact between relevant committees, or between the Senate and the European Parliament, and insufficient contact between the TLD and the SLG. TLD officials have complained that they do not have access to the EU–US Summit. The limited reach of the TLD in the US Congress is demonstrated by the fact that a senior staff member for the Subcommittee on Trade in the House was unaware that the TLD existed. It was argued that, 'If we are out of the loop as trade people, they may be mis-targeting resources.' The TLD fails to raise awareness of relevant people and cannot compensate for the domestic interests of Congress, for example in the banana dispute (see Chapter 7). Commission officials have described the TLD as a 'dialogue of the deaf' and TLD officials admit that while the dialogue has the potential to defuse disputes, such as the hush kits case, it has not solved any policy disputes.[49]

In short, the Early Warning System is mostly a bureaucratic tool that seeks to raise awareness. It has yet to bring legislators together, thus undermining its capacity to act as a concrete dispute prevention or resolution forum. European and American policy makers accept that the Early Warning System, as exercised by the NTA institutions, will not be a solution to all 'political' transatlantic disputes – such as the banana or beef cases – but argue that increased dialogue between experts could defuse technical disputes. Expert level contact through, for example, the Biotechnology Forum, is regarded as useful for preventing a fully blown dispute over GMOs.[50] At this stage of transatlantic integration it may well be true that the Early Warning System has done little more than 'give these experts a dose of "transatlanticism"' (Frellesen 2001).

Decentralised policy setting and shaping

To summarise, this chapter has outlined the existence of a transgovernmental policy process that functions around the intergovernmental summits. This section seeks to determine the extent to which transgovernmental actors are involved in policy setting and policy shaping. It is argued here that the existence of dense, sub-summit level networks illustrates the important role that transgovernmental actors play in the policy process.

First, while intergovernmental actors 'make' the decisions that establish policies through history making agreements, transgovernmental actors, at a ministerial level, 'set' transatlantic decisions by signing policy agreements between the EU and the US. For example, the Mutual Recognition Agreement was 'set' by the USTR and the then DG I Commissioner; the Positive Comity Agreement was set by the US Attorney General, the Federal Trade Commission, the Commissioner for Competition and the President-in-Office of the Industry Council and in the case of the Implementing Arrangement for Co-operation in the Fields of Metrology and Measurement Standards, agency directors for the National Institute of Standards and Technology and the EU Commission's Director-General for Research 'set' the transatlantic policy.

The limited number of transatlantic agreements signed suggests that a small number of actors actually set agreements, but many more transgovernmental actors play a role in shaping transatlantic decisions through the institutions characterised in this chapter. When asked the general question, 'who shapes transatlantic decisions', interviewees returned a wide range of responses. Some pointed to domestic agencies – the USTR, the State Department, DG Trade, DG External Relations, and actors such as the Article 133 Committee and the Council Working Groups – others to individuals. For example a Commerce Department official suggested that Deputy Assistant Secretary of Commerce for Europe, Charles Ludolph was instrumental in getting the MRAs moving in the US, while a US State Department official credits one anonymous official with keeping US interest in combating trafficking in women. Most indicated and went to great lengths to explain the roles played by NTA institutions. Thus, the second question addressed by this section, why do these transgovernmental institutions matter?

The intergovernmental summit

To recap, the EU–US summit is the focal point of the transatlantic calendar. It has two main functions: Intergovernmental actors use the summits to discuss topical issues, political hotspots and trade disputes. On a technocratic level it is the place for policy initiation and policy output. As an event, the summit creates the impulse to produce deliverables. In short it is a decision 'making' forum.

The EU–US summit is highly criticised, particularly in the EU, where there has been a push to make it a more effective policy producer. It is argued that the summit structure undermines the quality of NTA deliverables. Deliverables lack substance because the pressure to produce them leads officials to try to coordinate as long a list of potential deliverables as possible.[51] Prior to 2001 these summits were held biannually which meant that officials were under constant pressure to produce deliverables. However, many argued that the frequency of the summits led to 'NTA fatigue', and many statements and declarations were superficial or simply recycled.[52] One Commission official argued that the process had become 'a conveyor belt where deliverables get resold or turned into sudo deliverables'.[53] In 2001 the Commission convinced the Council to accept an annual rather than a biannual summit, meaning that only every other Council Presidency is able to participate in a summit meeting.[54]

EU–US summits are where 'big decisions' are made, but the scope for intergovernmental decision taking is limited by time constraints. The Commission Communiqué (2001) made the case for summits being more focused, having clearer priorities and a limited number of strategic policy themes. The need to 'manage' the dialogue highlights the important role played by the NTA institutions at a sub-summit level, specifically the Senior

Level Group. The densest contact takes place at lower levels between the political and economic working groups. In what resembles a pyramid structure the SLG connects the 'expert' level and the 'political' level. It pulls the NTA process together.

Transgovernmental institutions

The importance of NTA institutions is further highlighted by the fact that transatlantic decisions are complicated by technical as well as political differences. Even where the EU and the US agree at an intergovernmental level to pursue cooperation, facilitating joint action is difficult. Both the EU and the US have demonstrated 'capabilities–expectations gaps' in different policy sectors. For example, US officials argue that the weak EU JHA pillar blocks more aggressive EU–US cooperation under the global challenges chapter of the NTA, whereas EU officials argue that the US federal system blocks cooperation on TEP services.[55]

Given the many obstacles to policy coordination, caused, for example, structural differences, the NTA institutions are designed to get experts talking and to get transgovernmental actors to assess how the EU and the US can cooperate under the 'mandate' of the NTA. The vast range of working groups, which are unparalleled in any other dialogue, identify areas where the EU and the US can coordinate efforts. The SLG is the filter of the process. It is a cross-cutting institution that brings together political and economic officials and facilitates inter-agency coordination. Overall, one Commission official argues, 'It means getting bureaucrats to work on new subjects and new challenges.'[56]

Like the summit, there has been some debate recently on the effectiveness of the NTA institutions. In principle the SLG should serve as the 'engine room' of the NTA, driving the process by seeking out deliverables and elevating them to the political level. Others have argued that the SLG is more like a waiting room or a 'mailbox', particularly for issue areas that do not make it onto the summit agenda. In addition it has been argued that the SLG could be more fruitful if there was better follow up on deliverables.[57] However, enforcing the follow up of all issues is time consuming and resource intensive. The Commission (2001) argues that the NTA process should be adjusted to increase the managerial role of the SLG and to give the NTA Task Force a more operational responsibility. The push from the Commission to decentralise more 'shaping' duties is demonstrated by its argument that, 'The Senior Level Group should provide the oversight and drive while the Task-Force is responsible for monitoring and ensuring the operational follow-up' (European Commission 2001).

Finally, the Early Warning System outlined in the previous section demonstrates the need to fortify stronger conflict resolution and prevention systems in EU–US relations. Although in theory the system is designed to foster dialogue and exchange information which may prevent future conflicts, for example over hush kits, in practice the system is most likely to address technical, rather than political issues controlled by bureaucrats. Although legislators can potentially play a crucial role in the Early Warning System, the system as it is designed does not foster enough contact between NTA institutions and legislators. The weak TLD and the domestic orientation of the US Congress is also blamed for the ineffective system. In reality it is legislators that have a more vested interest in protecting domestic over international or transatlantic interests.

Networks, technocrats and transparency

The new type of governance employed at the transatlantic level marks a distinct change from traditional diplomacy. Decisions are now being made by a variety of actors at various levels of decision-making. What has developed is both a bottom-up and a top-down process. Much more emphasis has been placed on decision 'shaping' and 'setting', thus a degree of control over the decision-making process has been transferred to the transgovernmental level.

Transgovernmental communication is seen as a means of facilitating increased cooperation because technocratic decision setting and shaping lowers the threshold for disagreement between actors, in part because the NTA process is designed to find areas where the EU and the US can cooperate. In short it de-politicises issues by placing them in the hands of policy experts. Undemocratic decision-making has been somewhat intentionally melded into the transatlantic policy-making process. As discussed in Chapter 2, some of the steps towards transatlantic institutionalisation were purposely designed not to attract attention. They are bureaucratic agreements that avoid legislation and side-steer Congress. The method of institutionalisation used by the EU and the US is comparable to European integration by stealth. Thus, like the EU, transatlantic decision-making encounters similar problems of legitimacy.

The nature of the policies pursued by the NTA further illustrates the function of bureaucratic decision taking. New technology and concentration on regulatory standards means that the policy-making process has become very technocratic and tends to yield debates high above the head of average citizens. Policy networks and epistemic communities have been employed to assist decision-makers. The need for 'expert' consultation and the employment of transgovernmental rather than strictly intergovernmental networks means that policy makers often rely on non-elected bodies to 'shape' decisions that affect the general population. Still, many transgovernmental institutions deal with 'low' rather than 'high' security issues. Coordinating humanitarian aid, law enforcement cooperation and education can be facilitated by dialogue between policy experts rather than politicians.

Technocratic decision-making under the NTA has highlighted the need for transparency in the process and the input of civil society. Chapter 4 identifies how transnational networks have been brought into the NTA as a means of increasing transparency in the policy-making process, thereby securing the wider legitimacy of transatlantic decisions.

Conclusion

The transatlantic mechanisms created in the process of institutionalisation have led to the creation of dense networks between the EU and the US. These networks, in turn, became transatlantic decision-making forums. Here, communication between EU and US counterparts forms the closest thing there is to a transatlantic 'policy process'.

The transatlantic structure, however, has had to accommodate different competencies of decision-making in the EU and the US and thus separate processes have been established. As a result, there are multiple layers of contact in the transatlantic dialogue, represented by three different branches of governmental dialogue. While the EU–US summit is the intergovernmental forum for decision-making, many transgovernmental actors influence the process in a shaping and setting capacity at the sub-summit level. These institutions, particularly the Senior Level Group, formulate the impulse for cooperation by seeking out deliverables, and by producing a forum for conflict prevention under the Early Warning System.

As noted in Chapter 2, the capacity of the NTA process to facilitate cooperation and prevent conflict is highly criticised. This chapter discussed the limits of the NTA institutions. It was argued that the ability to defuse political disputes and to make transatlantic policies rests on the political will of intergovernmental actors. Many more actors have a capacity to shape and set the policy details under the 'mandate' of policy reach established by history making decisions. The need to coordinate many different tiers of policy shaping highlights the important role that NTA institutions play in 'managing' the transatlantic dialogue.

Finally, the technocratic nature of bureaucratic decision shaping and setting has raised some questions about the legitimacy of the process. Chapter 4 discusses transatlantic attempts to 'legitimise' the process by giving transnational actors an institutionalised role in shaping transatlantic policies.

Notes

1 These summits were held biannually up until 2002 and annually after that.
2 The attendance of EU–US summit fluctuates depending on where the summit is held. For example the US Secretary of State attends, but other US Cabinet members may not if the summit is held outside Washington DC. The Vice President attends only when the US hosts the summit.
3 Interview, Commission official, Brussels, 1999; US Mission Official, Brussels, 1999.

4 Interview, Commission Secretariat official, Brussels, September 1999.
5 Interview, US State Department, Washington DC, October 2000.
6 Interview, Commission official, Washington DC, October 2000.
7 Interview, Council Presidency, September 1999.
8 This sentiment was expressed in 20 different interviews with EU and US policy officials between July 1998 and May 2001.
9 Similar accusations have been made about banana negotiations which also took place in December 1998 (see Chapter 8).
10 The European hosted summit is held in the capital of the member state which holds the European Presidency. Interview, Commission official, Brussels, September 1999.
11 Expressed in interviews with US State Department and Commission officials, Brussels, September 1999 to October 2000.
12 Interview, Commission, Brussels, September 1999.
13 Interview, US Mission official, Brussels, September 1999.
14 Interview, Commission official, Brussels, September 1999.
15 Interview, TACD Secretariat, London, January 2000.
16 Interview, US NGO, Washington, October 2000.
17 One Commission official even joked that the deliverables were created to remind summit leaders why they had to attend the summits. Interview, Commission Secretariat, Brussels, September 1999.
18 Interview, TABD September 1999; interview, Commission official, Washington DC, October 2000.
19 Interview, Commission Delegation, Washington DC, October 2000.
20 The Troika format traditionally included the Commission, current Council Presidency, the predecessor and successor. Under the Amsterdam Treaty, entered into force 1 May 1999, however, the 'new' Troika includes the Presidency, the Commission and the new CFSP High Representative, Javier Solana Madariaga.
21 Interview, Council Secretariat, Brussels, September 1999.
22 Interviews, Council Secretariat and Finnish Presidency, Brussels, September 1999.
23 Before the structural changes made by Prodi to the Commission in 1999, the Commission typically put forward the appropriate DG's Chef de Cabinet (Interview, Commission official, Brussels, September 1999).
24 This practice has not been overly effective, as fewer people access government web sites than media sources. One Commission official summed up the public scope of the SLG report by describing its purpose as 'all to convince the six or seven academics who care to read the report'. Interview, Brussels, September 1999.
25 Interviews with EU and US officials, Brussels, September 1999. See also Frellesen (2001).
26 The Finnish delegation sent the Director General for the Department of External Economic Relations, and the Germans were represented by the head of the External EU Department and the head of Bilateral Desk for German–American relations. The Austrian delegation sent the head of North America Positions, and the British presidency was represented by Dick Stay, the head of External Relations and the man who services council work. Interview, Commission official, Brussels, September 1999.
27 Interview, US Mission official, Brussels, September 1999.
28 Interview, US Mission official, Brussels, September 1999.
29 Interview, EU Commission official, Brussels, September 1999.
30 In June 2001 a Commission official noted, 'The TLD is in a state of "impasse" after the election of the new US Congress. The EP is working to reactivate it.'
31 Interview with Commission and European Parliament September 2000 and US TLD,

October 2000.

32 Interviews with Commission officials, Brussels, September 1999.
33 Interviews with US Mission officials, Brussels, September 1999.
34 Interview, USTR, October 2000.
35 Interviews at the US State Department, USTR, Council Presidency, and Council Secretariat, 1999–2000.
36 Interview, US TABD, Washington, March 2000.
37 Interview, Commission officials, Brussels, September 1999.
38 Interview with former member of the US delegation to Washington, Brussels, September 1999.
39 Interview, USTR Official, October 2000.
40 Interview, European Parliament Secretariat, September 1999.
41 Interview with Commission official, Brussels, September 1999.
42 Quoted from 'Jaw-Jaw', Financial Times Online, 23 June 1999, www.ft.com.
43 Interview, Commission official, Brussels 1999.
44 Interview, UK Foreign Office, January 2000.
45 Interview, Commission delegation, Washington DC, October 2000.
46 Interview, TLD Secretariat, Washington DC, October 2000.
47 Interview, US Congress, Washington, October 2000.
48 Interview, European Parliament, September 1999.
49 Interviews with US, EU TLD officials and Commission officials, September 1999, October 2000.
50 Interview, House Subcommittee on Trade, October 2000.
51 Interview, Commission official, September 1999.
52 Arguments to this effect made by Commission officials in Brussels, October 1999 and Washington DC, October 2000 as well as a Finnish Council Presidency Representative, Brussels, September 1999 and a US State Department Official, Washington DC, October 2000.
53 Interview, European Commission, Brussels, September 1999.
54 Interview, European Commission, Brussels, October 1999.
55 Interviews, US Mission, Council Secretariat and Commission, September 1999.
56 Interview, Commission Delegation, Washington DC, October 2000.
57 Interview, US State Department, Washington DC, October 2000.

4

Transnational policy shaping

The institutions created by the New Transatlantic Agenda (NTA) have increased the scope for transgovernmental actors to influence transatlantic decisions. This chapter examines how the NTA and the Transatlantic Economic Partnership (TEP) have also encouraged the build up of transnational networks. Ad hoc dialogues between, for example, educators and scientists were sponsored through the NTA process as a way of 'building bridges' across the Atlantic. This chapter focuses on interest groups that were formally invited to participate in the policymaking process, including the Transatlantic Business Dialogue (TABD), the Transatlantic Consumer Dialogue (TACD), the Transatlantic Environmental Dialogue (TAED) and the Transatlantic Labour Dialogue (TALD). The chapter discusses the implications of the input of business and 'civil society' into the transatlantic decision-making process and questions whether these dialogues point to a 'decentralisation' of transatlantic decision 'shaping' to private, transnational networks. It is argued that while all of these dialogues clearly participate in the process, only the TABD is a true policy 'shaper'.

The main aims of this chapter are to analyse the institutionalisation of the networks, the level of formal access they are given to transatlantic decision takers and the impact they have on transatlantic decisions. The organisation and orientation of the dialogues is discussed, as is the frequency of contact with transgovernmental and intergovernmental actors. Measuring the 'impact' of these dialogues is more difficult. As this research is interview driven, the success of these dialogues is measured by the impact that both their members and EU and US officials 'perceive' them to have had on the transatlantic policy process.

Finally, in relation to the wider discussion on the institutionalisation of the transatlantic relations, this chapter questions why the transatlantic dialogues make a difference to the transatlantic policy process. What encouraged the transatlantic architects to offer government sponsorship of private networks, particularly in the US where this runs against the norm? It is argued that the dialogues were seen as useful additions to the NTA process first, as a way to gain effective policy solutions, and second, as a means of making the policy process more open and transparent.

The first section examines the TABD. The second looks at the TACD and TAED, and the third section discusses the TALD, or lack thereof. Each section outlines the creation of the dialogues, their structures and policy recommendations, their access to, and impact on, the transatlantic process. The fourth section assesses the capacity of these groups to serve as policy advisors. It is argued that the inclusion of multiple groups with a variety of interests and varied access to the process creates problems for policy 'setters', but that issue orientated, multi-dialogue task forces are one way to facilitate consensus building between the dialogues.

The Transatlantic Business Dialogue

The Transatlantic Business Dialogue is the most established of the transatlantic dialogues. It was conceived (in 1994) and launched (in 1995), before the NTA and is now considered to be a major success story of the new transatlantic dialogue.

The TABD was the invention of US Commerce Secretary, the late Ron Brown.[1] A formal business dialogue was seen as a means of securing greater US business support for the Commerce department, which was under threat from Congress, and a way to boost the impact of European business on EU level negotiations. The TABD was also conceptualised as a way to secure greater support for the US in transatlantic negotiations. As Cowles (2001b: 232) argues, 'US government officials were convinced, moreover, that their negotiating position would coincide much more closely with the US–EU business communities stance than would that of the European Commission'.

Although the creation of the TABD was initially controversial in the US, the main challenge was to gain European support for the process.[2] European business lacked organisation at the EU level (see Cowles 2001b: 238), and the Commission's DG I initially opposed the creation of a business dialogue without labour, consumer or environmental dialogues. The Transatlantic Policy Network (TPN), a dialogue between legislators and businesses, was influential in getting European industry and officials involved. It was able to draw on its extensive European business contacts, and enlist the support of active Transatlantic Policy Network (TPN) members, such as Ford, Xerox, Daimler Chrysler, EDS and AOL.[3]

In the end, it was the support of US Commerce Secretary Brown, Commissioner Brittan (External Relations) and Commissioner Bangemann (Enterprise) that facilitated the inauguration of the TABD. They invited industry leaders to comment on the creation of a transatlantic business forum. The Commerce Department and the Commission also actively participated in the first TABD meeting in Seville.[4]

Despite differences between European and American business approaches to the dialogue, the launch was deemed a success and the group reached consensus on over 70 joint recommendations. A few months later roughly 60 per cent of the TABD recommendations resurfaced in the NTA and the Joint Action Plan noted the governments' intent to take the recommendations of the TABD into consideration when creating the New Transatlantic Marketplace (see also Cowles 2001a).

How the TABD works

The TABD is not a traditional lobbying organisation. Rather, it is a forum for consensus reaching between European and American business with the aim of boosting trade and investment. The overall purpose of the TABD – from a governance perspective – is to assist the government in facilitating trade liberalisation.[5] As one TABD official argued, 'Industry consensus is a policy tool'.[6] Since its creation the TABD has aimed to promote integration between the EU and the US by providing progress reports indicating where American and European industry feel cooperation is both necessary and feasible.[7] It then exerts political pressure on USTR and the Commission to follow up on recommendations. The TABD also participates in the Early Warning System, expanding its policy reach to areas of potential dispute. It is credited with convincing the Commission to push back policy changes on metric labelling and a gelatine ban, both of which had the potential to erupt into EU–US trade disputes.

Throughout the 1990s, the TABD became both highly institutionalised and increasingly organised. Despite the insistence by its participants that the TABD is a process as opposed to an organisation, it has nevertheless developed into a transatlantic 'institution'.[8] It has held annual CEO meetings since 1995,[9] established two small secretariats (with less than five permanent staff) in Washington and Brussels and appointed rotating company chairs (CEOs), one American one European, to lead the dialogue in rotating annual terms.[10]

The TABD chairs are just a fraction of the many companies who have a stake in the TABD. Growing participation, from an initial 60 to 200 CEOs, gave the process broader legitimacy. The TABD is carried by a number of companies who, as active members, participate more regularly in specific policy sectors through working groups. A TABD official admits that in some sectors the number of companies involved is small, but that, 'in general if a corporation lends their CEO to something, they are highly engaged'.[11] Membership of the TABD is open, but it has been criticised in the past for excluding certain sectors – such as generic pharmaceutical firms and small and medium sized enterprises.[12]

The TABD is led by rotating chairs (see Table 4.3), each of which has played a role in developing the dialogue.[13] The build up of TABD structures – including a leadership team, a steering group, issue managers and expert level groups – points to a growing interest in effectively managing the process (see table 4.1).[14] The aim of these structures is to 'create more energy in the dialogue by focusing CEO and government attention on more defined and actionable issues'.[15] The leadership team encourages TABD members to bring forward projects that are specific and detailed in order to prevent the TABD developing into a chat shop.[16] In addition, the other structures are designed to focus on technical issues, create 'ready made' policy solutions and elevate them on to higher political agendas.

The TABD process centres around the annual CEO conference, which typically takes place a month before the EU–US summit. The meeting is used first, to identify areas of business consensus, and second as a forum for CEOs to meet with high level officials in the US Administration, the Commission, Congress and the European Parliament.[17]

The TABD chairs have presented their recommendations at numerous EU–US summits, but while these meetings are useful for publicity and even for short discussion of key issues, it is not the real point of access for TABD members. The importance of expert level talks is demonstrated by the appointment of issue managers and working level government contacts. Expert discussions are incorporated, with the results of the CEO dialogue, in the CEO Conference Report. Another mechanism that incorporates both CEO level and 'expert level' input is the Mid Year meeting and annual TABD Scorecard, which monitors government follow up on TABD proposals. Further policy recommendations are produced as a result of frequent working group and issue group meetings. Each issue manager has an EU and US government contact and the US Administration has even created an interagency task force to work with the TABD.[18] The TABD structure results in dense levels of formal and informal government–business contacts.

What an impact

Establishing a causal relationship between TABD recommendations and transatlantic policy output is troublesome, not least because much contact between the TABD and the EU and US governments is conducted informally or behind closed doors.[19] Government response to policy recommendations is arguably important, but do the acknowledgement of those proposals, the initiation of policy changes, or implementations of recommendations define success?

The TABD is arguably an important part of the business community,[20] a powerful lobby[21] and an important player in the NTA process.[22] One TABD participant suggested that concrete action had been taken on at least two-thirds of its proposals. US Vice President Al Gore reaffirmed that success claiming that the governments had implemented 50 per cent of the TABD's 129 recommendations.[24] The TABD is credited with providing leadership and direction in NTA negotiations and facilitating the MRAs, the Safe Harbour Agreement and multilateral agreements on intellectual property rights and

Information Technology.[25] A Commission official argued that, 'the TABD plays an important and positive role. It helps determine priorities, keeps us on track and makes us deliver on time or else explain why we cannot'.[26] The *Journal of Commerce* stated, 'Organised, plugged-in and persistent, the business dialogue has been setting the tone for trade talks between Brussels and Washington.'[27] Cowles (2001a: 230) contends that, 'the TABD has played a critical role not merely in setting the agenda for transatlantic trade discussions, but also participating in US-EU negotiations and shaping domestic-level support for their agenda.'

A number of TABD members initially complained about the slow government response to many of its proposals, but they came to realise that full implementation of its recommendations would be timely (see Cowles 2001b). A TABD participant argued that, 'members are permanently grumbling about the reaction time, but we are still on board'.[28] Generally, TABD participants are impressed with the level of access that TABD membership allows and the impact that the dialogue has had on the policy process. The benefits to one company – EDS – were summarised by a representative who argued that,

> Taking TABD leadership has both provided credibility for EDS staff in their consequent and subsequent involvement in actual negotiations with government, and led to tangible results. For example, the ongoing moratorium on imposing tariffs on E-commerce would probably not have occurred without the TABD or some other vehicle.[29]

Some Commission officials have downplayed the importance of the TABD, particularly in response to claims that it has played a dominant role in the policy process vis-à-vis other dialogues. In particular, Commission officials have argued that the TABD is not as important as it perceives itself to be. It has been accused of being self-congratulatory and a product of government rhetoric.[30] A USTR official argued that, 'things are not just happening because the TABD says so'.[31] Nonetheless, even sceptics agreed that the TABD was 'shaping' if not 'making' policy. One NGO argued, 'even if they are not as powerful as they say, they still have extra clout.'[32]

The consumer and environmental dialogues

Building 'people to people' links was identified by the NTA as an important tool for securing broad public support for the transatlantic partnership. Originally, the idea was to create a civil society dialogue that could incorporate business, trade unions and citizens associations.[33] The TEP invited consumer and environmental groups to participate in the process 'on issues relevant to international trade as *a constructive contribution to policy-making*'.[34]

The decision to include consumers, environmentalists and workers in the transatlantic dialogue was the result of pressure from NGOs, the European Commission and eventually the US State Department. The success of the

TABD sparked criticism from the NGO community, which in 1995 argued that the decision-making capacity of the TABD within the NTA was unbalanced by an absence of civil society input.[35] The initial push from NGOs for access to the TABD was denied, but NGO lobbying efforts raised awareness in the EU and US administrations of the growing need to legitimise the process.[36]

Table 4.1 The TABD structure after 2001

Policies	*Mechanisms*	*Process*
CEO priority issues Capital markets Dispute management Expert level dialogue Networked economy Regulatory policy WTO SME perspective	**Leadership team** CEO level	**Annual conference** CEO plenary
Expert groups, Issue managers Aerospace, automotive, climate change, cosmetics customs, dietary supplements, EETIS, export controls and economic sanctions, heavy equipment industries, intellectual property rights, international personnel mobility, medical devices, taxation, pharmaceuticals, recreational, marine, refrigerants, telecommunication services	**Steering groups** Expert groups Issue managers	**Mid year report** Leadership input Steering group input **Working level** Issue manager/ NTA Task Force

Consumers International (CI) lobbied the Commission, particularly DGI, which Cowles (2001a: 242) contends, had previously advocated participation from the 'wider public interest'. The Commission's mandate to support consumers and environmentalists increased with the Amsterdam Treaty, and DGI gained support for civil society dialogues from the Health and Consumer Protection and Environmental Protection DGs (Bignami and Charnovitz 2001: 24). Growing opposition from the US NGO Public Citizen to the TABD and increasing demands from environmental groups put pressure on the US State

Department.[37] Finally, NGOs used formal channels to respond to the US Federal Register notice on the TEP.[38]

Although the main push for the civil society dialogues came from the Commission, the State Department was crucial in securing US funds for the consumer and environmental dialogues. Unlike the business dialogue, the NGO dialogues could not be launched without a financial commitment from the governments. Funding was found with relative ease on the European side where the Commission had a history of funding NGOs. However, the US government does not generally fund the private sector. In this case the US Information Agency (USIA) within the State Department was able to find funds for both the TACD and the TAED under a scholarship budget line subject to approval by the Senate Finance Committee.[39] Consumer International – the designated grant receiver for the TACD – was given roughly $60,000 from USIA and 110,000 euros from the Commission. The US based National Wildlife Federation (NWF) and Brussels based European Environmental Bureau were given $100,000 from USIS and 200,000 euros from the Commission.

Government sponsorship of the TACD and TAED in general and the use of public funds specifically enabled, but also undermined, the initial attempts to build both dialogues. Unlike European NGOs, many US groups were not accustomed to receiving public funds and few organisations allowed government funding.[40] US NGOs feared that the consumer dialogue and environmental dialogues were attempts to legitimise the liberalisation policies employed under the New Transatlantic Marketplace. The Corporate European Observer (CEO), which had developed into a 'TABD' watchdog, argued that the consumer and environmental dialogues symbolised attempts to 'green-wash' the TEP.[41] TAED and TACD members objected to being hired to patronise government policies or to act as 'contracted civil society'.[42] The TAED, which contained no pro-globalisation NGOs, stressed that its creation in response to bilateral government initiatives under the NTA was in no way intended to legitimise these procedures (TAED Press Release, 3 May 1999). The European Environmental Bureau (EEB) stressed in its funding application to the Commission that, 'financial support for the TAED should not lead to management of the agenda of TAED by the sponsors, but rather by the participants'.[43] Public Citizen President Ralph Nader tried to block the creation of the TACD by arguing that it would create the 'illusion of consultation and participation' and be misused as a public relations ploy.[44]

The divide within the consumer dialogue on the issue of trade liberalisation surfaced at its first meeting in September 1998, which was attended by roughly fifty consumer groups. The meeting was overshadowed by the dispute between Public Citizen (led by Ralph Nader), which opposes trade liberalisation, and Consumer Union (led by Rhona Karpatkin), which views it as a means of increasing consumer choice.[45] A 'devastating' speech by Nader and three outbursts from American consumer groups during the first meeting led one EU official to argue that, 'the meeting was a disaster. The groups needed to figure out how to organise themselves'.[46] In the end, the vote to establish the TACD was won by a narrow margin. Faced with the decision to be on the inside or outside of the process, Public Citizen became a Steering Group Member.[47]

The TAED experienced similar, if not as dramatic, challenges in getting off the ground. It held its first official meeting in May 1999. Again, there was some disagreement on whether government officials should participate (see Bignami and Charnovitz 2001). An American NGO indicated that, 'there was a lot of hesitation at first about the TAED on the US NGOs side, and there is still a great deal of uneasiness about what the governments have in mind for these dialogues'.[48]

European NGOs pushed hard for the TAED. The letter of invitation sent to NGOs asking them to join the dialogue claimed that the TAED could increase the effectiveness of cooperation and joint action among groups, provide highly effective mechanisms for challenging concerns to policy makers and enable NGOs to serve its members and the public with up to date information. TAED membership was officially opened to all NGOs, but no attempt was made to recruit 'free market' environmentalists (Bignami and Charnovitz 2001: 40). Public Citizen also took a TAED Steering Committee seat. Friends of the Earth (1999) argued that TAED members should monitor the use of the TEP to promote a new WTO Round, which unbalanced power relations between actors in the process.

The difficult births of the TAED and TACD highlight differences in approaches to private–public relations in Europe and the US. Most problems setting up the dialogues stemmed from the culture of interaction between NGOs and the US Administration, which is generally described as 'hostile', 'adversarial' and guided by 'great distrust'.[49] One US State Department official pointed out that, 'The concept that TACD should make decisions with the US government goes against everything US NGOs stand for.'[50] The US Administration is required to publicly seek and accept comments from non-governmental actors under the Federal Administrative Procedures Act, but many NGOs were not accustomed to receiving government response to their recommendations unless they had demonstrated the capacity to block trade initiatives or make a public impact (Bignami and Charnovitz 2001: 41). The result is that American NGOs are more accustomed to using lawsuits than dialogue to shape policy.[51]

The initial response of American officials to the TACD and TAED demonstrated the poor relationship between NGOs and the US government.[52] Early problems with the TACD were attributed to its management by USTR, which was accused of being critical and belittling of the dialogue.[53] Part of the problem was that the TACD coordinator was charged with fostering a dialogue that – at times – went against the grain of USTR's trade agenda. The shift of the TACD co-ordinator to the State Department – where the TAED was co-ordinated – helped to foster better dialogue. TACD officials argue that the State Department was more diplomatic and granted consumers more meetings.[54] The Bureau for Business and Economic Affairs, led by Tony Wayne, and the Under Secretary of State for Global Affairs, Frank Loy, are credited with supporting the dialogues and overcoming gaps between NGOs and the US Administration.

Still, the general perception is that TAED and TACD were quickly able to gain a better rapport with the Commission. European NGOs have a better working relationship with each other and with the Commission because private–public dialogue is arguably an important part of the European decision-making process. European groups are described as having a more 'cordial' relationship with the Commission in part because the Commission generally works under the assumption that it needs civil society input.[55] One US official argued that, 'there is greater sympathy among both sides of consumers for the way things are done in Europe. The EC has a different way of dealing with consumers. US Consumers believe they get more access and respect in Europe.'[56]

Once more, the Commission exerted pressure on US actors in the NTA Task Force and SLG meetings to establish the consumer and environmental dialogues, because the interests of civil society coincided with European positions on several looming trade disputes with the US. The TAED and TACD have made recommendations that support many of the Commission's policies on food safety, privacy, electrical waste and the Precautionary Principle.[57] A TACD official argued that, 'where there is EU–US policy stalemate, civil society comes nearer to EU positions. Politically it is in the interest of EU to have US consumer movement on its side.'[58]

In general, Commission support helped legitimise the TAED and TACD processes in the eyes of US NGOs, as groups in the US realised they could draw on the success of their European counterparts.[59] After initially releasing a joint press release that criticised the TEP Action Plan, the TACD and TAED began making policy recommendations, on a range of issue areas, to EU and US officials (see Table 4.4). TAED focused on safe energy sources, biotechnology, waste management and emissions standards.[60] The TACD, despite its shaky start, was also able to make over 20 concrete recommendations at its second meeting, focusing on e-commerce, food safety and multilateral investment rules.[61]

Organisation in the TACD and TAED

Institutionalising the consumer and environmental dialogues was a complicated task, because the shaky start to both dialogues delayed the establishment of organisational structures. American NGOs, less experienced in working at an international level, had to establish how to work together (Bignami and Charnovitz 2001).[62] Moreover, financial and time constraints made it difficult to encourage groups to take on managerial posts.

Figure 4.1 The TACD structure

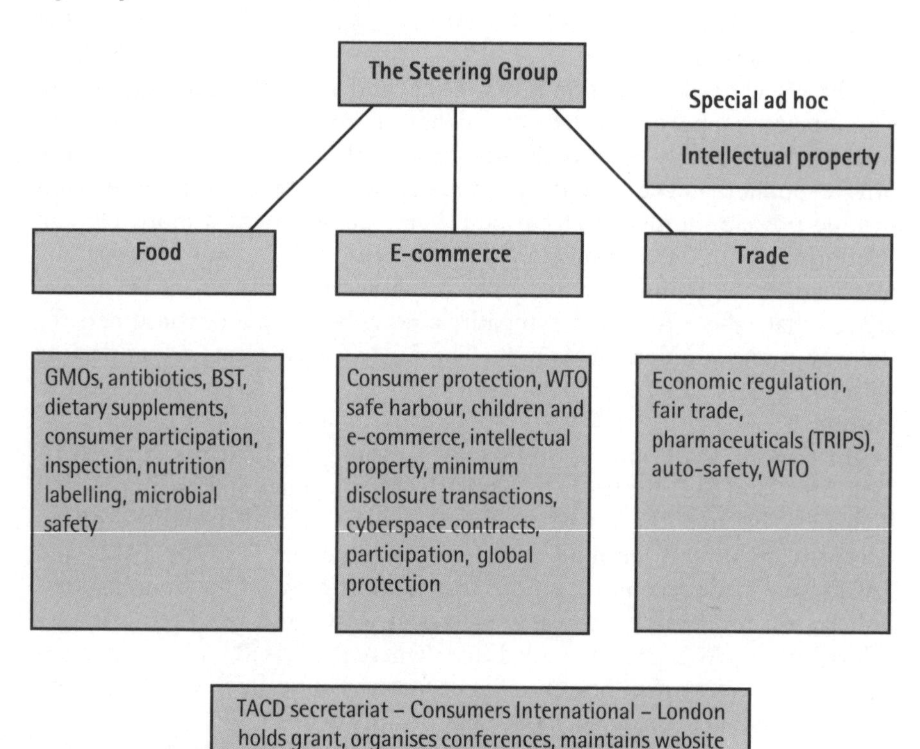

The TACD soon emerged as the most institutionalised of the civil society dialogues. The group established one secretariat, at Consumer International (CI) in London, because CI was an international NGO and was able to accept grants from the US government and the European Commission. The creation of a Steering Group put a core group of NGOs in charge of leading the dialogue, but individuals at CI are given the most credit for managing the dialogue.[63] Most of the other sixty consumer organisations participate in the TACD in the three working groups on food, electronic commerce and trade, and Issue Managers are appointed for each main issue in the working groups (see Figure 4.1). Each working group is co-chaired by EU and US managers who are in contact before annual general meetings to discuss the agenda, to commission reports, or identify areas for action. Within the groups, joint EU and US Issue Managers are charged with monitoring specific policy sectors. In general the groups interact more regularly through email list-serves.[64]

The TACD leadership has worked to produce effective mechanisms capable of producing concrete policy recommendations. It holds annual summit meetings similar to those of the TABD where working group and high level discussions are held with EU and US officials.[65] The Steering Group publishes a report of summit findings and presents them to the appropriate government officials before the EU–US summit. TACD also attended its first summit in December 1999.

The TAED established similar structures to the TACD. It has five working groups (see Figure 4.2) who meet in conjunction with the annual general meeting and carry out informal contact through Issue Managers. Certain working groups have designated issue co-ordinators for policy areas that overlap working groups. The Steering Group guides the dialogue and has decision-making authority over funding, budget activities and the output of TAED documentation. It meets at an annual general meeting, and holds additional strategy meetings throughout the year. Unlike the TABD and TACD, the TAED does not have a secretariat. Rather it has coordinators who perform the administrative functions of dialogue.[66] The TAED grant-holders (the EEB and the NWF) were the original coordinators, however by 2000 the US branch of the TAED could not find a member willing to take on the job.[67]

Despite early objections to the participation of government officials, EU and US officials have been well represented at TAED meetings, where both high level and expert level contact (between the working groups and officials) takes place.[68] Like the TABD and TACD the annual TAED meeting produces recommendations, which representatives had the opportunity to present to EU–US summit leaders in Washington (1999) and Lisbon (2000).

What impact?

The failure to fill vacancies in TAED posts demonstrates the lost momentum among US NGOs caused, in part, by TAED funding problems. In January 2000 the objection of Senator Jesse Helms, in the Senate Finance Committee, to funding for the TAED blocked the approval of funds, and stopped the State Department from issuing the grant. Effectively this action killed the TAED, because the Commission's budget line relied on 'matched' funds from the US government.[69] The funding problem overshadowed the May 2000 TAED meeting in Brussels, and in November 2000 the TAED announced a suspension of its activities.[70] John Hontelez, Secretary General of the EEB and member of the Steering Committee of the TAED argued,

> We have to stop our activities because the US government has not been able to provide its part of the necessary finances to run this dialogue. It has faced opposition in the Senate, and apparently, it is not giving it enough priority. The US government has always pretended the TAED is of great importance to them. This failure however does not confirm this.

The TACD and TAED were encouraged by the US Administration to seek private sources of funding before the suspension of the TAED. State Department officials indicated that the 2000 TACD grant, which managed to pass Congressional Appropriations, would be the last. Despite earlier claims that the US Administration and European Commission should work to fund the dialogue, US officials argued that public funding was never a permanent arrangement. One official argued, 'It is not US government policy to fund NGOs.'[71] The future of the TACD hinges on the capacity of the group to find private funding, which EU TACD officials have argued that they are aiming to do in order to continue the dialogue.[72] US TACD members were less optimistic about the future, and argued that first the impact of the dialogue needed to be evaluated.[73]

Figure 4.2 The TAED structure (2000)

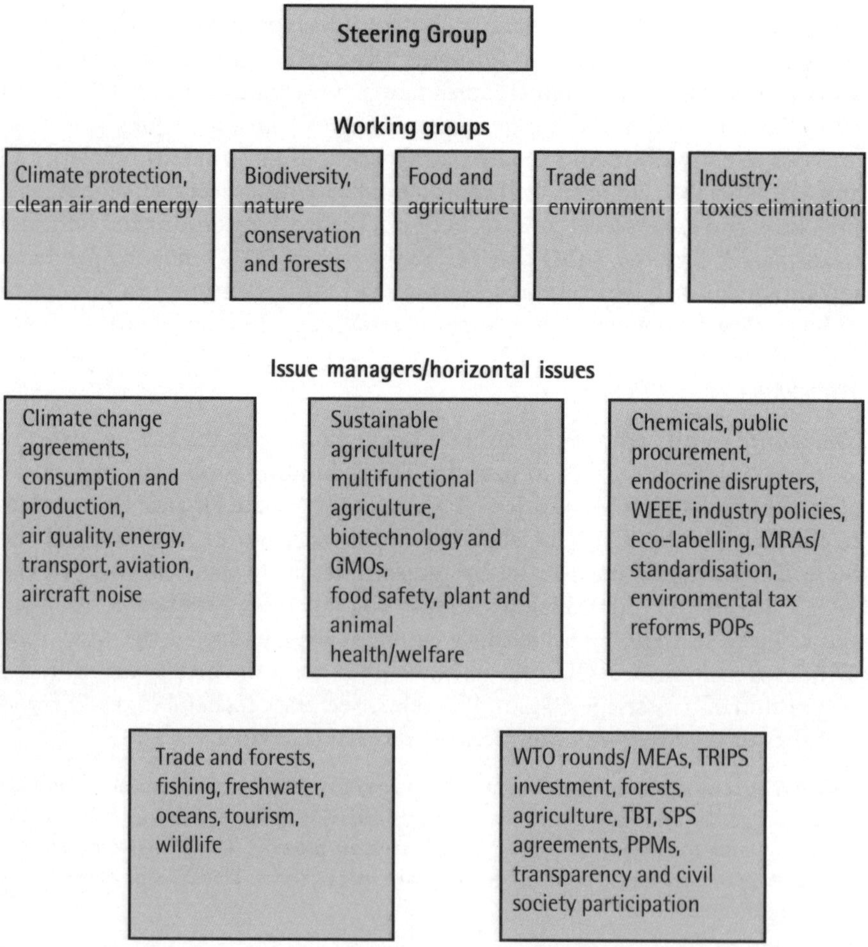

The future survival and success of these groups is directly linked to their capacity to add value to wider transnational social movements (see also Buck 2000). What, if any, gains were reaped through the creation of the dialogues? In accordance with their outlined objectives, the success of the TACD and TAED rests on the capacity of the groups to build dialogue between EU and US NGOs, to increase NGO access to EU and US officials and to shape policy output.

A major achievement of the TACD and TAED has been the build up of dialogues between European and American NGOs, which served as important sources of information sharing and networking. EU and US officials describe the dialogues as a 'learning process'.[74] American NGOs are learning from European NGOs about the EU and about European policies, and both sides are learning how they can harmonise strategies and simultaneously exert pressure on their governments. US NGOs have found allies in European consumer groups and, on many policies, in the European Commission.

The TACD, in particular, has been praised for overcoming differences between US NGOs.[75] As one official argued, 'the success of the TACD is just overcoming the Consumer Union–Public Citizen gap and getting American consumer groups on speaking terms'.[76] TAED representatives agree that the environmental dialogue has also jumpstarted cooperation. Another source suggested that, 'People are coming together. There is more common ground and no clear divide between European and American NGOs on trade.'[77] Environmental Protection Agency (EPA) officials agreed that transatlantic dialogue between the groups was significant, arguing that, 'first they must get comfortable at the table with each other because governments respond when constituencies are united and focused'.[78]

In one respect the dialogues have successfully fulfilled the objectives of the NTA: they have 'built bridges' across the Atlantic. The real test for participants, however, is their capacity to act as 'policy shapers'. Here the results are less visible. First, members of the TACD and TAED have complained about the level of access vis-à-vis the business dialogue. Second, consumers and environmentalists have argued that the civil society dialogues do not have the same influence in the decision-making process to that exerted by the TABD.

On the one hand the civil society dialogues have gained access to both high level and working level officials through the annual general meeting (see Table 4.2). The TACD and TAED each have contacts in the State Department and the US Mission in Brussels at a working level. Both have increased the formal level of access that consumers and environmentalists have to policy makers.[79] Bignami and Charnovitz (2001) argue that:

> Groups like Consumers International have, for years, hammered out common positions among member groups and taken these positions to the Codex, the United Nations, and various other international organizations. They have had observer status in the United

> Nations and the Codex (but not the WTO). They have educated the public and campaigned on various issues. Never, however, had they been promised direct, formal access to policymakers in the course of intergovernmental negotiations.

However, the access that consumer and environmental groups have gained is overshadowed by the comparable success of the TABD. Before the 1999 Bonn Summit the TAED and TACD wrote to summit leaders to request access, but the German Presidency, urged on by the US Commerce Department, refused invitations to the civil society dialogues.[80] The TAED and TACD – supported largely by the Commission – publicly denounced the unequal access given to the TABD. In response, the Washington 1999 Summit statement included an annex for equal handling of the dialogues.[81]

In general the change in summit procedures was seen as a symbolic win for the non-business dialogues, as EU–US summits are arguably not their best point of access.[82] Commission officials argued that private sector input would be more effectively aimed at working group level and have pushed for dialogue access to SLG rather than summit level meetings. One official argued, 'it is not much use if you haven't got your point across before then. They need to concentrate on early stages of policy decision-making where recommendations can be much more detailed. You have a better chance of influencing the expert than the political boss.'[83] However, access to transgovernmental actors is also a source of contention among the transatlantic dialogues. NGOs argue that the TABD gets higher level officials at its meetings, including the US Vice President and the WTO Director.[84] The TABD has a designated 'agency' that acts as its partner- the US Commerce Department – while the TAED and TACD have a small number of designated people within the State Department. Unlike the Commerce Department which has a responsibility only to corporations, a State Department official pointed out that, 'we cannot only take consumer or environmental consumers on board'.[85] The TABD also has crosscutting support from the US inter-agency committee that deals with its issues, and its members benefit from informal contact with governmental officials. One NGO official argued that, 'where TABD has more access is at a daily working level – lunches and receptions, meetings every month. It is a huge policy-lobbying machine.'[86]

The real problem with the NTA dialogue process is not just that NGOs do not feel like they have access to officials, because formal dialogue *has* increased through the TACD and TAED. Rather, the real gap between the TABD and the TACD is in the number of policy recommendations that have influenced transatlantic decision setters.[87] NGOs claimed that the success rates of the TACD and TAED – if measured against the TABD's 50 per cent rate – would be significantly lower.[88] Some argued that none of their proposals had been fully adopted. Others noted that NGO input had helped change the thinking on some policies, for example on the better access for medications in developing countries and greater contact over GMOs and product labelling.

Table 4.2 Formal access for the transatlantic dialogues

TABD	*TACD*	*TAED*
Regular attendance at EU–US summit	Limited access to EU–US summit	Limited access to EU–US summit
High level contacts at annual CEO meeting	High level contacts at annual general meeting in plenary	High level contacts at annual general meeting in plenary
Working group contact at annual CEO meeting	Working group contact at annual general meeting prior to plenary	Working group contact at annual general meeting prior to plenary
Mid year meeting	Steering group planning meeting	Steering group planning meeting
US interagency coordinators	TACD contact person in in State Department	TAED contact person in State Department
Regular issue manager – working level contacts		

Overall however, the dialogues have not produced the same concrete gains that the TABD has. The TAED Scorecard argued that government responses to recommendations (in grades from A to F) were significantly below average.[89] The TAED slammed the US government for its 'total failure to act' on a wide variety of issues.[90] Sixty-five consumer groups echoed the same sentiment, that the EU and the US had largely ignored consumer trade policy recommendations, in an annual report (TACD 2000a).[91] The message is that 'the overall impact of the TACD has not been enough, but we are encouraged by the achievements of the first few years and believe we can further establish the dialogue as an important part of transatlantic trade policy-making'.[92]

To summarise, the TACD and TAED have increased formal access for consumer and environmental NGOs, but the quality of access has been called into question. As one NGO observes, 'they are telling us what they are doing, rather than taking our advice. We have access but we don't learn specifics. TAED participants argue that US officials seem to be just going through the motions.'[93] The low key government response to TACD and TAED proposals fuelled claims that the governments were not taking the groups seriously – or as seriously as they take the TABD. Government officials stressed the importance of the TACD and TAED as dialogue structures. A State Department official argued, 'Whether or not their policies are adopted, they are widely understood and seriously considered.'[94] However, to participants faced with funding problems it is important that the TACD and TAED serve as more than 'talk shops'. The consensus is that talking is useful, but that the TACD can only gain support to continue if it is an efficient lobbying organisation. A

TACD official argued, 'Consumers and environmentalists are not downplaying dialogue, but they expect more concrete results, in part because TABD gets them.'[95]

Table 4.3 Active dialogue members

TABD	TACD	TAED
Price Waterhouse Coopers	Consumers International	European Environmental Bureau
Electrolux	Danish Consumer Council	Community Nutrition Institute
Xerox	Consumer Federation of America	World Wildlife Federation
United Technologies Corporation	US Consumers Union	German League for Nature and the Environment
Lafarge	US Public Interest Research Group	National Wildlife Federation
Suez-Lyonnaise	EuroCoop	Edmonds Institute
Daimler Chrysler	Kepka	Center for International Environmental Law
Philips Electronics	Italian Consumer Council	Biodiversity Action Network
Warner-Lambert	Public Citizen	Public Citizen
Tenneco		
Ford		

The Transatlantic Labour Dialogue

The goal of promoting cooperation on labour issues is found in the NTA and TEP. The economic chapter of the NTA makes broad reference to internationally recognised labour standards and employment issues. In May 1997 the AFL-CIO and ETUC agreed to initiate the dialogue under government sponsorship at the Bridging the Atlantic 'people to people' conference in Washington. A year later the TEP Action Plan outlined a number of commitments to increased dialogue on labour between workers, employers and NGOs and business and labour advisory groups (see also Knauss and Trubek 2001).[96]

The Transatlantic Labour Dialogue is the least developed formal NTA dialogue. The first meeting of the TALD, held a month before the TEP, coincided with an international labour summit. Its formal launch came with the submission of a joint statement to the EU–US Washington Summit in 1998. Its second meeting took place at an international (G8) meeting, and no official statement was ever released. The American Federation of Labour and the Congress of Industrial Organisations did issue a letter to President Clinton and Chancellor Schroeder before the Bonn Summit (June 1999). They agreed to support human rights clauses in international agreements and to broaden the labour agenda for the WTO. In December 2000, it issued its first real recommendations to EU–US leaders. Six months later, however, the TALD again appeared to be static.[97]

Table 4.4 Transatlantic dialogue policy positions

	TABD position	*TACD Position*	*TAED Position*
Biotechnology • Safety	Supports establishment of science-based proof that GMOs are harmful	Supports establishment of science-based proof that GMOs are not harmful	Supports establishment of science-based proof that GMOs are not harmful
• Labelling	Against GMO labelling	Supports mandatory labelling	Supports mandatory labelling
E-commerce	Supported safe harbour agreement	Opposed safe harbour/supports right to privacy	
Precautionary principles	Argues the PP should only be based on sound science	Favours use of PP in consumer, health, safety, environment regulations	Favours use of PP in consumer, health, safety, environment regulations
TRIPS	Supports full implementation of TRIPS	Against using TRIPS to block production of medicine in developing countries	
Climate change	Argues Kyoto emissions standards are non-tariff barriers		Supports implementation of Kyoto Treaty
The European Waste Electrical Equipment Directive (WEEE)	Identified as an Early Warning candidate		Supports WEEE and industry responsible for safe waste disposal
Participation and Regulatory Guidelines	Supports transparency and the Regulatory Guidelines	Supports transparency and the Regulatory Guidelines	Supports transparency and the Regulatory Guidelines

Hope for the recovery of the TALD was bleak, because its structure was flawed from the beginning. Knauss and Trubeck (2001) argue that the TALD lacked substantive expectations; was set up only as a small and quasi-private dialogue; was neither bilateral nor transatlantic and was a low priority for labour leaders.

First, although the TALD produced more substantive results in 2000, there was no sign of establishing an organisational structure, a secretariat or formal objectives. At the London meeting in 1999, labour leaders agreed to hold periodic reviews of the trade union dialogue, coordinate their positions on the planned Euro-American social and employment initiatives and initiate a Euro-American working group. None of these tasks was completed, and there was no subsequent commitment on behalf of the labour dialogue to pursue a transatlantic policy agenda.

The TALD is basically a dialogue between the AFL-CIO and the EUTC. Its meetings have included only a handful of people and have not even been held as separate events. Knauss and Trubeck (2001) note that, 'merely trying to find out what transpires at its meeting can be an exercise in frustration. In sum, there is little to indicate that either labour organisation has given the forum any serious attention.'

Those involved with the TALD agree that it is not a forum for policy shaping, and is only marginally a forum for dialogue. It is argued that the TALD is not transatlantic because the structure of international trade unions dialogue predates the NTA. The international orientation of global labour movements creates diplomatic problems for EUTC and AFL-CIO, and it was feared that a transatlantic based dialogue stood the risk of getting 'their [affiliates] noses out of joint'.[98] The international structure of the labour movement also explains the TALD's focus on multilateral rather than transatlantic issues. Most of the December 2000 statement focused on multilateral trade liberalisation, the MAI, sustainable development, the UN Rio +10 meeting and Aids Drugs to Africa (see Box 4.1).[99] The TEP is not viewed as a substantial policy forum. A TALD representative argued, 'Trade unions are exerting an inside track at the WTO level. If the bilateral level becomes more important, then the TALD will follow.'[100]

Consequently, the TALD is little more than a modest exchange between a European and an American labour federation. Given its lack of commitment and clear lack of influence, the labour dialogues – even more so than the consumer and environmental dialogues – cannot survive without government support. The labour movement is not willing to commit the resources to fund a transatlantic dialogue. One European labour representative argued that, 'You are not going to reinvent the trade union organisation for one-fifth the cost of a plane ticket. If they want us involved, they have to put their money where their mouth is.'[101]

The labour movements' resistance to be drawn into the NTA process means that the TALD has had no impact on transatlantic policy shaping.[102] One official even bluntly stated, 'There is no labour dialogue.'[103]

Box 4.1 The Transatlantic Labour Dialogue

Co-ordinators: AFL, CIO, EUTC

Meetings: London 1998 and Bonn 1999

Statements: May 1998, December 1998, December 2000 Summits

Interests: The MAI, GATS and public services, TRIPS and Aids drugs in Africa, sustainable development

Transnational decision shaping

The creation of the NTA dialogues has ensured that private actors have more access to transatlantic decision takers at both a high political level and a working level. While the civil society dialogues have all gained a formal role in the process, only the TABD has emerged as a true policy 'shaper'. A combination of factors contributes both to the effectiveness of the dialogues and the wide range of government responses to the recommendations.

Organisation, focus and funding

EU and US officials have, in the past, blamed a lack of cohesion, organisation and interest in the NTA process for the inequalities in actor access and policy adoption. The civil society dialogues, when compared to the business dialogue, have been characterised as weak, unorganised and plagued by internal bickering. There were claims that the TACD and TAED were less influential because they were new to the process. They have even been described elsewhere as 'toddlers in the policy playpen'.[104]

The ability of the private dialogues to organise themselves is directly linked to their capacity to produce cohesive proposals. Consensus among domestic groups and between EU and US actors is considered a major strength of the dialogues. The TABD is undisputedly the most developed transatlantic dialogue. It is highly organised and its proposals carry weight because they bear the approval of two hundred CEOs.[105] In short, the TABD is arguably a 'well oiled machine'.[106]

In contrast, however, it has been argued since the launch of the other dialogues, that strong management of the social dialogues was needed in order to overcome differences between groups.[107] One US official argued that, 'the TABD plays a different role than the other dialogues, which is to come to a common position and give recommendations. This is not what the other dialogues have done – they don't agree.'[108] Reaching consensus between NGO groups is more complicated because they are constituency based and have funding commitments to other organisations.[109] The civil society dialogues also had more trouble getting off the ground because of internal policy differences. Initially, US consumers groups were unable to agree on whether to start a dialogue, let alone agree on policy proposals.

To some extent the criticisms levelled at the civil society dialogues were warranted in the early days of their implementation, but the groups – excluding the TALD – recognised the need for organisation. The TACD, which was arguably the most incoherent after its first meeting, subsequently emerged as the most coherent civil society dialogue. Officials argued that the initial dispute between Public Citizen and Consumer Union was (mostly) set aside and that Consumer International and the Steering Group had worked hard to ensure that the consumer movement had a common face. The TACD – three meetings on – was described as very organised and very disciplined.[110] A dialogue that was earlier described as 'rude' and 'confrontational' was argued to be proficient. A US official observed that,

> If they are tearing their hair out they are not showing the governments. By the time they sit across from us, they are very, very professional. They do not wash their dirty laundry in public. The Steering Committee presents a united front. They spend a lot of time co-ordinating and they are coherent.[111]

Before its suspension, the TAED coordinators had also argued that the dialogue needed a more focused agenda, clear strategy and better organisation. A draft assessment of the TAED – presented at the 2000 meeting – emphasised the need to make the working groups more effective and criticised in particular the Trade Working group for failing to overcome internal differences. In response to vacant US posts, the report noted that, 'there are bottlenecks with regards to willingness to and/or ability of lead groups to invest sufficient time in co-ordination'.[112]

The orientation of the TAED and TACD's proposals has also distinguished them from the TABD. A credit to the TABD is its focus on policy details that are specific to the NTA institutions and the goal of the NTM. Although the TABD has a priority group that deals with the WTO, it has used global forums like the GBDe, to address multilateral issues. The TACD and TAED, on the other hand, have debated the need to allow non-transatlantic NGOs into the dialogues. Like the TALD, there has been a tendency for these dialogues to focus on multilateral or domestic rather than transatlantic issues. They have been accused of presenting broad proposals and of less effectively providing ready-made solutions. This is in part because they concentrate on issue areas where the EU and US disagree, for example over GMOs, BVT and beef. A TACD representative argued that, 'TABD is doing the governments' job for them. Civil society is not as focused on technicalities. It is about following reactions of process.'[114]

In reality, however, the TACD – more than the TAED – has successfully shifted the focus of the dialogue to address a number of 'transatlantic' policy issues. For example it has continuously emphasised the EU–US Safe Harbour

Agreement and employed research staff to follow the transatlantic MRAs. On the TAED it was claimed that, 'Broad proposals are still a problem. Contrary to business, many groups have less experience co-operating with each other. Each has its own agenda, and some recommendations reflect that.'[115] It was also argued that proposals – such as the demand to end multilateral disputes dealing with environmental legislation – could not be seriously addressed in the NTA. Rather, it was more appropriate 'to bring it to a stage where these dialogues can be used, we need to get to next stage – have more concrete, operational proposals'.[116]

Officials acknowledge that the quality of organisation and proposals is hindered by the funding problem encountered by the civil society dialogues. This obstacle is demonstrated by the suspension of TAED activities. A TACD official explained that NGOs cannot afford to hire researchers and lawyers to come up with policy setting details.[117] The lack of resources makes it harder for these groups to establish their own networks and to penetrate the established networks of 'working lunches' and drinks receptions in Brussels and Washington. The funding problem is also most acute because the future of the dialogues depends on it. Still, funding will be a permanent source of inequality. One MEP argued that, 'They will never have the same influence [as TABD]. They don't have the same money or clout.'[118]

Outsiders and insiders in the policy process

In many respects, consumers, environmentalists and industry are competing to influence transatlantic decision-making because they hold different – sometimes directly opposing – stakes in the process. The TACD and TAED share many of the same goals, which is reflected in a number of joint statements they have issued about the TEP and participation in the NTA process more generally. Furthermore, all of the groups have supported the implementation of the transatlantic regulatory guidelines, which highlight the need for transparency – and thus increased access – for the dialogues. However, Table 4.4 outlines a number of policy areas where the TABD holds different interests to the TACD and TAED. For example, the TABD and TAED disagree over the implementation of the Kyoto Treaty, because the TABD argued that emissions standards would adversely affect the competitiveness of industries. The TABD and the TACD disagree over the Safe Harbour Agreement because the TACD believes that the agreement does not adequately protect privacy. The TABD has identified a number of European environment directives – including the WEEE as possible Early Warning System candidates (TABD 2000).

The competition between the groups is demonstrated by their aims to counter-influence one another. Public Citizen helped organise protests of the TABD CEO meeting in Cincinnati in 2000. Lori Wallach, Director of Public Citizens' Global Trade Watch, argued in a guest article in the *Cincinnati Enquirer* that, 'TABD does not stand for Truly Appalling Backroom Deals, but it should.'[119] Both the TACD and TAED have emphasised the importance of monitoring the TABD. The business community returns the sentiment. Cowles (2001b: 263) argues that,

> Indeed, the US–EU business community tends to view the creation of 'other dialogues' in the US–EU relationship – the Transatlantic Labor Dialogue, the Transatlantic Consumers Dialogue, the Transatlantic Legislators Dialogue – not merely as an attempt to introduce civil society into US–EU relations, but also to counteract the growing influence of the TABD.

One of the biggest obstacles faced by consumers, environmentalists and labour unions is that their interests conflict with the agenda of the New Transatlantic Marketplace.[120] The TAED in particular consists of many groups that oppose trade liberalisation. Although there are many pro-liberalisation groups within the consumer dialogue, it has been noted that breaking down regulatory barriers – a goal of the NTA and the TABD – has the potential to undermine health and safety standards. One of the first actions of the TACD and TAED was to oppose implementation of the TEP Action Plan because of its inadequate commitment to sustainable development and transparency. As one official pointed out, 'the TABD says things the governments want to hear. Its interests are seen as more compatible with the goals of the TEP and the NTA'. Adding, on the other hand that, 'TAED argues against the WTO. No one wants to hear this.'[121]

The civil society dialogues have become 'outsiders' in the policy process in part because they challenge the legitimacy of the NTA. While all of the dialogues have argued the need for increased transparency in transatlantic decision-making, only NGOs have spoke out against the de-politicisation of issues. It is argued that social standards can only be protected if democratically elected bodies take decisions related to TEP in a transparent, participatory and accountable way. Opposition to the process as well as the policies means that, as one TACD official argued, 'they created monsters that do not now want to play by the rules'.[122]

Increasing transparency, finding consensus

The EU and the US have attempted to make the NTA process legitimate by bringing in different groups, laying out guidelines for equal access and encouraging public participation and transparency under the Joint Regulatory Guidelines. In addition, NTA and TEP policies must follow domestic channels of decision-making. In the US, public notices of agreements are posted in the Federal Register. The European Commission uses formal channels of communication under the Commission's Social Forum to gauge the wider public views on policies.

Competition between actors has complicated transatlantic decision-making. The threshold for consensus between groups is high because so many interest groups – with very different interests – have been given a formal role in transatlantic decision-making processes. Some officials have argued that inviting participation from the civil society dialogues has weakened the process because it undermines 'efficient' decision taking.[123] In response to this problem, transatlantic actors have sought ways to encourage the dialogues to reach consensus.

First, they supported the idea of 'multi-dialogue' meetings between business and civil society.[124] In 2000, the first multi-dialogue meeting was co-organised by European Partner for the Environment and the Luso Foundation with funding from the Commission.[125] The multi-dialogue meeting was launched to increase awareness of each other's activities and to explore mechanisms for understanding. All of the dialogues, barring the TALD, attended.[126] The meeting's concentration on one policy sector – Sustainable Development – helped focus the dialogue. Groups were also pulled into the dialogue by assurances that the meeting would not be used to negotiate any common positions but rather to allow groups to exchange views. Participants in the meeting were cynical about gaining any concrete results from the first meeting, but the second meeting held in January 2001 is a testament to the multi-dialogue's continued support.

Second, EU and US officials worked with different dialogues to establish cross interest policy networks or 'issue-orientated' task forces. The need to focus on cross cutting interest groups and specific policy problems was also addressed by the governments in the TEP. To date the most successful task force was the Biotechnology Consultative Forum which managed to produce agreed results from the science, business, academic and NGO communities. TACD members originally argued the Forum could not be used as a justification of consumer support.[127] However, the participation of an EU Steering Group Member helped balance the representation.

Finally, officials argue that the Legislators Dialogue could be a potential instrument for closer dialogue between the dialogues.[128] As discussed in Chapter 3, however, the TLD contact with the NTA process is underdeveloped. Five years into the process, the TLD has had good relations only with the TABD and little to no contact with the TACD and TAED. Its capacity to balance the dialogues is also undermined by the fact that the TABD is perceived to have more direct access to the bureaucratic process than it actually does.

Conclusion

This chapter sought to establish if and how the transatlantic dialogues have played a role in shaping decisions. It discussed the interaction between private actors in new transnational networks and between private and public actors at a number of levels – both transgovernmental and intergovernmental. Finally, it questioned the impact of private decision shaping forums on the overall process of transatlantic decision-making.

A number of themes arose in this examination of the transatlantic dialogues.

The motivations for inviting participation from the TABD and the civil society dialogues varied. The TABD, which was largely encouraged by the US government, was brought into the process to help facilitate the goals of trade liberalisation laid out in the New Transatlantic Marketplace. The TALD dialogue was brought in to advise the EU and US on aspects of the marketplace relating to labour issues. The consumer and environmental dialogues were pushed by the Commission to balance the interests of the process. The Commission found an ally in the TACD and TAED on policies where it was in dispute, or about to enter a dispute with the US, for example over GMOs, the WEEEs, and data protection. Encouraging civil society participation was also seen as a way to increase transparency in the Transatlantic Economic Partnership after the US government came under fire from domestic NGO groups worried about the de-politicisation of social and environmental regulations.

Increasing the participation of domestic groups at the transatlantic level has not necessarily made the process more balanced. Above all, there are wide ranges of interests covered by policy network. There is also a gross imbalance of power and resources between big business and civil society. While the TABD has been deemed largely successful in shaping policy and the TACD claims to have had some impact in shaping decisions, the TAED and TALD have been less effective. While the TABD has very much found itself an 'insider' in the process, civil society has remained somewhat on the 'outside'. The argument, thus, is that the TABD is the only formal dialogue, of the four, to exercise real decision shaping powers.

Notes

1 Brown (1994) argued, in a speech to the American Chamber of Commerce in Brussels, that EU–US business coordination on transatlantic trade issues was an important part of liberalisation.
2 Cowles (see 2001b and 1996) argues that American businesses, the State Department and the USTR were initially lukewarm to the idea. In particular the US agencies feared it was a way for the Commerce Department to shape trade negotiations.
3 The close relationship between the TABD and TPN is demonstrated in part by the fact that they share office space as well as contact lists.
4 Cowles (2001b: 243) notes, for example, that American businesspeople arrived at the meetings carrying Commerce Department briefing packs.
5 Interview, TABD participant, Brussels, September 1999.
6 Interview, TABD official, Brussels, September 1999.
7 It produces recommendations on specific policy sectors including but not limited to the Information Technology Agreement, E-Commerce, Intellectual Property Rights and the Mutual Recognition Agreements.
8 Interview, TABD participant, Brussels, September 1999. See also Cowles (2001a).
9 The meetings were held in Seville, in Chicago (1996), Rome (1997), Charlotte (1998), Berlin (1999), Cincinnati (2000) and Stockholm (2001).
10 The TABD chair companies provide office space for the American secretariat (in Europe

the secretariat is housed with the TPN) and provide the budget for TABD costs. The precise figure of the budget is difficult to pinpoint. It varies from year to year depending on the co-chair companies, and can vary from $250,000–$500,000. This sum funds the EU and US TABD offices, the secretariat salaries and TABD functions. However, the total costs of the TABD are difficult to quantify because the funding arrangement between the TABD and the participant companies are based on a 'loose structure'. Mid-year meetings, receptions and conference costs often have separate sources of funding (in the case of the conference there is local sponsoring from the host cities). Interviews, US and EU TABD participants, Brussels and Washington DC, October 1999, October 2000.

11 Interview, TABD Secretariat, Brussels, September 1999.
12 Generic firms initially complained that they had been kept out of the process, but were later brought into the TABD pharmaceutical working group, and Small and Medium Sized Enterprises (SME) were given a voice in the process through the Transatlantic Small Business Initiative and the priority group on SMEs. The Transatlantic Small Business Initiative was launched for companies that were outsized in the TABD. It holds summit meetings and operates on a working group structure, but is largely represented in the political arena by the TABD.
13 Cowles (2001a) notes for example that the Tenneco-Philips team (1997) tried to make the TABD more efficient by getting more companies involved at a higher level. Daimler-Benz AG and Warner-Lambert (1998) focused on the implementation of TABD recommendations and introduced the TABD Scorecard. Xerox and Suez Lyonnaise des Eaux tried to re-enforce small informal contact between CEOs and high level decision makers as well as expert level contacts between TABD participants and Agency Directors, such as the Secretary of Commerce.
14 Originally, the TABD was based on four working groups: (1) regulatory issues; (2) trade liberalisation; (3) investment; (4) third country relations. Following the Seville meeting 15 working groups were established. The Tenneco and Mead leadership (1997) introduced more issue managers to get more companies involved and put the working groups under three core areas – the Transatlantic Advisory Committee on Standards; Business Facilitation, and Global Issues. By 2000 the structure of the TABD expanded to five working groups and roughly 40 issue groups, each of which was also co-chaired by an American and a European company.
15 See www.tabd.com.
16 Interview, TABD participant, Brussels, September 1999.
17 Government attendees of the TABD summit have included the EU Commissioner for Trade, the EU Commissioner for Enterprise and Information Society, the US Commerce Secretary, the USTR, the US Vice President and the WTO Director.
18 The Commerce Department has at least three staff members in the Europe office who devote 50 per cent of their time to the TABD prior to its annual meeting. Interview, Commerce Department, October 2000.
19 Access to the annual meeting between officials and CEOs is closed to both the press and academic observers. Access became more restrictive with the Berlin CEO Conference as CEO demand for invitations increased. The author was offered access to the press core, but not to working group or plenary meetings in either 1999 or 2000.
20 Interview, Brussels, September 1999.
21 Interviews, TABD office and US Mission, Brussels, September 1999.
22 Interview, US Mission, Brussels, September 1999.
23 Interview, TABD participant, Brussels, September 1999.

24 Speech given to TABD at Charlotte Meeting, 1998.
25 See also Cowles (1996: 21): 'Economically, the TABD has provided government leadership with clear negotiating direction and has improved the prospects for trade liberalisation. Politically, the TABD has emerged as an important component of larger transatlantic relations'.
26 Interview, Commission Delegation, Washington, October 2000.
27 *Journal of Commerce*, 5 February 1998.
28 Interview, TABD participant, Brussels, September 1999.
29 Interview, TABD Participant, Brussels, September 2000 and email, June 2000.
30 Interview, Commission official, September 1999.
31 Interview, USTR official, October 2000.
32 Interview, US NGO, October 2000.
33 The idea rose out of a 1997 NTA 'building bridges' conference. See People to People Conference Report, 1997.
34 Italics added by author.
35 The TACD (Doc 1–99) argues that public interest groups demands since 1995 to participate in the process did not result in formal, or even inconsistent informal dialogue despite government support for the TABD.
36 Interviews, TACD Secretariat, London, January 2000. Commission Delegation, Washington, October 2000.
37 Interview, TACD Secretariat, January 2000.
38 A NWF Trade Discussion Paper 1998 argues that the TEP seems to be largely the result of TABD input.
39 Interview, TAED participant, Washington DC, October 2000.
40 The TAED had problems finding a US NGO to manage the grant before the NWF reluctantly agreed to accept the funds. Three-quarters of the TACD original Steering Groups' charters prohibited public funds. Interview, TACD Secretariat, via telephone March 2000; TAED official, Washington, October 2000.
41 CEO (1998a); (1998b), see also De Brie (1998).
42 Interview, European Commission Delegation, Washington DC, October 2000; TACD Secretariat, London, January 2000.
43 TAED (2000c).
44 See also Bignami and Charnovitz (2001).
45 Interview, European Commission Delegation and US State Department, October 2000. See also Bignami and Charnovitz (2001).
46 Interview, Commission Delegation, Washington DC, October 2000.
47 Interview, Commission Delegation, Washington DC, October 2000.
48 TIES interview with Jake Caldwell, April 1999.
49 Interview, TACD participant and USTR official Washington DC October 2000.
50 Interview, State Department official, Washington DC, October 2000.
51 Interview, TACD participant, Washington DC, October 2000. See also Cowles (1997).
52 The comments of one official demonstrate the extreme position that, 'There is nothing we can learn from TACD, TAED.' Interview, US Embassy, London, January 2000. Others argued that the TACD and TAED simply existed to oppose the TABD. Interview, USTR, Washington DC, October 2000.
53 Interview, European Commission Delegation, Washington DC, October 2000.
54 Interview, TACD Secretariat, London, January 2000.
55 Interviews, USTR, Washington DC, October 2000 and Council Secretariat, Brussels, September 1999; TACD Participant, Washington DC, October 2000.

56 Interview, USTR, Washington DC, October 2000.
57 Interviews, TACD Secretariat and US Embassy London, January 2000; Commission Delegation, TACD Participant, Washington 2000 and Council Secretariat and Commissioner, Brussels, September 1999.
58 Interview, TACD Secretariat, London, January 2000.
59 Interview, USTR and US State Department, October 2000.
60 To summarise, the TAED recommended the removal of subsidies for environmentally unfriendly energy sources (such as coal), demanded that sustainability assessments be applied to a number of WTO agreements and expressed its opposition to the multilateral Trade-Related Aspects of Intellectual Property Rights (TRIPs), Technical Barriers to Trade and Sanitary and Phytosanitary Measures (SPS) Agreements. It aired concerns about biotechnology, eco-labelling and the Precautionary Principle, the MRAs and Chemical and Electrical Waste Management, including Waste of Electrical and Electronic Equipment (WEEEs) It stressed transparency in transatlantic and multilateral decision-making, urged both governments to support the Kyoto Treaty and to stop challenging environmental legislation at the WTO. The message to the EU–US Summit, Lisbon, 31 May 2000 was that, 'Until such time as parity exists between environmental governance and multilateral trade rules, we demand that both the United States and the European Union immediately agree to mutual moratorium on WTO challenges and threatened challenges.'
61 The TACD has had a more technical focus on the transatlantic process because many consumer concerns are with regulatory issues. It made recommendations on consumer protection and E-Commerce, and in particular urged the EU and US to abandon the Safe Harbour agreement. It sided with the Commission on disclosure information for E-Commerce, argued GMOs should be labelled to ensure consumer choice, opposed the use of animal antibiotics and Bovine Growth Hormones and stated that the precautionary principle should apply in scientific cases where the evidence is not conclusive. While European scientists argue that the hormone is associated with different types of cancer the FDA claims Bovine Somatotropin, or BST presents a 'manageable risk'. The US supports using biotechnology while European governments have argued with consumers and environmentalists in favour of the precautionary principle and of mandatory labelling.
62 Interview, European Commission Delegation, Washington DC, October 2000.
63 Interviews, USTR and US State Department, Washington DC, October 2000.
64 Email correspondence, TACD Secretariat, June 2001; interview, US NGO, Washington DC, October 2000.
65 Government representatives at TACD meetings have included the US Secretary for Agriculture, the EU Commissioner for Health and Protection, US Congressmen, the Deputy USTR, Deputy Head of the Commission Delegation and NTA Task force level representatives.
66 Discussion papers, articles and updates are provided on the groups' web site, which is co-sponsored by the Transatlantic Information Exchange Service Network (see www.tiesweb.org).
67 A number of working group chair positions were also left open.
68 Past participants include the EU Trade Commissioner, the EU Environmental DG, the Assistant and Deputy Assistant Secretary for the Environment in US State Department and EU Council Presidency representatives. Some TAED members have complained about the absence of the USTR. A Steering Group Member argued that the USTR had been asked to attend, given the attendance of Trade Commissioner Pascal Lamy, but

refused on the basis that the USTR was not the same level as the EU Trade Commissioner. Interview, TAED, Brussels, May 2000.

69 Interview, US State Department, Washington DC, October 2000.
70 Interviews, TACD participants, Brussels, May 2000.
71 Interviews, US State Department, Washington DC, October 2000.
72 Interview, TACD Secretariat, London, January 2000.
73 Interview, TACD participant, Washington DC, October 2000.
74 Interview, Commission Delegation and USTR, Washington DC, October 2000.
75 Interview, Commission Delegation, Washington DC, October 2000.
76 Interview, Commission Delegation, Washington DC, October 2000.
77 Interview, US NGO, Washington DC, October 2000.
78 Interviews, Environmental Protection Agency, Washington DC, October 2000.
79 Interview, USTR, Washington, October 2000.
80 NGO groups argued that the Council Presidency was persuaded by the German Chancellor Schroeder, who hails from a largely industrial region. Interview, TACD Secretariat, London, January 2000.
81 It was agreed that EU and US authorities should meet formally with all of the dialogues at least once every six months, that working level contacts should facilitate routine interaction and that a rotating schedule for summit attendance should be put in place.
82 Rather, it has been argued that the summits serve as photo opportunities. Interviews, TAED and TACD participants, London (January 1999) and Washington DC (October 2000).
83 Interview, European Commission, Brussels, September 1999.
84 While government presence at TACD and TAED annual meetings has increased, NGOs argue that they do not have the same level of representation. One US NGO contended, 'We did not have the Vice President at our annual meeting. We are lucky to get one US Cabinet member.' Interviews TAED and TACD, Brussels, London, Washington DC, January 1999–October 2000.
85 Interview, US State Department, Washington DC, October 2000.
86 Interviews, TACD Secretariat (London) and two TACD members via email (January 1999–October 2000).
87 A TACD official notes, 'It is not that the structures are not working well, but that they are working better for the TABD.' Interview, TACD Secretariat, London, January 2000.
88 Interviews with European and American NGOs, London, Brussels and Washington DC, January, May and October 2000.
89 The Commission's response to GMOs received the highest mark (a C+).
90 TAED–TACD Press Release 'Transatlantic Consumer Dialogues Release Annual Reports, Slam Government for Lack of Responsiveness', 6 June 2000.
91 TACD press release, 'US & EU Consumer Groups Call for Swift Action to Balance Trade Dialogue, 30 March 2000.
92 Email correspondence with TACD Secretariat, June 2000.
93 Interview, American NGO, Washington DC, October 2000.
94 Interview, US State Department, Washington DC, October 2000.
95 Interview, TACD Secretariat, London, January 2000.
96 It also included a commitment to end child labour.
97 The 2001 EU–US Summit Statement from Gotenburg stated, 'We support the Transatlantic Environment Dialogue and the Transatlantic Labor Dialogue in their efforts to rejuvenate their activities.'
98 Interview, TALD, September 1999.

99 Although it should be noted that TALD did broach the subject of EU–US approaches to Burma.
100 Interview, TALD official, Brussels, September 1999.
101 Interview, TALD, Brussels, September 1999.
102 Interviews, European Commission, Brussels, September 1999; and US State Department, Washington DC, October 2000.
103 Interview, US State Department, Washington DC, October 2000.
104 Quoted in Peterson (2001a).
105 Interview, Council Presidency and European Commission, Brussels, September 1999.
106 Argued by TABD official, interview, Brussels, September 1999.
107 Interviews, European Commission, Brussels, September 1999.
108 Interview, US Mission, Brussels, September 1999.
109 See also Aaron *et al.* (2001) who argue that, 'when NGOS are brought together to discuss common issues but discover that they differ significantly in their political agendas and operating style, it can be a complicating factor'.
110 Interview, USTR, Washington DC, October 2000.
111 Interview, US State Department, October 2000.
112 TAED (2000c).
113 At a global level, the Global Business Dialogue on Electronic Commerce (GBDe) was launched in 1998 to develop a global consensus on the industry principles for the policy debates on electronic commerce. The GBDe share interests, overlapping membership and secretariat staff. Interview, TABD, April 2001. See also Cowles forthcoming.
114 Interview, TACD official, by telephone, June 2000.
115 Interview, Commission Delegation, Washington DC, October 2000.
116 Interview, Commission Delegation, Washington DC, October 2000.
117 Interviews, TACD Secretariat, London, January 2000.
118 Interview, European Parliament, Brussels, September 1999.
119 Quoted in 'Closed-Door process needs change', guest column in *Cincinnati Enquirer*, 19 November 2000.
120 One US official suggested for example that, 'the governments have accepted that consumer views are valid, but NGOs have not accepted that liberalisation is good'. Interview, USTR, Washington DC, October 2000. See also Aaron *et al.* (2001).
121 Interview, European Commission, Brussels, September 1999.
122 Interviews, TACD Secretariat, London, January 2000.
123 Interview, Commission Secretariat, September 1999.
124 The principles for government relations with the Transatlantic Dialogues calls for dialogue between the dialogues. Despite the government's encouragement, there was very little outreach between the dialogues before 2000. The Luso American Development Foundation (the secretariat of the Donors Dialogue) tried to organise a meeting in 1999 but failed to gain enough support from the dialogues or from the governments. The TACD argued that it needed to first get itself organised. Commission officials worried that the dialogue was exclusive. A TABD official argued that it clearly had different interests than the other dialogues. One participant noted that, 'this would mean compromise – that is the governments' job not businesses'. TAED and TACD members reiterated their suspicion of the TABD and the need for governments to strike a balance between interest groups. (Interviews with the European Commission, Brussels, September 1999; US State Department and US Commerce Department, Washington DC, October 2000.

125 The European Commission (DG External Relations) provided support for the project. Additional contributions to help cover the costs of the two US resource persons were provided by the US State Department and the Heinrich Böll Foundation. In addition, each of the dialogues covered the travel costs of their respective representatives.

126 The role of Ron Kingham – the former coordinator of the TAED – was influential in gaining TACD and TAED support for the meeting. Telephone correspondence, March 2000.

126 The US had chosen a consumer representative who was opposed by US consumer groups for having previously been employed by the GMO giant Monsanto Corporation. Interview, TACD Secretariat, via telephone, March 2000.

127 Interview, European Parliament, September 1999.

5

Anti-trafficking coordination in Eastern Europe

Globalisation and political instability in newly democratised states have given rise to global challenges that cross borders and elude national efforts to curb trafficking in drugs, nuclear material and migrants. The end of the Cold War ushered in a period of economic instability in Central and Eastern Europe (CEE), Russia and the Newly Independent States (NIS), creating social circumstances which gave rise to organised criminal networks. Weak democracies are unable to contain these networks, and Western democracies are increasingly unable to police their borders. Trafficking does not stem from Eastern Europe alone, but the rise of criminal trade from Eastern to Western Europe means that criminal activity originating in CEE inevitably crosses the borders of developed countries (Ruggerio 2000: 189).

The increased mobility of capital and people means that individual states, both developed and developing, are unable to adequately target international crime and international terrorism alone. The idea that cross border crime must be managed through national, regional and international cooperation became accepted wisdom throughout the 1990s. The US government set up FBI training centres in Budapest and Bangkok to train local authorities to fight transnational crime and terrorism. The EU set up Council working groups to deal with terrorism, police cooperation and organised crime under the Justice and Home Affairs Pillar. At the international level, in December 2000, 189 states signed the UN Convention on Transnational Organised Crime. A transatlantic framework for increased law enforcement cooperation was created under the global challenges chapter of the NTA.

This chapter examines EU–US cooperation in combating trafficking in women as a case study of joint cooperation in law enforcement, fighting global challenges and transatlantic policy-making. In 1997, and again in 1999, the EU and the US coordinated two anti-trafficking information campaigns. The first was in Ukraine and Poland and the second in Bulgaria and Hungary. A third, Russian campaign was also being considered. EU–US cooperation in trafficking in women is an important indicator of the factors that instigate and impede cooperation in the area of Justice and Home Affairs. Trafficking in women is not only an issue of transnational crime, but also of human rights, migration, and labour.

Transatlantic cooperation in the area of trafficking in women is distinct, first because it is rather low key in terms of visibility when compared with economic cooperation under the NTA. EU–US policy on trafficking in women is much less integrated than it is for example in the case of the Mutual Recognition Agreements (see Chapter 6). Second, the implementation of joint projects in this area affects the EU and the US only indirectly, because the transatlantic anti-trafficking information campaigns are run in third countries. Thus, in contrast to the MRA case, the interest of outside states that are affected by the transatlantic information campaigns directly impacts how the EU and the US can cooperate.

This chapter seeks to explain the decision-making process that led the EU and the US to join forces in fighting trafficking in women. First, it questions why the EU and the US chose to cooperate in this area: What informed the intergovernmental 'political decision' to cooperate on trafficking in women? This question is addressed in the first section, where the national and international political climate on trafficking in women is discussed in relation to the decision to establish a transatlantic policy on trafficking in women. Here it is argued that the EU and the US were able to cooperate on trafficking because it was framed as a human rights issue as well as a law enforcement policy.

Once it is established why a joint policy on trafficking in women was pursued, the focus of the chapter turns to how transatlantic officials chose to cooperate. The second section questions how prominent transgovernmental actors are in setting and shaping the policy on trafficking in women. In addition, this chapter asks if there has been a shift of decision 'shaping' powers to transnational actors. The third section examines the role NGOs played in shaping the decision-making process. The final section questions the significance of transatlantic cooperation on trafficking in women, both in the context of the international movement against trafficking and the global challenges pillar of the NTA. What does this case study tell us about the larger NTA political agenda and the scope for cooperation in the field of Justice and Home Affairs?

The political decision to target trafficking

At the May 1997 EU–US Summit in The Hague, US President Clinton, Commission President Santer and the Dutch Council Presidency agreed to cooperate on trafficking in women and issued a statement committing both sides to work together to combat the problem. The details of the project were finalised six months later and announced at the following summit. Two years later the EU and the US endorsed a second project, and in 2001 negotiations for a trafficking information campaign in Russia were underway. This section seeks to explain the political or 'intergovernmental' decision to pursue cooperation in this area and it questions why transatlantic leaders chose to address this particular global challenge.

This chapter does not give an in depth analysis of the nature of the problem of trafficking in women. Rather, it concentrates on the intergovernmental response to the problem. More extensive coverage of illegal trafficking in migrants is found mostly in the sociological literature.[1] Trafficking in women is a well documented problem that is both global and extensive. It is a governance problem that has been tackled at the national, EU, transatlantic and international level. The International Organisation of Migration (IOM) (2003) believes that as many as two million people are trafficked each year, and it is estimated that trafficking in women and children is a business that generates $7–12bn annually (OSCE 1999).[2] The Congressional Research Service notes that trafficking in women and children is considered the largest source of profits for organised crime after drugs and guns (Miko 2000).

In order to determine why the EU and the US have chosen to highlight trafficking in persons as a global problem, we must first identify the problem. Defining trafficking in women is difficult, as many different interpretations exist. For some it is important to make a distinction between trafficking and smuggling. Martin and Miller (2000: 969–70) argue:

> Trafficking in persons means the recruitment, transportation, transfer, harboring or receipt of persons, either by the threat or use of abduction, force, fraud, deception or coercion or by the giving or receiving of unlawful payments or benefits to achieve the consent of a person having control over another person.

A broader definition is given by Hughes (2000: 627–8) who acknowledges that many women initially consent voluntarily to work abroad in the sex industry, but without the knowledge that they face physical abuse, exploitation and enslavement. Her definition includes trafficking, which 'may be the result of force, coercion, manipulation, deception, abuse of authority, initial consent, family pressure, past and present community violence, economic deprivation or other condition of inequality for women'.

Varying definitions of trafficking highlight different aspects of the problem. The rise of voluntary illegal migration to the EU and the US creates problems of border control more generally. The desire of persons to migrate illegally due to economic conditions means a criminal market has emerged for smuggling migrants. The line between smuggling and trafficking is blurred in the trade in women. Trafficking is an immigration problem because many women seeking work (both legal and illegal) in the West agree to be voluntarily smuggled across borders, only to find themselves trapped into trafficking schemes. NGOs, the IOM and academics question the voluntary nature of involvement in trafficking networks, because as Hughes (2000: 636) argues 'Even women who voluntarily travel to engage in prostitution do not anticipate the level of manipulation, deception, and coercion to which they will be subjected.' The international definition of trafficking put forward by the UN Protocol on Trafficking acknowledges that trafficking in persons occurs even when payments are given or received to achieve the consent of a person having control over another person.[3] Thus, fraud and deception as well as coercion and abduction constitute trafficking.

The point is that trafficking is a multifaceted problem for states. First, it is linked to smuggling, which means that it is a border control problem, particularly for the EU whose perimeter is shared with a main supply region. The involuntary movement of persons aggregates the problem for states because trafficking is a violation of international law and international norms banning slavery. Trafficking in women is both a transnational crime and a human rights violation. In short, EU and US interest in combating trafficking in women is linked to all three dimensions of the problem: it is an immigration/migration issue, a law enforcement violation and an infringement of human rights.[4]

A criminal market built on abusing human rights

One way to approach the problem of trafficking in women is to analyse it as a transnational crime, which is driven by the demand for an illegal market in women (Hughes 2000; Schloenhardt 1999; Taylor and Jamieson 1999). In market terms, the trade is driven by a demand for women sex workers in the West and a supply of impoverished women and criminal networks in the East. The direct impact of the crime is not just that it crosses borders but that the EU and US are the main destination points for trafficked persons. The demand for trafficked women exists mainly in countries with thriving sex industries, including Germany, the Netherlands and the US.[5] The criminal market exists for the involuntary trade in women because sociologists note that there is a demand for prostitutes that could never be supplied voluntarily (Hughes 2000).

Three factors facilitate the criminal market for the trafficking trade. First, globalisation and political instability drive the supply side of the market. Globalisation increases the mobility of persons, which facilitates trade, and free capital allows criminal money to be moved easily throughout the world. In short, 'Privatisation and liberalisation of markets have created wider and more open marketplaces throughout the world' (Hughes 2000: 630–1). New technology, specifically the internet, has increased communication and resulted in rapid and unregulated movement of human capital (Stoecker 1998; 1999).

The globalisation of capital has made it difficult for individual states to combat the problem of trafficking, but illegal markets have emerged within countries in part because there are not appropriate laws in place (Schloenhardt 1999). Newly developing democracies lack the legal capacity to protect trafficking victims and prosecute traffickers, and demand countries have only a recent history of criminalising the traffickers rather than the trafficked.[6]

The free movement of capital and people and increased communication through advanced technology facilitates the movement of people and funds, which in turn propels the trade in trafficking in women. Trafficking is an attractive business because the profits from trafficking in human beings rivals that of drug trafficking but the penalties are minimal. For example, while the sentence for drug trafficking in the UK is up to twenty years imprisonment, the sentence for trafficking in humans usually carries a two to three year sentence.[7] In the US the statutory maximum for involuntary servitude is ten years, as opposed to a life sentence for trafficking 10g of LSD (O'Neill 1999: 43). The traders in this illegal market consist of amateur traffickers, small groups of criminals as well as international trafficking networks (see Scholenhardt 1999). However, it is widely acknowledged that organised crime largely fulfils the role of supplier (Taylor and Jamieson 1999).

Organised criminal networks are able to exploit the trade in trafficked women because countries with developing economies and emerging democracies fill the supply side of the market. Traditionally, Asian countries were the lead suppliers in the trafficking trade, but the post-Cold War transitions to democracy and private market economies in CEE, the NIS and Russia created new markets for transnational crime in general and illegal trafficking in women specifically. Difficult economic circumstances fuelled illegal activity and forced people to seek work abroad. The illegal trade in women increased, note Martin and Miller (2000), because women bore the brunt of economic restructuring. In Ukraine, for example, IOM notes that women represent up to 90 per cent of the newly unemployed.[8]

Trafficking in women is a law enforcement problem, because it involves the illegal transport of people across borders as well as kidnapping, forced labour and slavery.[9] However, it is a difficult problem to confront on a criminal level, because international law enforcement cooperation is superficial and international human rights laws are rarely enforceable. Little to no action was taken against traffickers prior to the 1990s despite the United Nations' (UN) 1948 Universal Declaration of Human Rights, which claims 'No one shall be held in slavery or servitude'. It is the classification of trafficking in women as a human rights violation, however, which helped gain momentum for international anti-trafficking movements. The international, national and indeed transatlantic responses to trafficking prior to 2000 addressed the problem through education and aid rather than criminal prosecution. It was the combined interest in trafficking in women on a migration, human rights and law enforcement platform that made bilateral and multilateral action possible.

Anti-trafficking policy responses

International interest in targeting trafficking in women is demonstrated by its prominence on the agenda of the UN and the Organisation for Security and Co-operation in Europe (OSCE).[10] Trafficking is addressed in the Stability

Pact for South Eastern Europe (1999). The 2000 UN Convention Against Organised Transnational Crime includes a Protocol on Trafficking in Women, which is designed to help governments share information about organised crime and increase their ability to prosecute traffickers.[11] International organisations have encouraged national governments actively to target trafficking in women through human rights legislation, but the UN Protocol represents the first international step towards criminalising trafficking in women.

A number of factors prompted US domestic action on trafficking in women. McBride Stetson (2000) believes that trafficking in women came onto the US public agenda from the 'top down'. She argues that the international human rights angle on trafficking in women prompted the Executive Branch's involvement, which eventually led to Congressional action. Specifically, the characterisation of trafficking as a women's issue as well as a human rights issue helped push it on to the US policy agenda.[12] The precedence for US involvement on trafficking in women was the creation of an Interagency Council on Women in 1995 by President Clinton. The Interagency Council worked with the State Department in creating an anti-trafficking 'czarina',[13] and in establishing representatives in charge of tackling the issue of trafficking in women in the Justice Department, Health and Human Services and the US Agency for International Development. McBride Stetson (2000: 18) argues that the Interagency Council, 'which is staffed primarily with femmocrats, is the linkage between the UN's Commission on the Status of Women ... on the one hand and the federal policy makers in Congress on the other'.[14]

Interest in targeting trafficking in women also came from the 'bottom up' through US NGOs. Women's groups and human rights groups actively encouraged the US Administration and the US Congress to act on trafficking. The US Administration held briefings with members of the NGO community to discuss trafficking and many NGOs worked with Republican Representative Chris Smith, who sponsored the US Trafficking Victims Protection Act 2000. Finally, NGOs solicited media attention in order to raise public awareness to the problem.[15]

The Clinton Administration's commitment to trafficking in women was secured in March 1998 when the President issued the policy document 'Steps to Combat Violence Against Women and Trafficking in Women and Girls'. The document identified trafficking as a 'fundamental human rights violation' and outlined a three-tiered approach to combat trafficking in women and children. The Clinton Administration pledged to work towards *preventing* trafficking through the education of women and local authorities and job skills training, *protecting* victims through funding regional assistance of victims and finally *prosecuting* the traffickers. It included a commitment to work abroad with source, transit and destination countries to prevent trafficking and protect victims. At home, Congress's Trafficking Against Women Act of 2000 incorporated the 'three p's' into domestic legislation, with additional

Box 5.1 Transatlantic efforts to combat trafficking in women

- **Joint Action Plan, 1995** committed the EU and the US to cooperate in the fight against trafficking in women and illegal immigrants.
- **Ministerial Meeting, April 1997 in The Hague:** Ministers agreed to begin work on trafficking in women information campaigns and put trafficking on the EU–US Summit agenda.
- **EU–US Summit May 1997:** EU and US Summit leaders agreed to pursue joint co-operation on trafficking in women.
- **November 1997:** The transatlantic information campaigns are launched in Poland and the Ukraine.
- **EU–US Summit, December 1997:** The SLG report announced that the information campaigns had been launched in Poland and the Ukraine, and a trafficking in women statement is released as a summit deliverable.
- **April–June 1998:** The first information campaigns were implemented.
- **The SLG Report, May 1998** stated that US law enforcement officials and the EU Multidisciplinary Group on Organised Crime should evaluate whether to expand the initiative to discourage trafficking.
- **EU–US Summit, December 1998:** EU and US leaders formally agreed to extend information campaigns to Bulgaria and Hungary.
- **Transatlantic Conference on Trafficking in Women, July 1998:** A transatlantic conference was held in Lviv, Ukraine to evaluate the success of the Polish and Hungarian information campaigns.
- **SLG, June 1999** reported that law enforcement cooperation continued to combat trafficking in women and children despite delays in planning the Bulgarian and Hungarian campaigns.
- **October 1999:** planning stage of Bulgarian and Hungarian campaigns began.
- **January–June 2000:** implementation of Bulgarian and Hungarian campaigns began.
- **November 2000:** US Trafficking in Women Act was passed.
- **December 2000:** The UN Protocol on Trafficking in Women was signed in Palmero.

provisions for strengthening the punishment for traffickers and sanctions against foreign governments failing to meeting minimum standards in combating trafficking.

Two less normative factors dictated an EU level response to the problem of trafficking in women. First, the new supply source of trafficked women affected the EU much more directly than the US. While the US was dealing with roughly 45,000–50,000 trafficked women a year, the EU had to contend with an estimated 500,000.[16] The geographical location of this new supply meant the problem was right at the doorstep of the EU. One US official argues, 'For the EU trafficking is definitely an immigration issue ... you cannot separate it from the political debate on asylum and harmonisation.'[17]

The precedence for EU immigration policy in general and trafficking in women policy specifically was set by the creation of the Justice and Home

Affairs (JHA) pillar in the Maastricht Treaty. The Treaty of Amsterdam introduced a new institutional framework for dealing with organised crime at the EU level and moved migration policy for the first time into the Commission's negotiating competency. This move allowed the Commission to take more direct action through the DAPHNE[18] project and the STOP programme. The DAPHNE project funds NGOs who deal with violence against women and children while the STOP[19] programme coordinates initiatives to fight against trafficking in human beings. European level policy in this area has been directly targeted at the applicant states, which are the source of trafficked women.[20] Finally, the Council Framework Decision on Trafficking (2002) encourages the member states to adopt a common legal definition of trafficking in persons and to harmonise minimum penalties.

Intergovernmental interest in trafficking

We have established that trafficking is of interest to states because it is linked to migration, human rights and law enforcement policies and that the EU and the US have demonstrated their interest in fighting trafficking at a regional, national and international level. The US has also pursued bilateral cooperation on trafficking in women with individual member states including Italy and Finland. EU–US cooperation was secured at the transatlantic level through the NTA framework. The NTA Joint Action Plan identifies trafficking in women as a specific global challenge in the context of immigration and asylum in 1995. In 1997, post Amsterdam, EU and US ministers decided that they should take steps to coordinate their anti-trafficking efforts in Europe. Both partners were already pursuing individual anti-trafficking programmes and, for the most part, there was no clear ideological divide on the issue of trafficking. Thus, it was identified as an area where resources could be pooled and efforts organised to combat the problem. The political decision to go ahead with a joint trafficking project was announced at the EU–US Summit in May 1997 in The Hague. It was there that transatlantic leaders 'made' the decision to establish a transatlantic policy on trafficking in women.

Transatlantic anti-trafficking policy

The intergovernmental decision to establish a transatlantic policy response to trafficking in women explains *why* the EU and the US decided to cooperate in this case. Transgovernmental level decisions are examined here in order to determine *how* the EU and the US decided to cooperate. The focus is on the administrative decisions that 'set' the transatlantic anti-trafficking policy.

While the political decision to cooperate on trafficking came from the top down, the details that established the information campaigns were derived from the bottom up. The issue of trafficking in women rose up through the ranks of the dialogue structure, from the NTA institutions to the ministerial meetings and finally the EU–US Summit. Coordination of EU and US efforts to cooperate were handled through NTA institutions such as the NTA Task Force and the Senior Level Group. The majority of contact, however, was made on an ad hoc and informal basis. In reality, it was a small group of people who co-facilitated EU–US cooperation in this area.[21] Key contact persons in the US Mission, DG Justice and Home Affairs and DG External Relations established and maintained the dialogue on trafficking. The concept of an information campaign and the details of the transatlantic project were derived at the working group level, and close cooperation between US law enforcement and the EU Multidisciplinary Group on Organised Crime preceded the decision to expand the transatlantic anti-trafficking initiative (SLG 1998a).

EU and US foreign ministers effectively 'set' the policy on trafficking in women, but their decisions were directly based on the input of lower level transgovernmental actors who were charged with finding a way that the EU and the US could work together. NTA institutions were key in providing a focus for transatlantic efforts to combat trafficking in women. The SLG tracked the progress of the information campaigns and was thus able first, to keep momentum going for the process by highlighting ongoing work in Task Force and SLG meetings and second, to serve as a problem solving forum. One US official notes that when obstacles arose, the NTA Task Force and the SLG 'kicked in', and that the NTA process helped accelerate decisions over funding problems.[22] One EU official notes that it was the NTA Task Force that provided political guidance to the coordinators of the process.[23] Policy 'shaping' decisions were affected by domestic structures, bureaucratic processes and the political will of both the EU and the US as major 'demand' states, along with the cooperation of the supply states where the information campaigns were run. The project thus required that officials accurately gauge the capacity for cooperation between the EU and the US on trafficking in women.

Three key transgovernmental decisions are addressed here; first the decision on where to target transatlantic efforts, second, the details of the transatlantic policies and third, who would implement the transatlantic campaign.

Where to co-operate?

In assessing where to launch the anti-trafficking information campaign, policy makers had to determine both where these campaigns were needed and where they were most likely to have an impact. Each country chosen for the transatlantic campaigns was either a source or transit country for trafficking networks, a country where local government authorities showed commitment to address the problem and where non-governmental infrastructure existed to implement the campaigns.[24]

The campaigns target major supply or transit states largely responsible for the movement of women from Eastern to Western Europe. Ukraine and

Russia are two of the poorest countries in Europe, and the trafficking of women from this region is so widespread that it has been nicknamed the 'Natasha Trade' (Hughes 2000). Bulgaria is another source country, where an estimated 10,000 women each year are trafficked to Northern and Southern Europe.[25] Poland is both a demand and a transit country. The US Embassy reports that 70 per cent of Ukrainian women working in the sex industry in Poland are there under duress and are controlled by the Agencija Tovazhyshka prostitution ring (Hughes 2000). Women from many of the newly independent states are also moved through Poland and Hungary into the EU.

Government cooperation is essential in this type of EU–US project because implementation takes place within the territory of sovereign states. In short, government cooperation is necessary because host states can be sensitive about law enforcement cooperation and foreign government funding.[26] One US official notes that before the campaigns were run host states were even sensitive to outside queries about the problem of trafficking.[27] Once EU and US intervention in host states was established, there were also concerns among some CEE and Russian officials that trafficking was taking up more time and attention than other areas of law enforcement.[28] Finally, there were concerns that the burden of targeting trafficking was misplaced. Source and transit countries have pointed the finger of blame back at the West and argued, 'First, you deal with the demand!'[29]

The countries chosen for the first campaign were both states that expressed interest in addressing the problem of trafficking. The Ukrainian and Polish governments had shown a commitment to confronting migration problems and working cooperatively to protect potential victims (see IOM 1998). The Polish and Hungarian governments had extra incentive to cooperate with the EU on trafficking given their positions in the first wave of European enlargement. In fact the EU showed preference for working with countries that were in the fast track for EU accession.[30] The EU-instigated cooperation with Russia, under the EU–Russia Partnership, proved to be more difficult.[31] The low level of commitment to the problem, sensitivity to outside involvement and the bureaucratic structure of the Russian government held up the negotiations. In addition there is no 'carrot', in the form of European membership, to lure Russian cooperation. However, US legislation that warrants sanctions against countries not adequately addressing the trafficking problem could prove more persuasive.[32]

Finally, the existence of civil society, particularly a strong NGO presence or field level support for international organisations, was a prerequisite for running the anti-trafficking information campaigns. Each country where the EU and the US have cooperated had a non-governmental infrastructure capable of implementing the campaign at a local level and the support of the IOM. The IOM was able to draw on NGO subcontractors in Ukraine where more research and advocacy has been done on trafficking in women by non-governmental organisations than in any other source country (Hughes 2000). The existence of the well-established anti-trafficking NGO La Strada was a factor in the EU decision to use Poland as a host state. Policy proposals submitted by IOM field offices in Bulgaria and Hungary shaped the transatlantic decisions to cooperate in those countries. Finally, although Russia has a less established civil society than other host states, Russian based advocacy groups such as the Mira Med Institute and the Moscow Center for International Defence have expressed an interest in working with local authorities to combat the problem of trafficking.

Table 5.1 Anti-trafficking implementation partners

Parallel trans-atlantic information campaigns	*Campaign I*	*Implementation partner*	*Campaign II*	*Implementation partner*
EU-sponsored	Poland	La Strada	Hungary	IOM
US-sponsored	Ukraine	IOM	Bulgaria	IOM

How to co-operate?

Transgovernmental actors played a crucial rule in gauging what type of cooperation was possible and how the EU and US could jointly address the problem of trafficking. The information campaign was conceived as a way to target trafficking in women on the supply side by raising awareness of potential victims and local authorities. The aim of the information campaign was to train authorities and to build on the NGO structure in order to gain information about trafficking trends, recruitment methods and potential deterrents to the trafficking trap.[33] These campaigns stress prevention rather than law enforcement cooperation, the emphasis being on research and strategy definition in the first phase and information dissemination in the second.

To claim that the EU and the US successfully pursued 'joint action' on trafficking in women is somewhat deceptive. It is more realistic to describe the campaigns as 'separate but parallel' projects. EU and US officials acted together to coordinate efforts, but the administration of each campaign was carried out separately. According to EU and US officials, different bureaucratic structures and funding arrangements dictated the way the EU and the US could jointly manage the problem. Logistically, it was easier to support different projects, but joint coordination was desirable to avoid overlap. Parallel campaigns were chosen so that comparisons could be made between the two.[34]

The EU and the US did agree to match funds (approximately), coordinate timing and effectively employ implementation partners. The US State Department's Bureau of Population and Migration put forward $382,000 in Ukraine and $400,000 for the Bulgarian campaign. The Commission matched the funds with 250,000 euros for the Polish project and 268,000 euros for Hungary.[35] The differences in internal funding mechanisms made coordinating payments difficult. Both EU and US officials agree that generally it is much easier for the US to deliver funds than it is for the EU. On the US side, the State Department was able to allocate funding for this project out of the Bureau of Population Refugees and Migration's budget. On the EU side, the Commission ran into problems with the original funding for Poland. They tried to fund the campaign using Phare money set aside for human rights, but were subject to a number of conditions set out by the Council of Ministers. While US officials were keen in the first case to distribute the money before the end of the fiscal year, the Commission was unable to match the funds in time and implementation of the project was delayed by six months.[36] To avoid later delays the subsequent project was funded through a Commission budget, a line that is approved by the European Parliament rather than the Council, and thus subject to fewer restrictions.[37]

Choosing implementation partners

Funding issues also dictated why the EU and the US decided to use different implementation partners in the first information campaigns. The EU chose to work with the non-governmental organisation La Strada in Poland because the Commission had a history and practice of working with NGOs. In addition the EU funding structure made it easier to fund NGO projects.[38] US budget rules made it more practical to fund the campaign in the Ukraine through an international organisation. The International Organisation on Migration was originally chosen because it was already working in the Ukraine and because it had a good working relationship with local officials and NGOs. The second campaigns were both run through the IOM because it was determined that it had, with its larger size and support structure, done a more comprehensive job. The IOM also had a better working relationship with the government, particularly in Bulgaria where La Strada has not had a habit of working with government officials.[39]

In summary, the EU–US information campaigns against trafficking in women are an example of policies which were officially 'set' by high level transgovernmental actors (ministers) but heavily shaped by lower level transgovernmental officials (US Mission, State Department and Commission officials) who made crucial decisions on where, how and with whom the EU and the US would cooperate. The small number of staff dealing with trafficking, however, meant that government officials relied heavily on information from non-governmental sources. Thus, it is important also to examine the role of NGOs and international organisations in 'shaping' policy on transatlantic trafficking in women.

Shaping the transatlantic anti-trafficking policy

NGOs and international organisations have played a crucial role in the global anti-trafficking movement. On the US side, there is an active dialogue between government and human rights, women's rights and religious NGOs on trafficking in women. In particular the Global Survival Network, Human Rights Watch, the International League for Human Rights and the Coalition Against Trafficking in Women have worked closely with both the US Administration and the US Congress.[40] Feminist and human rights NGOs worked with Republican Chris Smith of New Jersey, who sponsored the anti-trafficking bill in Congress, and the US Administration held briefings with members of the NGO community to discuss trafficking.[41] The Under-Secretary of State for Global Affairs, Frank Loy recognised the important role played by NGOs in a testimony to Congress in 1998. His department's web page provides links to roughly ten NGOs, including Anti-Slavery International, the Traditional Values Coalition and the International Human Rights Law Group.[42]

The Commission's original communication on trafficking in 1996 also noted that combating trafficking would require the involvement of NGOs. That same year the Commission invited EU and US based NGOs to the anti-trafficking conference it hosted in Vienna. Many European NGOs including La Strada (in Poland, the Czech Republic, Bulgaria and Ukraine); Phoenix (in Germany); the Foundation Against Trafficking (STV) (in the Netherlands) and Payoke (in Belgium) have established a habit of cooperation with the Commission. Under the Daphne project the Commission funded forty-nine different NGO projects.[43]

At the international level, transnational networks work in both OSCE and UN forums. NGOs actively participated in the OSCE Human Dimensions Seminars and the Vital Voice Conference in 1997. The Human Rights Caucus was created of about ten European, American and Asian NGOs to shape the negotiations of the UN Protocol on Trafficking. NGOs also keep each other informed on individual projects. One US NGO representative notes that email contact across the Atlantic is constant.[44]

While NGOs may broadly shape the international and domestic decision on trafficking, there is no evidence of an institutionalisation of political non-governmental actors within the NTA. Despite the lack of a transatlantic specific NGO network, there is evidence that non-governmental actors shape the transatlantic anti-trafficking campaign both from the top down and the bottom up. Networks of NGOs did participate in different decision-making forums, and the two implementation partners were directly responsible for shaping the transatlantic decisions. In this case, however, the main policy 'shaper' was an international organisation.

Transnational policy shapers

The IOM was highly influential in determining both where and with whom the EU and the US would cooperate. It submitted proposals for potential information campaigns across CEE and the NIS, and the location of its field offices helped shape the decision on where to cooperate. Feedback from the IOM on the first campaign also influenced the transatlantic decision to implement campaigns in both Bulgaria and Hungary. Poland is the only case where an NGO – La Strada – managed a campaign, but the IOM also subcontracted work out to private actors in Bulgaria, Hungary and Ukraine.[45]

This case study supports the argument that transnational actors have played a role in shaping the decision-making process on trafficking in women. It does not, however, point to an institutionalisation of transnational decision-making structures. The limited ad hoc or sub-contracted use of NGO resources at the transatlantic level is indicative of the fact that private actors play a less formal role in shaping decisions under the political chapters of the NTA.

Increasing the anti-trafficking dialogue

Would the transatlantic global challenges framework benefit from a more institutionalised role for transnational actors through, for example, an anti-trafficking dialogue, similar to the TACD or TAED? What, if any, would the benefits of a formal transnational dialogue be in this sector?

The role of NGOs in preventing trafficking and protecting trafficking victims is undoubted. In addition to providing governments with information and raising awareness, NGOs can fulfil crucial services such as victim assistance. Gramegna (1996) argues that NGOs have a 'leading role' to play in offering counselling, care and assistance to trafficked women. In many countries what limited assistance there is for victims of trafficking is provided almost exclusively by NGOs. One OSCE (1999: 14) report states that, 'where legislation and institutions are weak, or where police and other authorities are complicit to trafficking, NGOs may be the only institution taking effective steps to prevent trafficking or to protect victims'.

The role of NGOs is especially important because private actors are able to fulfil functions that governments and the IOM cannot always provide. In particular NGOs are needed to establish a direct link between victims and local authorities. Johnson (1999) argues that EU member state governments should recognise the fact that private NGOs are sometimes more able to provide necessary services, because they serve as a buffer between governments and victims. The OSCE (1999: 21) report notes that victims who receive support from NGOs are more likely to cooperate with law enforcement and serve as potential witnesses. In addition NGOs provide a crucial service to governments and the IOM by providing them with valuable information about traffickers and the trafficked. In short, one European NGO argues, 'NGOs play a crucial role in the information campaigns because they are the source of first hand information, they have the direct access to victims of trafficking, but also have a broad based knowledge of local conditions – political, economic and social – needed to implement the campaigns'.[46] The importance of maintaining a link between the public and private sector is an underlying theme in the NTA. Many NGOs have expressed the need to forge a formal dialogue between non-governmental and governmental actors similar to those that exist in the economic chapter of the NTA. Steve Warnath (1998) of the President's Council on women notes that, 'In discussions with NGOs, various government officials and others we have heard that it would be helpful to convene a series of meetings in different regions of the world to facilitate government, NGOs and private sector co-operation in developing of regional strategies of prevention, protection and enforcement.' Speaking at the launch of the Hungarian information campaign, the EU Commissioner for Justice and Home Affairs Antonio Vitorino stated the campaigns should, 'stimulate the building up of important networks and partnerships between police, judicial and social authorities as well as with NGOs and other actors of civil society'. NGO representatives have argued that groups like La Strada have to be integrated into the decision-making process because they know the most. In addition, a case can be made for creating a more direct and formal role for NGOs in the decision-making process because there is a degree of distrust between NGOs and the IOM.[47]

Three barriers stand in the way of institutionalising a transatlantic trafficking dialogue. First, some NGOs, particularly at the local level, are unwilling to work directly with governments or with the IOM.[48] There is some scepticism in the NGO community about the use of the IOM, given its mandate as a migration organisation. In addition some organisations are sceptical of local authorities and feel they alone are better able to provide protection to victims. Many fear that victims, rather than traffickers, will be criminalised under domestic legal systems (OSCE 1999: 21). Second, determining which NGOs to fund could prove difficult given clear ideological differences across groups. For example, US feminists disagree with the language used in the UN Protocol on Trafficking.[49]

Despite these barriers to institutionalisation, however, building a stronger link with civil society on the political dialogue could reap the same benefits that the economic dialogue has from the TABD, the TAED and TACD. Institutionalising the political dialogue further through, for example, an anti-trafficking dialogue would elevate the NTA's policy of 'building bridges' in political sectors.

The impact of information

This section evaluates the implications of the information campaigns both in a transatlantic and an international context. It seeks to explain the shortcomings of both the transatlantic and international response to trafficking in women, highlighting factors such as the sensitivity of international law enforcement cooperation and the weak JHA pillar in the EU. Yet, despite these shortcomings, it argues that the transatlantic information campaigns represent a significant effort under the NTA to fight global challenges.

Low-key cooperation

The information campaigns run in parallel by the EU and the US are an example of fairly low key cooperation in the area of Justice and Home Affairs. Transatlantic cooperation against trafficking in women was limited in this case to dialogue and co-funding. The campaigns concentrated on education, or prevention, rather than protection of victims and prosecution of traffickers.

It is widely accepted that prevention campaigns will not dramatically curb the number of trafficked women from CEE and the NIS unless the root causes of trafficking are addressed. One NGO official argues, 'you can tell one thousand women that they will be trapped in prostitution but it is counter-productive. Many knew they would be working in sex work, but they need the money to send back home.'[50] Even prosecution will not deal with voluntary migration pursued out of desperation. Trafficking in women is a problem that is directly linked to the poor economic and social circumstances that accompany the transitions to democracy and a private market economy. These are problems that the EU and the US are dealing with both individually and together under the NTA chapter on promoting human rights and democracy and through the Stability Pact for South Eastern Europe.

Given the fact that cooperation between the EU and the US on trafficking was limited to prevention rather than protection or prosecution, the question remains, how significant was the campaign? The information campaigns are criticised for not getting to the root of the problem by failing to address poor economic conditions and the lack of legal economic migration, and for not providing witness protection and extended stays for trafficking victims.[52] One US official argued that the campaigns were defined by rhetoric rather than action.[53] Another added that the EU and the US would always be capable of doing more individually than together because funding restrictions on each side meant that independent revenue would be needed eventually.[54]

Despite the limited nature of joint cooperation however, it is worth examining the EU–US campaigns in the context of the larger anti-trafficking movement. Policy makers argued that the decision to pursue a second and third round of the information campaigns is evidence that the projects have had worthwhile effects on the ground. One of the most significant aspects of the transatlantic information campaigns is that they increased awareness of the problem both externally and internally. First, the joint campaigns reiterated EU and US commitment to addressing the problem of trafficking.[55] An IOM official in Hungary noted that EU–US backing for the IOM information campaign in Hungary raised the profile of the project. Another official noted that the considerable coverage of the Ukrainian project had 'helped create a sense of urgency' about the problem of trafficking (Escaler 1998). The EU–US sponsored information campaigns also paved the way for further action on trafficking in women in the countries where they were run. The Commissioner for Justice and Home Affairs, Antonio Vitorino (1999) argued that 'previous campaigns have proved to have had considerable spin-off effects such as setting up of permanent co-ordination structures to work with the problem on a permanent basis'.[56] One US official added that these campaigns helped ensure that the host countries acknowledged the problem of trafficking and led to more 'open will' between the host states and the EU and US.[57] Finally, the transatlantic trafficking campaigns fulfilled greater NTA commitments, by helping to forge contacts between EU and US officials dealing with trafficking and with the IOM and local NGOs. The information campaigns have allowed officials to gain experience working with NGOs and governments and build further bridges in this area. The joint EU–US initiative is seen in the international community as part of a necessary step to strengthen cooperation and coordination efforts among relevant governmental, intergovernmental and non-governmental institutions (IOM 1998).

Anti-trafficking under the NTA

This case study sheds some light on the nature of political cooperation under the NTA. The Joint Action Plan contains transatlantic commitments to combat global challenges such as organised crime, terrorism and illegal immigration. Although the information campaigns are a step towards combating this illegal trade in persons, actual law enforcement cooperation has been limited. Nonetheless, it is worth examining what this case tells us about the capacity for the EU and the US to jointly address 'global challenges' cooperation and vice versa.

Cooperation in this chapter of the NTA is less integrated then in others. Funkt (unpublished: 35) identifies two factors which limit the capacity of the EU and the US to cooperate in fighting global challenges. First, he argues the preservation of state sovereignty and the poorly defined institutional role of EU actors in the area of Justice and Home Affairs has obstructed international law enforcement cooperation. The trafficking case is a prime example. By focusing on prevention the EU and the US chose to pursue a policy that only affected the sovereignty of the host country. Cooperation between the EU and the US is kept non-controversial to avoid member-state or Congress intervention.

Second, the weakness of the EU's third pillar is blamed more generally for a lack of US cooperation on political issues. Justice and Home Affairs Policy was only established with the Maastricht Treaty and migration issues moved in community competence through the Treaty of Amsterdam.[58] On a technical level, funding coordination in the trafficking case was difficult due to multi-level decision-making in the EU. Cooperation on protection and prosecution was inhibited because both the EU and the US were in the process of introducing new domestic anti-trafficking policies before 2001.[59]

Despite the limitations of the NTA's global challenges chapter, the trafficking case is significant in the context of the development of the NTA more generally. First, the information campaigns are the only co-funded policy project under the global challenges chapter of the NTA. Co-funding is a concrete deliverable, not just a commitment, and it represents a deeper level of integration. Second, the anti-trafficking campaigns represent the first operational activity within the migration dialogue established by the NTA. Despite the limited nature of the cooperation on trafficking in women, the original campaigns have served as a stepping-stone to additional projects across CEE and Russia. The information campaigns demonstrate how dialogue between Justice and Home Affairs officials can produce concrete results. One US official argued, 'I would like to think the success of these efforts will help pave the way for other global challenges'. That said, it was added that, 'it will be hard to replicate the kind of focus we achieved on such a specific area. Part of this has to do with the complex relationships on other global issues and the difficulty in matching specific goals.' The trafficking in women case is an example of how the EU and the US can pool resources and organise efforts to combat global challenges, even if only on a small scale. The cooperation on combating HIV/AIDS in Africa is a more recent example of how the EU and US officials have learned to share knowledge and coordinate resources to maximise their use.

Conclusion

In conclusion, the case of EU–US cooperation on trafficking in women draws many parallels with the other case studies discussed in this book. First, the trafficking case shows that the potential for cooperation is greater where bureaucratic control is exercised and Congress and member state involvement is minimal. The case analysed in this chapter is one in which the Commission and the US Administration have pursued a joint project that is both non-controversial and in the joint interest of Western states. By dealing with the supply side of trafficking through prevention campaigns in CEE, the EU–US information campaigns do not impinge on the sovereignty of either US domestic legislators or the national governments in the member states.

Nonetheless, it is clear that domestic institutions and the newness of Justice and Home Affairs policy in both the EU and the NTA limit how deeply the EU and the US can cooperate on political issues. The EU–US information campaigns are criticised for not addressing the prosecution of traffickers or the protection of victims. It is important to view these campaigns as an important stepping-stone both for the anti-trafficking movement and for the migration and law enforcement dialogue under the global challenges chapter of the NTA. New national, EU and international laws could increase the scope for cooperation on protecting victims and prosecuting traffickers on a transatlantic scale. The dialogue already established between Justice and Home Affairs officials in Europe and the US means that transatlantic policy on trafficking has room to grow under the NTA.

Notes

1 See Hughes (2000); Ruggerio (1997); Taylor and Jamieson (1999).
2 Hughes (2000: 627) argues that it is difficult to know exactly how many women have been trafficked because the trade is secretive, women are silenced, the traffickers are dangerous and not many agencies are counting.
3 The full definition of trafficking used by the UN Protocol on Trafficking (2000) includes, 'the recruitment, transportation, transfer, harbouring or receipt of persons, by means of the threat or use of force or other forms of coercion, of abduction, of fraud, of deception, of the abuse of power or of a position of vulnerability or the giving or receiving of payments or benefits to achieve the consent of a person having control over another person, for the purpose of exploitation'.
4 Trafficking is also a gender issue and a racial issue because the majority of trafficked persons are women and minorities (see Steffenson 2004).
5 Hughes (2000: 646) notes that Germany and the Netherlands are the most popular destinations for trafficked women in Europe because prostitution is legal. O'Neill (1999: 13) reports that the sex industry is among the primary sources of trafficked women in the US.
6 An OSCE (1999) report states, 'In the vast majority of destination countries, trafficking is approached primarily as an illegal migration or prostitution problem. Consequently, most law enforcement strategies target the people who are trafficked, not the criminal networks that traffic them. Assuming the State intervenes at all, it is the victims who are arrested and deported while the traffickers continue to operate with near-impunity. Few victims – in the destination country or upon return to their country of origin – receive any assistance, protection, or legal remedy against their traffickers.'
7 In the UK trafficking in persons was not a criminal offence until the introduction of the Sexual Offences Act (2004). Prior to this most traffickers were charged with living off the earnings of a prostitute, which carries an average sentence of three years (maximum possible is seven years) (interview with UK NGO). See also Kate Holt, 'Captive Market', *The Sunday Times Magazine*, 18 February 2001.
8 IOM (1997).
9 See Miko (2000)
10 The OSCE's commitment to combat trafficking is seen in the Moscow Declaration (1991), the Stockholm Declaration (1997), the Human Dimensions Seminars (1997–

99), the 2000 Action Plan and the creation of an Advisor on Trafficking in the Office of Democratic Institutions and Human Rights (ODIHR).

11 The stated purpose of the UN Protocol on Trafficking in Women is: (i) to prevent and combat trafficking in persons, paying particular attention to women and children; (ii) to protect and assist victims of such trafficking, with full respect for their human rights; (iii) to promote cooperation among State Parties in order to meet these objectives.

12 Both Secretary of State Madeline Albright and First Lady Hilary Clinton repeatedly stressed their commitments to women's issues during the Clinton Administration.

13 The formal title for the position is the Deputy Director and Senior Advisor on Trafficking in the US State Department.

14 McBride uses the word 'femmocrats' to highlight the strong presence of women's rights supporters.

15 For example, the *New York Times* ran an article in January 1998 based on a report by the Israeli Women's Network and a video documentation of trafficking compiled by the Global Survival Network. Telephone Interview, US NGO, March 2001.

16 These figures are rough estimates as no one is really sure how many people are being trafficked. For more statistics see the US State Department Trafficking in Persons Report (2003) or the IOM (2003) report on migration.

17 Interview by telephone, US State Department official, February 2001. For a more detailed discussion on the EU's preoccupation with 'people smuggling' see Den Boer and Wallace (2000: 517). Note that 'people smuggling' became a major preoccupation of EU law enforcement agencies in the late 1990s.

18 The programme sets up and reinforces European networks and the implementation of pilot projects, the results of which can be disseminated and shared throughout the EU. Activities focus on two principal areas: exchange of information and cooperation networks on an EU level and the raising of public awareness and exchange for best practices (DG JHA, 'Fight Against Organised Crime', www.euractiv.com).

19 The STOP programme supports training and information measures, studies and exchanges for those responsible for the fight against such forms of exploitation, including judges, public prosecutors, police, civil servants or the public services responsible for prevention, victim support or fighting these phenomena.

20 Candidate countries are encouraged to take a more pro-active attitude towards prostitution, giving women victims some support and helping to establish non-governmental organisations which can help these women. See http://europa.eu.int/comm/justice_home/news/8mars_en.htm, 'Trafficking in Women'.

21 Interview, US State Department officials and EU Commission officials, September 1999–May 2001.

22 Interview by telephone, US Mission official, Brussels, February 2001.

23 Interview, EU Commission official, DG External Relations, May 2000.

24 Interview, IOM official, Budapest, April 2000; interview by telephone, US Mission official, Brussels, February 2001.

25 The Balkans are the largest rising source of trafficked persons to Western Europe (see IOM 2001a).

26 Argument made by Commission official, DG External Relations, May 2000.

27 The interviewee argued that until recently you could not mention the 't' (trafficking) word in some of these countries. Interview by telephone, US Mission official, Brussels, February 2001.

28 Interview by telephone, US Mission official, February 2001; interview, Commission official, DG External Relations, Brussels, May 2000.

29 Interview, US Mission official, February 2001.
30 US officials pointed out that the EU had expressed an interest in dealing directly with countries in the first wave of enlargement. Interview, US Mission official, Brussels, January 2001; US State Department official, Washington DC, August 2000.
31 It should be noted that while the EU's Partnership with Russia is designed to cross over into more concrete joint action, the US involvement, at least on a transatlantic level, is restricted to the information campaign.
32 Interviews, EU Commission official, External Relations, Brussels, May 2000; and US Mission official, Brussels, February 2001.
33 Interview, EU Commission official, Brussels, May 2000.
34 Paragraph based on interviews with a high-ranking DG External Relations official, Brussels, September 1999; EU External Relations official, Brussels, May 2000; US State Department official; Washington DC; August 2000; EU Commission official, Washington DC, October 2000; US State Department official, Washington DC, October 2000; US Mission official, Brussels, September 1999; US Mission official, Brussels, February 2001.
35 Figures are approximate and are taken from interviews, the US Population Refugees and Migration website and EU JHA website.
36 Interview, Commission official, Brussels, May 2000.
37 Interviews, US Mission official, Brussels, February 2001; US State Department official, Washington DC, August 2000; US Mission official, Brussels, May 2000.
38 NGOs must go through a formal application process and compete for funding at the EU level, but La Strada was already being funded by the Commission.
39 It was also thought that the projects would be more comparable if the same partner implemented them. Interviews, US Mission official, Brussels, February 2001; US NGO, Washington DC, March 2001.
40 The Coalition Against Trafficking in Women was formed by a number of women's rights groups including Equality Now; Planned Parenthood; International Women's Health Coalition; National Organization for Women; Women's Environment and Development Organisation; Catholics for a Free Choice; Sisterhood is Global Institute; National Black Women's Health Project; Feminist Majority; Center for Women Policy Studies. See McBride Stetson (2000: 6).
41 In a meeting held on 22 February 1999, the President's Interagency Council on Women held a briefing with over 120 representatives from the NGO community to discuss among other things the Council's initiatives to combat trafficking in women and girls. See US State Department, Highlights from NGO Public Briefing Meeting, 22 February 1999.
42 See www.usinfo.state.gov/topical/global/traffic.
43 Over 400 proposals were received under the Daphne project.
44 Interview, US NGO, Washington DC, March 2001.
45 IOM relied on Winrock International to facilitate interaction among women's NGOs and worked with La Strada in Ukraine.
46 Interview, European NGO, (via email) 2001.
47 This distrust stems from the fact that the IOM is a government sponsored body dedicated to organised migration. Interview, US NGO, Washington DC, March 2001.
48 Interview, US NGO, Washington DC, March 2001.
49 They argue the reference to 'forced prostitution' in the definition advocates prostitution and allows traffickers to use consent as a legal loophole. See 'The Clintons' Shrug at Sex Trafficking', *Wall Street Journal*, 10 January 2000. Response to 'The Clintons' Shrug at Sex Trafficking', 12 January 2000 (http: www.catw.org); interview with US NGO,

Washington DC, March 2001.
50 Interview, US NGO, Washington DC, February 2001.
51 Interview, US NGO, Washington DC, February 2001.
52 Interview, US State Department official, Washington DC, October 2000.
53 Interview, high-ranking US State Department official, Washington DC, October 2000.
54 Interview, US State Department Official, Washington DC, October 2000.
55 Interview, US Mission official, Brussels, February 2001.
56 Speaking notes, launch of Hungarian information campaign, November 1999.
57 Interview, US Mission official, Brussels, January 2001.
58 For a more comprehensive overview of the development of JHA policy see Den Boer and Wallace (2000).
59 One US official argued, 'Because JHA co-operation on the EU level is just being developed, the US still relies extensively on bilateral relations with member states, making co-operation, particularly in law enforcement, very complex.' Interview, US Mission official, Brussels, February 2001.
60 Interview by telephone, US Mission official, February 2001.

6

The Mutual Recognition Agreements

Ultimately the goal of the New Transatlantic Marketplace is to create a barrier-free marketplace through further liberalisation of trade in goods, services and investment. A major part of that market opening strategy is to implement agreements that eliminate non-tariff barriers to trade. The Customs and Co-operation Agreement (1996); Mutual Recognition Agreement (1997); the Science and Technology Agreement (1997); the Positive Comity Agreement (1998) and the Veterinary Equivalency Agreement (1999) are examples of agreements that aim to reduce barriers to trade in the form of regulatory, customs and competition standards.

This chapter examines the Mutual Recognition Agreements (MRAs), signed in six sectors in 1997 and under negotiation in six additional sectors, in the larger context of the transatlantic partnership. The MRAs are of economic significance because they eliminate redundant testing and certification costs affecting $180bn in trade.[1] Politically, the MRAs represent a spillover of integration from the European single market. The MRAs have the potential to spark further integration within the transatlantic process because they symbolise confidence building between trade officials and regulatory authorities. These agreements are important for understanding the nature of the interaction between the partners, because joint decision-making in the MRA process carries wider implications for transatlantic governance.

Decision-making in the MRAs is examined here as a case study of economic policy-making under the NTA framework. Like the anti-trafficking information campaigns, the MRA were pursued under the NTA framework and monitored by transatlantic institutions. They represent a policy sector where transgovernmental networks of trade officials exercised considerable control over the development of the policy and where new networks of regulatory officials formed to shape policy details. The MRAs are also a test case for the policy shaping capacity of private, transnational networks, particularly the TABD, in the transatlantic policy process.

The Mutual Recognition Agreements also highlight the importance of decision-making in a system of multi-level governance. The MRAs, unlike the anti-trafficking information campaigns, were controversial in the domestic arena because they directly affect the enforcement of domestic health and safety standards. Transatlantic institutions, which are comprised mainly of political and trade officials, had to negotiate with regulatory authorities in the MRA process. The competition between trade and regulatory officials was particularly fierce in the US, where regulators were unaccustomed and initially opposed to the principle of mutual recognition (see also Steffenson 2005). In this case, it can be argued that the US rather than the EU suffered from a capabilities–expectations gap.

This chapter questions how the MRA negotiation process was managed under the NTA and to what extent this transatlantic dialogue was able to accommodate the interests of different actors. It is argued that transatlantic institutions played a crucial role in facilitating decisions which made, set and shaped MRA policy. The difficulty lies in the fact that these sets of actors were charged with finding a policy that could accommodate not only their transatlantic counterparts but rival domestic agencies as well. In this respect the MRA case also bears resemblance to the banana dispute discussed in Chapter 7.

This chapter is approached in the following way. The first section examines the political decision to pursue the MRAs at a transatlantic level. The second section discusses how domestic actors and transgovernmental actors set and shape policy and the third section examines the role of private networks in the process, examining NGO claims that the process lacks transparency and accountability. The final section looks at the significance of the MRA negotiations in the larger context of the NTA.

The political decision to pursue MRAs

Regulatory cooperation is crucial to improving market access because different standards and certification procedures often form non-tariff barriers to trade. The purpose of Mutual Recognition Agreements is to remove the barriers that result from additional or different conformity assessment requirements on either side of the Atlantic. The concept of mutual recognition denotes the acceptance of US product or service tests in the EU without duplicate testing, and vice versa. In theory this means products can be 'approved once, accepted everywhere in the transatlantic marketplace'.[2] A 'full equivalence' MRA would allow both EU and US regulatory agents to accept the standards of their counterparts. Nicolaïdis (1997a: 1) argues, 'The "recognition" involved here is of the "equivalence", "compatibility" or at least "acceptability" of the counterpart's regulatory system, the "mutual" part indicates that the reallocation of authority is reciprocal and simultaneous'. In practice, however, the first EU–US MRAs established only far more modest regulatory cooperation.

The intergovernmental decision

The political impetus for Mutual Recognition Agreements came from the top down. Intergovernmental actors laid out the intention to pursue an agreement on mutual recognition certification and testing procedures in the New Transatlantic Agenda (1995) and the Transatlantic Economic Partnership (1998) (see Box 6.1). The NTA included the aim 'to conclude an agreement on mutual recognition of conformity assessment [which includes certification and testing procedures] for certain sectors as well as the intention to identify other sectors for further negotiation'. The first set of MRAs (signed in 1997) included annexes in telecommunications, medical devices, electromagnetic compatibility, electrical safety, recreational craft and pharmaceuticals (see Box 6.2). The aim was to eliminate duplicate testing and inspection procedures to enable products to be certified once, locally. Importantly, these agreements maintain domestic regulatory standards, but they allow foreign conformity assessment bodies to become certified inspectors so that products can, for example, be tested in the EU for export to the US. Transatlantic leaders announced their intention to expand mutual recognition to the testing and approval of services – architecture, insurance, engineering – as well as new goods – road safety, cosmetics and marine safety – in the Transatlantic Economic Partnership. The TEP outlined plans to extend mutual recognition to professional certification and in the case of marine safety to negotiate a full equivalence agreement or MRA + for marine safety equipment.

Box 6.1 A chronology of the MRA negotiations

(1995) NTA and NTA Action Plan outline the intention to pursue MRAs.

(1996) The Senior Level Group identifies eight sectors for possible MRAs.

(1997) The MRA Agreement is signed including 7 annexes.

(1998) TEP and TEP Action Plan announce the spread of MRAs to new goods sectors and services.

(1999) The TEP Steering Group announces a draft framework agreement for service MRAs in architecture, engineering and insurance as well as the intention to begin negotiations in marine safety.

(2000) The first MRAs – in recreational craft, EMC and telecoms – move into the operational phase while sectors such as pharmaceuticals and medical devices miss deadlines for implementation.

Box 6.2 The MRA annexes

MRA Set 1: NTA (signed in 1997)	*MRA Set II: TEP (negotiations began in 1998)*
Goods	**Goods**
Telecommunications,	Road safety
Medical devices	Cosmetics
Electromagnetic compatibility	Marine safety (MRA +)
Electrical safety	**Services**
Recreational craft	Architecture
Pharmaceuticals	Engineering
	Insurance

Mutual interest in mutual recognition

Mutual recognition is a method of trade liberalisation that is both an alternate and complimentary approach to other methods of regulatory cooperation, but how did mutual recognition come on to the transatlantic policy agenda and why was it chosen over other market opening strategies, especially harmonisation? Intergovernmental actors had a number of motivations for pursuing mutual recognition in addition to and as an alternate for a strict harmonisation strategy. Put plainly, the MRAs are a means of achieving increased market access at the lowest political cost.

First, it can be argued that MRAs, unlike harmonisation, reduce the cost of redundant testing procedures for both manufacturers and government agencies (see also Nicolaïdis 1997a: 3). It can be argued that the MRAs save not only corporations, but also regulatory agencies both time and resources (see Ives 1997: 32). A 1996 US government briefing reported that mutual recognition could save the Federal Drugs Administration $1.5m in the pharmaceutical sector alone.[3]

The political costs of mutual recognition are also less than of harmonisation. Because mutual recognition fits into the new transatlantic framework, it is a contractual norm rather than a legal proceeding. Thus, mutual recognition is negotiated by bureaucrats rather than legislative authorities (Nicolaïdis 1997a: 1). MRAs, for the most part, bypass US domestic legislation, thus making them easier to negotiate. Mutual recognition is also easier to achieve than harmonisation because it requires only a limited transfer of authority. MRAs do not require regulatory agents to change their domestic rules, nor do they require the transfer of authority to a supranational body (Nicolaïdis 1997a: 4). Thus, they are even less likely to attract negative attention from the US Congress or the EU member states.

Finally, the European Union had a vested interest in 'exporting' mutual recognition to its trading partners (see also Steffenson 2002, 2005). Nicolaïdis (1997a; 1997b) points out that the EU–US mutual recognition negotiations are an example of both normative and strategic spillover from the European single market. She argues that in negotiating MRAs with countries outside the Union, the EU has made mutual recognition a symbol of European integration. More strategically, it has been able to shape the environment of transatlantic negotiations, because the Commission has experience negotiating both internal and other external MRAs.

The onset of mutual recognition within the new transatlantic marketplace has sparked a further breakdown of regulatory barriers to trade in a number of sectors. The US National Institute of Standards and Technology and the EU National Measures Institute signed an agreement extending mutual recognition to test reports, calibration and measurement certificates provided for regulatory compliance. The Veterinary Equivalency Agreement extends the principle of mutual recognition to animal standards. Furthermore, the conclusion of the first phase of the MRAs enabled intergovernmental leaders to set the precedent for the negotiations in three new goods and three new service sectors. Most notably, coastguard officials have been able negotiate full mutual acceptance of certification standards for marine safety equipment.

Political obstacles to the MRAs

Mutual recognition in the transatlantic marketplace is not used with the same depth or scope found in the European single market because a number of factors have blocked further and faster integration. First, transatlantic institutions lack the depth to oversee and enforce the MRAs. European mutual recognition has been established legally in the EU through the Cassis de Dijon case, and is legitimately enforced by the European Court of Justice. The transatlantic relationship, on the other hand, lacks the overarching institutional capacity to enforce mutual recognition.

Second, distinct political and cultural systems dictate different negotiating styles in the EU and the US. Drawing on the logic of the single market, the EU pushed for an agreement that would cover full mutual recognition of standards equivalence. However, US trade officials acknowledged that full MRAs would not be compatible with domestic legal systems in many sectors (Ives 1997: 28; Vogel 1998). USTR negotiators took the position that a less ambitious, but more pragmatic strategy should be pursued.

The EU and the US also disagreed over where to apply mutual recognition. US negotiators argued in favour of sector by sector negotiations. They feared that including too many regulatory agencies would lower the threshold of the agreement. EU negotiators on the other hand hoped that an overarching framework agreement would spark negotiations in more sectors (Ives 1997; Nicolaïdis 1997a; 1997b; Egan 2001a; 2001b). In the end, the Commission was able to insist that the pharmaceuticals annexe be included in return for annexes on telecommunications and recreational craft (Horton 1998: 648).

Another barrier to MRA negotiations stems from the EU and US regulatory processes, which are defined by different institutional structures and legal requirements. The US federal structure has complicated both the negotiations and implementation of the agreements, because the national level is bound legally to respect the rights of individual states, particularly in services sectors.[4] EU officials have accused the US regulatory bodies of 'not being able to deliver'.[5]

As a result of two distinct and equally complex procedures, many actors – both private and public – play a role in setting and shaping regulatory policy. Intergovernmental actors made the decision to include MRAs in the NTA and TEP frameworks, but the policy details were derived from negotiations between transgovernmental actors and in consultation with transnational actors. The following two sections elaborate on the role played by these actors. Each points to competing forces at work in the MRA process. One consists of transgovernmental actors fighting over their sovereign right to control the regulatory process, the other is made up of transnational actors struggling to obtain information and subsequently exert influence over international standards.[6]

Foreign trade and domestic regulatory negotiations

The USTR Charlene Barshefsky and former European Commissioner Leon Brittan signed the first EU–US Mutual Recognition Agreements in 1997, thus effectively setting the policy for MRAs.[7] The Office of USTR and DG I (now DG Trade) aided by the US Commerce Department and DG III (now DG Industry) played a large role in setting and shaping the overarching umbrella agreement. However, the complexity of both EU and US regulatory systems dictated that many transgovernmental actors had a role in shaping the individual annexes. The NTA and the TEP delegated the task of facilitating mutual recognition to trade officials within transatlantic institutions, but the technocratic nature of mutual recognition and the need for confidence building also led to the entrenchment of transatlantic regulatory networks. The MRA negotiations are an interesting case study for multi-level governance because they highlight competition between transgovernmental networks that promoted the MRAs as a means of trade liberalisation, and the domestic regulators, particularly in the US that fought to protect their regulatory autonomy.[8]

Regulatory autonomy in a trade driven process

Both EU and US regulatory systems involve a complex interplay between many different department agencies, standards setting bodies and legislative bodies. Negotiation and confidence building in the MRA process was complicated by the clashing interests of regulatory and trade officials and by the institutional 'mismatch' of the EU and US regulatory systems. Two main differences surfaced in the MRA negotiations: contrasting systems of regulatory accountability and cultures of regulatory autonomy (Nicolaïdis 1997a). Institutional asymmetries were a source of conflict in the MRA process, because, notes Stuart Eizenstat, 'We found that we have entirely different regulatory regimes' (quoted in Cowles 2001b: 225). The fierce protection over autonomy exercised by the Food and Drug Administration (FDA), in the medical devices and pharmaceuticals annexes, and to a lesser extent the Occupational Safety and Health Administration (OSHA), in the electrical safety annexe, led to claims that US regulatory agents were, 'obsessed with giving up sovereignty'.[9]

The accountability of EU standards was brought into question because EU regulatory authorities rely more on private Conformity Assessment Bodies (CABs) for product testing standards than their US counterparts. US regulatory agents, particularly the FDA, were opposed to the EU system of private CABs. The medical device negotiations were prolonged because the FDA was initially unable and unwilling to transfer regulatory authority to third parties. While the EU argued that private third party assessment bodies should be able to certify in accordance with FDA standards, FDA officials claimed they could not delegate the ultimate authority to approve the private third party reports or manufacturing facilities inspections (Ives 1997: 30). FDA opposition was only curbed when the FDA Modernisation Act (1997) altered the scope of FDA control and allowed delegation of authority to third party assessment bodies (Egan 2001b: 15).

Nicolaïdis (1997b: 19) argues that contrary to US fears, there is a very symbiotic relationship in the EU between the private and public sector and that accountability is high because the European Organisation for Testing and Certification – a government agency – oversees CABs. Two main organisations, Comité Européen de Normalisation (CEN) and the Comité Européen de Normalisation Electrotechnique (CENELEC), coordinate various national standards bodies and over forty regulatory organisations (see also Egan 2001a: 8–9).

On the other hand, it can be argued that accountability is not as visible in the US system where there is no authoritative body in charge of regulatory agents. US regulatory policy is both highly fragmented (see Egan 2001b) and decentralised (see Cowles 1997). The US system relies heavily on voluntary conformity from over four hundred federal and state, trade and industry associations, scientific and technical societies. The American National Standards Institute (ANSI) does serve as an 'administrator' and 'coordinator' of the private sector voluntary standardisation system, however Egan (2001b: 24) notes that the ANSI does not set standards itself and that not all standards bodies are members.[10] Thus, EU officials worried about capacity of the US to guarantee regulatory quality given the lack of accountability (see also Nicolaïdis 1997b; Egan 2001b: 14). To compensate for this problem the National Institute on Standards – an agent of the Commerce Department – created the National Voluntary Conformity Assessment Program to accredit conformity assessment in the US.

EU officials believed US accountability was further threatened by the autonomous role of many US regulatory agencies. The Federal Drug Administration, the Federal Communications Commission, the Federal Aviation Agency, the Defence Department and the National Institute on Standards and Technology (NIST) all operate separately and are governed by individual statutes from Congress. The high degree of autonomy experienced by US regulatory agencies means that sovereignty is guarded very closely. According to Cowles (1997: 35) 'the statutory independence of the agencies meant that regulatory officials had their own independent mindset and turf to defend as well'.

Generally, rivalry between trade and regulatory agencies stems not only from competition over regulatory authority, but because the trade and regulatory officials inherently perform different functions and have different goals. Ives (1997: 29) adds that negotiations were difficult because 'A successful negotiation requires regulatory authorities to co-operate with trade officials ... But the agencies almost speak different languages – the regulators in scientific terms, the trade agencies in economic terms.' One US NGO simplified the divide by arguing, 'One builds things, the other knocks things down.'[11]

Conflict between trade and regulatory officials was particularly cumbersome in the US. A delicate balance between the European Commission (both DGI and DGIII), national regulatory bodies and the private sector had already been met within the single market requirement. US regulatory agents, on the other hand, did not have the same experience with MRAs and some were 'less comfortable' with the notion of mutual recognition.[12] Clashes between trade and regulatory officials are most evident in the medical devices and pharmaceutical annexes of the MRA, where the FDA has US domestic authority, and in the electrical safety annexe, which is under the jurisdiction of OSHA. While the FDA was not opposed directly to mutual recognition, it did express concern about the transfer of authority to private actors, EU regulatory agents and US trade officials. FDA officials were keen to demonstrate that the 'legal authority to regulate is placed with FDA, not Commerce, not USTR'.[13] The FDA argued that the statutory authority of the agency could not be delegated to other bodies. Within the NTA process, State Department and USTR officials sought to convince the FDA that MRAs did not affect their statutory mission. Under the Modernisation Act of the Federal Food, Drug and Cosmetic Act (1997) Congress instructed the FDA to support USTR in reaching agreement with the EU on all products under the FDA's jurisdiction. However, this mandate gave the FDA flexibility to determine that the agreements would not lead to a reduction in standards levels (Merrill 1998: 742).

Regulatory officials were initially opposed to setting up a joint EU–US committee to oversee conformity assessment because of the potential opportunity for trade agencies to dominate (see Ives 1997) and opposed the negotiation of an overarching umbrella agreement or 'EU packaging' of the annexes driven by USTR. Sharon Holston, Deputy Commissioner for External Affairs for the FDA testified in front of the House Committee on Commerce, Subcommittee on Oversight and Investigations that, 'There were clearly times during the negotiations when DG-I negotiators operated under the assumption that trade issues were paramount in the negotiation. It was made clear to them, however, that for legal and policy reasons health and safety issues would govern.'[14] FDA also requested a Memorandum of Understanding (MOU) with USTR to secure clear authority for the FDA in the sectoral annexes and to ensure that the USTR's role was restricted to 'observer' in Joint Committee meetings where FDA annexes were discussed.[15] A FDA official argued, 'on anything that affected FDA, we were in charge'.[16]

The FDA views the MRAs as a 'contract for service' to EU regulatory bodies.[17] In such an agreement the role of a trading partner is not that of law maker but rather that of information source or service provider (Merrill 1998). FDA is still accountable to Congress for standards in sectors included in the MRA, thus it has a vested interest in assuring that mutual recognition partners maintain the same level of equivalence. MRA negotiation and implementation was delayed, however, because most member states failed to gain the confidence of the FDA during the transitional period. Some argue that a superior regulatory culture prevents the FDA from cooperating with the EU simply because it believes FDA standards to be the highest in the world.[18] One FDA official argued that, 'FDA has a proud history. [Initially] we felt no need to play in this – we are used to being authoritative.'[19] Further, the FDA had problems accepting the equality and equivalency of standards across the 15 member states. One FDA official commented, 'FDA knew Europe was not "whole".' A US trade official affirmed the American perception that, 'Portuguese standards are not the same as those in the UK.' As a result of a lack of confidence between the FDA and member state regulatory officials, the UK was the only EU member state to meet FDA approval by the December 2001 deadline for implementation.[20]

Ultimately the MRAs seek to reduce the cost of exporting to producers and the cost of duplicate testing for domestic regulators, however, making domestic systems MRA 'ready' is also costly. FDA officials argue that the agency had spent 'significant' amounts promoting the MRAs out of 'nominal budgets'.[21] Misunderstanding over the cost of processing applications for conformity assessment under the MRA led to 'differences in interpretation' between OSHA and the Commission and delayed the approval of European CABs capable of implementing OSHA assessments. OSHA claimed that it was able to charge fees for processing applications for conformity assessment under the MRA, but the Commission argued that OSHA ran the risk of duplicating fee assessment (OSHA 2000).

Further conflict in the MRA negotiations resulted from the domestic orientation of US regulatory agencies and their lack of experience with the EU single market system. Conflict arose over the FDA's refusal to accept European certification of testing reports in lieu of the full reports.[22] FDA officials argued that their statutory authority required FDA officials to review the full reports, which caused 'enormous difficulties' with EU officials in the MRA negotiations. A FDA official argued, 'there was a lot of pressure not to hold to this position – they thought we were being arbitrary'.[23] Further problems arose because both the FDA and OSHA could not, unlike the EU, accept documentation provided in foreign languages. Although three European companies had applied for OSHA approval to certify electrical products, two were not considered because the applications were made in French and Spanish. One OSHA official argued, 'We're a domestic health and safety agency, we don't do translations' (Alden 2001).

Balancing the trade and regulatory camps

The conceptualisation of an EU–US MRA did not originate within the NTA process,[24] however the intergovernmental decision to pursue the agreements brought mutual recognition into the NTA decision-making process and put transatlantic actors at the 'steering wheel' of the negotiations. Transatlantic institutions played a key role in pushing negotiations ahead and striking a balance between trade and regulatory authorities. First, it was the NTA process that drove the MRA negotiations forward. The MRAs were the result of endless negotiations of experts through the transatlantic institutions before the EU–US Summit where the MRA framework agreement was announced.[25] The Senior Level Group and the TEP Steering Group charged trade officials with monitoring the process, identifying achievable goals on a sector by sector basis and setting a number of deadlines for practical tasks. The TEP Steering Group also took recommendations from the transatlantic dialogues, and initiated information exchanges between EU and US experts.[26] Under the NTA process regulatory agents in the annexes were tied into the umbrella time frame and trade authorities maintained control over the overarching process. One USTR official argued that the NTA, 'essentially put USTR in charge of what they should be, management of the issues'.[27] The NTA process pushed domestic regulators to meet deadlines, and one FDA official noted, 'we've been able to accomplish much more than we thought'.[28]

In addition, the MRA umbrella agreement created new transatlantic 'institutions' to facilitate the MRAs. First, it established a new transatlantic process for designation of procedures for mutual conformity assessment. European and American domestic actors were joined in Designating Authorities which were assigned to each sector in the MRA agreement. For example, in the medical devices sector the FDA and member state regulatory bodies were charged with approving and then monitoring private conformity assessment bodies in the EU and the US and to exchange information on the acceptability of such bodies.

Second, despite initial objections from US regulatory agencies and NGOs a Joint Committee of EU and US officials was created. This committee is responsible for making sure that the agreement functions. It thus serves an administrative role and as an extra 'check' for conformity assessment bodies. The Joint Committee provides a forum for discussion and helps coordinate the negotiation of extra sectors. Finally, on a working level, six Joint Sectoral Committees were also established to assist the Joint Committee and oversee technical implementation. Each of these committees played an important part in the confidence building process. It was the motivation of market access that drove the process forward and helped overcome the staunch protectionist positions of many domestic regulators. These new institutions are a forum for information sharing and problem solving. In short, they establish a pattern of cooperation between EU and US officials and trade and regulatory agents.

The argument being made here is this: trade officials and regulatory agencies clashed in the MRA negotiations because each had a different stake in the process. Regulators sought to protect the level of domestic standards and the authority to establish these standards. Trade officials fought to reduce different testing procedures as a barrier to trade and to keep the MRA process moving. Despite these centrifugal forces, the new level of transgovernmental institutionalisation provided a forum for managing the process. A working relationship was established whereby trade officials maintained control over the umbrella agreement and regulatory agents retained authority in the individual annexes.

Table 6.1 MRA institutionalisation

Institution	*Role*
Designating Authorities	Approve and monitor CABs
Joint Committee	Coordinate the negotiation, transition of annexes between trade and regulatory agents
Joint Sectoral Committee	Oversee technical implementation
Conformity Assessment Bodies (CABs)	Conduct certification testing

Transnational interest in the MRAs

The MRA negotiations also demonstrate the capacity of actors to shape transatlantic policy. The TABD, the TACD and the TAED endeavoured to shape MRA decisions. Given their conflicting goals, the business and social based dialogues formed separate alignments with the regulatory and trade camps. The TABD naturally aligned with the trade camp while consumers and environmentalists reiterated regulators' fears about lower health, safety and environmental standards.

TABD input

The TABD was a staunch supporter of the MRAs from its creation in 1995.[30] MRAs benefit industry because they seek to eliminate costly duplicate testing procedures, thereby reducing the cost of exporting. These regulatory agreements will affect exporting companies directly, as a typical US manufacturer may spend $50,000–100,000 annually complying with foreign regulatory requirements (see Stern 1997).

The TABD lobbied the MRA negotiations on both a political and technical level. First, it created the Transatlantic Advisory Committee on Standards (TACS) made up of industry experts from the working group on regulatory cooperation to investigate ways that regulatory standards could be harmonised on a sector by sector basis. Within four months of its creation the TACS was able to provide EU and US officials with a clear outline of where EU and US industry felt MRAs were feasible.[31] The TACD was able to provide the EU and US governments with specific information that could facilitate mutual recognition in a number of sectors.

On a political level, the TABD exerted constant pressure on the EU and the US to meet these proposals.[32] At the TABD conference in Chicago, EU and US officials agreed to a deadline for agreement on MRAs in the original sectors by 31 January 1997. When this deadline slipped, TABD publicly criticised the US Administration and the Commission for failing to conclude the agreement. The TABD chairs sent letters to US President Clinton and EU President Santer and stepped up their campaign through frequent meetings with officials, exerting pressure on the Administration through the US Commerce Department. The TABD became deeply embedded in the MRA decision-making process (see also Cowles 2001a; 2001b), and had representatives present when the agreements were finally signed in June 1997 (TABD 1998). The *Financial Times* reported, 'The key to final approval of the MRA was the Transatlantic Business Dialogue' (19 June 1997).

After the agreements were signed, the TABD continued to monitor the progress of the annexes in the transitional phase of the MRAs. The TABD Scorecard (issued mid year since 1998) identifies government successes and failures in the individual MRA sectors. The TABD (1999, 2000) has publicly criticised the delayed implementation of the medical devices and electrical safety annexes, and warned that failure to implement all of the annexes on time would undermine credibility of the entire process.

Trade officials have continually praised the TABD for its role in the MRA process. Numerous high-ranking officials have highlighted the role of the TABD, and even the TEP agreement notes its contribution. Commissioner Brittan (1998), 'noted the vital input of TABD'. US Commerce Secretary Daley argued, 'TABD said it was important, we heard them and we acted.' President Clinton (1996) thanked the TABD, 'for their leadership in achieving these agreements' and USTR Barshefsky (1997) claimed, 'We could not have achieved this [MRA] package without the Transatlantic Business Dialogue.' EU Trade Commissioner Lamy (1999) told TABD members, 'It is quite clear that I have much less influence over the process now than when I participated in it as a member.'[33]

TABD's influence in the MRA process was most recognised among trade officials at a political level. Commerce and USTR officials argued that TABD played 'a huge role' in the MRA process.[34] FDA officials admit that they briefed the TABD during the negotiations but they downplay the dialogue.[35] The TABD has an ally in USTR and Commerce, because its goals are trade, not regulatory in nature. The divide is a natural phenomenon because trade officials, businesspeople, regulators and the civil society dialogues do not have parallel interests in the MRA process.[36] For example, TABD pushed for the decentralisation of regulatory cooperation between the EU and the US, a policy directly opposed by the FDA and the NGOs.[37] A TABD advisor argued that US regulatory agencies and civil society networks, who oppose the transfer of authority to business, were obstacles to the international liberalisation of regulatory standards (Stern 1996).

TACD and TAED concerns

The EU–US MRAs are a controversial issue in the US NGO community. Unlike European NGOs that had experience with mutual recognition in the single market, many American NGOs did not understand what the MRA were trying to achieve.[38] An EU official argued that American NGOs had learned from Europeans through the TACD and the TAED.[39] But many US members continued to oppose the MRAs both on a political and technical level. On a political level, these groups teamed up with the FDA in opposing 'delegated governance', trade control over the regulatory process, and the influence of the TABD.[40] On a technical level the TACD and TAED expressed concerns about a downward spiral of health and safety standards and the cost to consumers and government agencies.

Despite attempts by the trade official–TABD coalition to convince NGOs of the safety of MRAs,[41] many groups held 'deep reservations' about the agreements (see CEO 1998b). In short they argued that MRAs could lead to a downward spiral or lowest common denominator of health, safety and environmental standards (de Brie 1999, TACD 1999: 3). The TACD specifically lobbied the government to abstain from negotiating MRAs in health and safety sectors. A TACD (2000b) briefing paper stated 'Equivalence-based mutual recognition is inappropriate for use with substantive standards.'[42]

A second opposition to the MRAs is the cost of negotiation and implementation. It is estimated that just one sector (pharmaceuticals) cost the FDA $10m to comply with the MRA agreement.[43] NGOs argue that the benefits of MRAs are direct to producers, and that the costs should therefore be covered by the private, rather than public sector. One TAED (2000b) paper maintained that, 'Given such a hefty price tag for this annex and the MRA as a whole, a case must be made directly to consumers on both continents who must be assured that there will be an improvement in their public health and safety protection to justify this cost.' The TACD also vocalised opposition to the transfer of authority away from regulatory agencies and the domestic system. NGOs fiercely opposed incorporating a voluntary conformity assessment system where the transfer of regulatory authority would shift from agencies like the FDA to private conformity assessment bodies in third countries (CEO 1998a, 1998b; TAED 2000). It is argued that, 'The delegation of tasks under the MRA to conformity assessment bodies in another jurisdiction runs the risk of de facto privatisation of government responsibilities' (TACD 2000a).

Consumers and environmentalists have teamed up with US regulatory agents in supporting strong national regulatory bodies. Furthermore, TACD and TAED members sided with US regulatory agencies against the creation of the Joint Committee. Like the FDA and the FCC, consumer and environmentalists were hesitant to create an influential body which could be potentially dominated by a trade agenda rather than social standards (TACD 2000b). A TAED official argued that at the core of their concerns was the fact that 'suddenly trade negotiators are in charge of regulatory policy'.[44]

A TACD briefing paper also raised concerns that the MRAs would effectively transfer domestic regulatory policy to the sphere of international trade policy. It is argued that moving MRAs into the scope of foreign trade put a cloak of secrecy over the negotiations (TACD 2000a and b). It also feared that Congressional oversight would be limited because the MRAs are an executive agreement and are thus not subject to ratification. The MRAs were negotiated outside the scope of the EU or US legislative process, with Congress and the European Parliament having only marginal involvement in the negotiations.[45]

Non-governmental organisations have also directly opposed the privileged access that TABD had to the MRA negotiations. The special relationship between the TABD and the Commerce Department in MRA negotiations was a particular fixation of US regulatory officials and NGOs. Supported by the Environmental Protection Agency, they argued that the role of the TABD in the MRAs bordered on violating the US Administration Procedures Act and the Federal Advisory Committee Act (TACD 2000a and b; 1998; TAED 2000b). One TACD member argued, 'Our biggest fear is that the MRAs *are* TABD.'[46]

Contrary to the TABD, the perceived input of TACD and TAED in the MRA negotiations was limited. Not one interviewee argued that either dialogue played a significant role in the output of policy. These groups became involved in the MRA discourse late in the game because they were created only after the first set of MRAs had been agreed. The TACD did not produce a briefing paper on MRAs until late 2000. A TAED statement was drafted for the May 2000 annual meeting, but MRAs were not picked up as a major 'issue area' by the Trade Working Group.[47] The resource gap discussed in Chapter 4 highlights additional differences between business and civil society. Whereas the TABD has a specific committee with extensive industry resources that concentrates on regulatory cooperation, TACD relies on a small number research staff and TAED on two 'issue managers'.

Civil society access

The TABD, TACD and TAED agree on two aspects of the MRA negotiation and implementation process, albeit for completely different motives. First, both consumer and business groups favour the US position of sector by sector negotiations. Consumers feared a framework approach would result in the spillover of MRAs to additional sectors whereas the TABD worried that the difficulty of negotiating an overarching strategy would prevent agreement in all or additional sectors.[48] Second, both pushed for more transparency in the rule making process in order to gain increased access to government negotiations. The TABD wanted access to joint sectoral meetings and to be included in the process to set up monitoring mechanisms (TABD 1999). The 2000 mid year report suggested that the rule making process should be more open to industry and that TABD should be able to comment on government guidelines before they are implemented (TABD 2000). It was also argued that TABD should play a formal role in the formation of a monitoring body for compliance with the agreements (TABD 1999). TACD and TAED members complained about the lack of adequate time for response for public comment. TACD (2000a and b) papers state, 'MRAs remove important regulatory processes and issues from the public realm and place them behind the opaque screen of foreign affairs.'

Government officials recognise the need to promote transparency, but deny conducting closed negotiations. Rather they stress that TACD and TAED have been briefed on MRAs, that Federal Register Notices have been published, that general public meetings have been held by USTR on the TEP and on auto safety and that the TEP Steering Committee (2000) calls for proposals from all dialogues. Transparency is not technically a problem in either domestic system. Any person can comment on ongoing regulatory procedures due to the US Administrative Procedures Act because notices have to be published in the Federal Register.[49] In the EU different parties are invited to provide input to Commission officials, for example through the Social Policy Forum. Cowles (1997: 13–14) argues that the transatlantic regulatory process does pose more problems, because there are no rules governing access. To gain credibility Egan (2001b: 32) argues that MRAs must be put into a legal framework that is approved by the European Parliament and the US Congress.

The MRAs in the context of the NTA

The MRAs have been hailed the most concrete deliverable produced by the NTA process. Economically and politically the MRAs represent a step towards integrating regulatory systems in order to produce an open transatlantic marketplace. Conflict in negotiating and implementing the MRAs, however, demonstrates the obstacles faced by MRA negotiators.

First, the limited scope of the MRAs, especially when compared to mutual recognition within the EU, highlights fundamental differences in the EU and US regulatory systems. Delays in the transition and implementation periods of the MRA annexes can be attributed to a 'mismatch of systems' and the struggle for autonomy not only between EU and US regulators, but between regulatory bodies and trade officials, particularly in the US. A number of officials on both sides of the Atlantic expressed concern with delayed implementation of the agreements, particularly in the medical devices and pharmaceutical annexes. In both of these sectors the FDA was responsible for holding up negotiation and implementation of the MRAs due to conflict over certification reports and levels of equivalency.[50] In the services sector negotiations of a framework agreement have been delayed because the US federal government does not have the authority to override state certification standards. One Commission official explains, 'it is frustrating for Europeans who say you [the US] agreed to do it and now you cannot deliver'. In this respect, it can be argued that the US suffers from the capability–expectations gap, which is usually attributed to the EU.

Still, the MRA process is an important case study that provides insight into the capacity of NTA institutions to produce policies or concrete deliverables. One EU trade official argued that the NTA structure was crucial to the MRA negotiations because the process needed political oversight. EU and US political officials argued that the NTA process was a way of 'getting technical people to do technical things'. NTA institutions are a way of managing the dialogue between regulators and trade officials and accommodating the international interests of trade and political officials as well as the interests of domestic actors.

Another benefit of the MRAs is the bridges the process builds between EU and US regulators and trade officials as well as the business and NGO communities. The confidence building process between EU and US officials is arguably an important part of the process. An EU official argued, 'Slowly, slowly we build dialogue. To get MRA convergence we build trust between regulators on equivalency assessment.' The MRAs are also an example of a learning process where US regulators, businesses and NGOs learn from their counterparts in the EU who already have experience of working with Mutual Recognition Agreements in the single market. Building confidence between regulators, trade officials and civil society is a step in securing and expanding the mutual recognition and harmonisation of standards that affect trade. The agreements themselves are a step in building the new transatlantic marketplace. Phase two or the 'next generation of MRAs' builds on confidence established between the EU and the US and goes further than the first phase by implementing full equivalency in marine safety and the MRA in services. A Commerce department official argues, 'The MRAs are the first step in broader liberalisation of trade through mutual recognition and harmonisation of health and safety, environmental standards'.[51]

The MRA process is of interest in this discussion on the transatlantic dialogue because the interaction of actors under the framework of transatlantic institutions is an example of dialogue through transgovernmental and transnational networks. Like the trafficking in women information campaigns, the MRAs demonstrate a delegation of decision setting and shaping to a range of transgovernmental actors, thus supporting the argument that the NTA has led to decentralisation in the decision-making process. The role of transnational actors in shaping MRA policy is also apparent. Unlike the trafficking in women case, the MRAs also represent a more controversial policy, which is characterised by competition between domestic actors and international negotiators. In this respect the MRAs also share characteristics with the banana dispute (see Chapter 7).

Conclusion

This chapter discussed the institutionalisation of new dialogues, the decentralisation of decision setting and shaping and the increased influence of private actors in MRA negotiations. Regulatory policy is a tricky sector because it deals with two politically sensitive subjects: the autonomy of regulatory authorities and the sovereignty of states to control domestic standards.

The roles of domestic, transgovernmental and transnational actors in MRA negotiations were outlined above. What emerged during MRA negotiations were two coalitions: one made up of US regulatory agents and the TACD and TAED, the other of trade officials and the TABD. The first fought against decentralisation and privatisation of standards for fear that agencies like the FDA and the OSHA would lose authority to foreign companies, thus leading to reduced levels of social protection. The TABD and trade officials supported the reduction of costs in order to facilitate trade and fulfil the goals of the New Transatlantic Marketplace.

In the end the influence of the latter is more visible. The FDA was forced to modernise, and thus accept the authority of EU private conformity assessment bodies and MRAs were negotiated in areas addressing health and safety issues despite NGO objections. The MRAs made the TABD an even greater success story and the USTR and Commerce had a big deliverable to report to the EU–US summit.

Conflict between and among trade and regulatory officials highlights the importance of the NTA process. Although MRAs had been discussed before 1995, the creation of NTA institutions and the political commitment to MRAs outlined in the agreement injected focus into the negotiations. NTA institutions such as the Senior Level Group and the TEP Steering Group provided political oversight for the negotiation and transition phases of the MRAs. However, while trade officials drove the process forward and were responsible for setting the overarching umbrella agreement, agencies such as the FDA and OSHA retained control over policy details in annexes where they had regulatory authority. The MRAs did not transfer authority from regulatory to trade officials, but rather gave USTR and NTA officials the job of delegating tasks to the appropriate domestic actors.

Notes

1 The MRAs for conformity assessment cover an estimated $50bn in trade while the services MRAs are expected to extend to $130bn. US Mission website www.useu.be/issues/mra0116.html.
2 This phrase was adopted by the TABD as a slogan for the MRAs. See www.tabd.com.
3 Based on the assumption that each Good Manufacturing Practices (GMP) pharmaceutical plant inspection the FDA performs costs the agency $100,000 and 150 such inspections are performed in the EU each year (see White House 1996b).
4 Interview, UK Foreign Office, London, January 2000.
5 Interview, European Commission, DG Trade, Brussels.
6 This point was made by a US Mission official in an interview, Brussels, September 1999.
7 EU decision-making procedures require Council ratification which was given on 22 June 1998. The negotiation of the second set of MRAs were not concluded in a timely manner.
8 The interplay between foreign trade and domestic regulatory agencies is also well documented in Steffenson 2002 and 2005.
9 Interview, UK Foreign Office official, January 2000.
10 Including prominent organisations such as the American Society for Testing Material and the International Institute of Engineers (IIE) (Egan 2001b).
11 Interview, TAED official, Washington DC, October 2000.

12 Interview, USTR official, Washington DC, October 2000.
13 Interview, FDA official, Maryland, October 2000.
14 Statement by Sharon Smith Holston, Deputy Commissioner for External Affairs, Food and Drug Administration, Department of Health and Human Services, Before the Subcommittee on Oversight and Investigations Committee on Commerce, US House of Representatives, 2 October 1998.
15 FDA official argued, on the Joint Committee, that 'we wanted to make certain that we are spokesperson'.
16 Interview with FDA official, Maryland, October 2000.
17 One official argued, 'the United States enters into an agreement with a trading partner under the expectation that the trading partner will take steps to help FDA perform its primary function of applying domestic legal standards to products imported into the United States'. Interview, FDA, Maryland, October 2000.
18 See Millen (1998).
19 Interview FDA, Maryland, October 2000.
20 Alden and Bowen (2001), *Financial Times*.
21 Interviews with FDA officials, Maryland, October 2000.
22 Interview with FDA officials, Maryland, October 2000; EU Commission Delegation official, Washington DC, October 2000.
23 The FDA finally agreed that it would 'normally' be able to accept certification. FDA interviews, Maryland, October 2000.
24 The FDA began discussions with the Commission as early as 1992.
25 Interview, Council Presidency official, Brussels, September 1999.
26 In 2000 meetings were held between expert architects and engineers with the aim to facilitate service MRAs in these sectors (TEP Steering Group 2000).
27 Interview, USTR official, Washington DC, October 2000.
28 Interview, FDA official, Maryland, October 2000.
29 Argued by TABD official, interview, Brussels, September 1999.
30 While some officials have argued that MRA negotiations existed before the TABD was created, arguably the most progress was made after the creation of the TABD.
31 In May 1996 it released a progress report listing priority areas for regulatory cooperation (see www.tabd.gov).
32 Interviews, USTR official, Washington DC, October 2000; US Commerce official, Washington DC, October 2000.
33 For a list of more supportive comments for TABD see, 'What They've Said About TABD', www.tabd.com/resources/content/quotes.html.
34 Quoted from EU Delegation official, interview, Washington DC, October 2000.
35 FDA interviews, Washington, October 2000.
36 Interview, US Commerce official, Washington DC, October 2000.
37 TABD supported FDA reforms, in order to make the agency more compliant with the EU regulatory system of private conformity assessment (Stern 1997).
38 One EU official argued that on the 'European side everyone knows about MRAs because of the single market, but US NGOs believed the US Administration was telling lies.' Interview, European Commission Delegation, Washington DC, October 2000.
39 Interview, EU Commission Delegation, Washington DC, October 2000.
40 One TACD member argued, 'we have better communication with FDA'. Interview, US NGO, Washington DC, October 2000.
41 Trade officials actively tried to portray the MRAs as environmental, consumer and labour friendly. When the MRAs were signed Barshevsky argued, 'The real winners

today are manufacturers, workers, and consumers, both in America and in Europe who will see reduced costs, increased jobs, and a better standard of living' (1997). At the TACD's second meeting in February 2000, the EU Head of Unit for DG Trade argued that by facilitating trade MRAs would benefit consumers by creating lower prices and greater choice (Petriccione 2000).

42 EU and US officials have argued that MRAs do not undermine health and safety because they do not change existing domestic standards. However, a TAED (2000) draft paper states that 'mutual recognition allows for imprecise, subjective comparison of what may be vastly different democratically achieved regulatory standards'. In addition, it is argued that there are no adequate provisions for amendments, termination, dispute resolution, public participation or congressional oversight.

43 TACD (2000b).

44 Interview, US NGO, Washington DC, October 2000.

45 The European Parliament has supported the MRAs, but continually fought for more input and consultation with the European negotiating team (European Parliament 1998). A Senate staff member argued that the MRAs are not an issue that have been focused on. Interview, Washington DC, October 2000.

46 Interview, US NGO, Washington, October 2000.

47 Although an earlier Commission response to the TAED's 1999 recommendations about the MRAs received a response from the Commission stating, 'Due to the very nature of the MRAs [they avoid the duplication of testing and certification], they do, per se, affect the environment.'

48 Egan (2001a) notes this is already the case with the umbrella agreement, where problems with sectors such as medical devices and pharmaceuticals hold up negotiation and implementation of other sectors.

49 Federal register notices posted by the FDA and USTR are available on their websites; www.fda.gov; www.ustr.gov.

50 To summarise, the problem stems from the fact that the FDA does not recognise the certification and regulatory requirements of the internal market as a single system. US officials criticise the EU for lacking overarching regulatory institutions. EU trade officials argue that the FDA is too stringent in requesting specific language rather than general principles. Interviews, European Commission, Brussels and FDA, Washington DC, September 1999–October 2000.

51 Interview, US Commerce Department official, Washington DC, October 2000.

7

The banana dispute

The main focus of this book has been on cooperation between the EU and the US. Although the NTA has been established as an administrator and facilitator of transatlantic agreement, it has not eliminated conflict between the partners, particularly on the economic front. Trade disputes cover less than 2 per cent of total transatlantic trade,[1] but media coverage of disputes is far more extensive than it is for EU–US summits or transatlantic agreements.[2] Hush kits, bananas, beef, genetically modified crops and foreign sales corporations have overshadowed the TEP, the MRAs and indeed the larger transatlantic partnership. Despite increased transatlantic dialogue between EU and US actors, these disputes have prompted warning reports of looming trade wars throughout the 1990s.[3]

The transatlantic banana dispute has attracted worldwide media attention.[4] Generally the case is of interest because it has erupted over a product which is not grown in significant quantities in either the EU or the US. It is a case that appears, at least on the surface, to pit big American corporations against small Caribbean farmers. Ultimately the dispute is of both economic and political consequence. On an economic level, the dispute represents a struggle for market access. On a political level this dispute is about the rules governing the internal trading system, and thus concerns the legitimacy and capacity of the institutions that manage it. The dispute is of interest to a broader analysis of EU–US relations, because it tests the capacity of both transatlantic and multilateral institutions to diffuse conflict.

Again, the interest lies with the institutionalisation of the dialogue in general and of transatlantic decision-making specifically. The banana negotiations differ from the MRAs because transatlantic institutionalisation has not affected how private actors influence the governance process. Rather, corporations have relied on traditional lobbying through domestic institutions. Nonetheless multinational corporations and transnational networks of Caribbean farmers and EU banana operators have shaped policy decisions.

The constraints of existing bilateral and multilateral trading arrangements and the avid interest of domestic actors on both sides of the Atlantic are key to understanding why the EU and US entered a trade dispute over bananas and why the dispute spiralled out of control for almost a decade. The first section maps the development of the dispute through five EU banana regimes. The second focuses on domestic input into the US negotiations, while the third section considers the Commission's negotiating mandate in light of commitments to ACP countries, the member states and domestic banana operators. The final section considers the wider implications of the dispute by questioning what impact the banana dispute had on the larger transatlantic partnership and the WTO.

The balance between 'fair trade' or 'free trade', as championed by the two partners, is a highlighted theme throughout the chapter. Two popular views of the EU–US dispute are examined: one depicts the US as a 'bilateral bully', the other portrays the EU as a multilateral 'rule breaker' (see Box 7.1). This chapter seeks to test which, if either, scenario accurately illustrates the role each side played in the dispute.

Box 7.1 Depictions of EU and US roles in the banana dispute

Scenario I: Bilateral bully versus Third World protector

EU officials have described the EU banana regimes as development policy, not trade policy. Throughout the banana dispute it was argued that the EU banana regime protected the economies of small, third world, banana producing states. According to this logic the US has been deemed a 'bilateral bully' for pushing around not just the EU, but small Caribbean states and even its 'partners in crime', the Latin American banana producers. The US decision to impose 'unilateral' sanctions before the WTO ruled on the revised banana regime and to introduce Carousel Retaliation met harsh reaction in the public arena. The media, particularly in countries that strongly supported the regime, such as the UK, generally supported the governments' decision to support 'poor Caribbean farmers' and supermarkets reacted to public opinion by introducing voluntary labelling of free trade bananas.[5] The EU banana regime also gained general support from non-governmental organisations mobilising against globalisation and brought the implications of the banana dispute into the larger debate on the cost of free trade.

Scenario II: Multilateral trade enforcer versus rule breaker

US officials rejected the idea that the EU was acting as a third world protector and instead portrayed it as the enemy of multilateral rules.[6] It was argued that that the EU member states were not protecting the Caribbean farmers, but rather their domestic banana operators who benefit from the EU licensing scheme. The USTR Barshefsky argued, 'This is absolutely a trade issue. This is nothing more than the taking of a number of import licenses from US distributors of Latin bananas and handing them over to European companies in a discriminatory manner'.[7] Under this scenario the EU image of a third work protector is replaced with that of a 'multilateral rule breaker'. The EU was chastised for failing to produce a WTO compatible regime despite three multilateral rulings. The US, on the other hand is the enforcer of multilateral trading rules and the protector of liberalisation.

A history of the banana dispute

The banana dispute stems from the European Community regulation on banana imports initiated by the Lome Convention in 1975, which established preferred access to the European market for African, Caribbean and Pacific (ACP) bananas. Subsequent re-negotiation of Lome and several EU Banana Protocols ensured that ACP states maintained their traditional access to the European market. Five separate banana regimes were renegotiated during the dispute (see Box 7.3). Each regime used tariff quotas and licensing schemes to alter market access for Latin American and Caribbean banana producers and transformed the practices of banana operators within the EU (see Box 7.4).

Member state regimes

Although Lome established access for ACP exporters, levels of access were determined by individual member states prior to 1993.[8] In reality three tariff regimes emerged.[9] Germany maintained duty free imports for both ACP and Latin American producers. The Benelux countries, Ireland and Denmark all imposed a 20 per cent duty on all imported bananas. Finally, France, Italy, Spain, Greece, Portugal and the UK offered duty free import for ACP states.

In 1993 Latin American banana producing countries requested a GATT panel to challenge this third regime. They argued that the system gave preference not only to ACP states, but also to domestic producers and operators.[10] The GATT ruled against the European banana regimes, but the decision was of little consequence. The EC was able, under GATT rules, to block the panel decision from being adopted because the member states were already undergoing reform to create a single European policy on banana imports. They argued the new regime would comply with the internal requirements of the Single European Market and the external requirements of the 4th Lome Convention.[11]

The restrictive tariff rate quota

In July 1993 the EC began implementing a single market in bananas under Council Regulation 404–93. It set up a three-tiered banana regime with duty free quotas for ACP banana producers and a two-tiered tariff structure for Latin American, or 'dollar bananas' (see Table 7.4). The single European policy on banana imports maintained the traditional divide in the market. Latin American producers were encouraged to keep but deterred from trying to increase their share. ACP countries had a substantial tariff advantage, but faced new competition from Latin American producers (see also Stevens 2000: 342–3).

Again the Latin American producers took issue with the quotas reserved for ACP states.[12] Five Latin American countries, this time supported by the US, took the new banana regime to the GATT in late 1993. The real complaint was the new licensing system.[13] US multinationals, particularly United Fruit Corporation, argued that the category 'A' licences were especially restrictive for the Latin American banana producing countries that had not cut deals with the EU.[14] The allocation of import licences also created a monopoly for European firms, and further restricted the quantities that US companies operating in Latin America could distribute in Europe.

The EU managed to block a second GATT panel report in 1994. However, the creation of the WTO in 1995 introduced new rules that prevented the EC from blocking panel findings and provided new procedures for dispute resolution, which included approving the challenger's use of retaliatory sanctions. Thus, a third challenge to the EU banana regime made by the US, Mexico, Guatemala, Honduras (and later Ecuador) in April 1996 carried more weight. In May 1997 the Dispute Settlement Body (DSB) gave the EU until 1 January 1999 to make its banana regime compliant with WTO rules.[15]

The 'non-restrictive' tariff quota

On 1 January 1999 the EU began implementing another banana regime based on a revised tariff quota system (Regulation 1637/98 and 2362/98). This regime made the allocation of licences less restrictive and increased the Latin American quota. The new licensing scheme did not distinguish between ACP and Latin American producers per se but rather based new quota levels on a favourable historical reference period (1994–96), when the EU had guaranteed ACP imports.[17]

US officials argued that the changes to the regime were cosmetic and accused the Commission of making only a token gesture to bring the regime in line with international trade laws.[18] Believing it was still not WTO compliant, the US proceeded first, to publish a list of intended sanctions in the Federal Register and second, to file another request for a WTO panel in November 1998, two months before the new EU regime was implemented. Following its implementation, the US sought WTO authorisation to impose over $500m in retaliatory tariffs.

In March the WTO Dispute Settlement Body (DSB) announced it needed more time before ruling on the compatibility of the new EU regime. The US proceeded with plans to impose 100 per cent tariffs on a range of items, but agreed not to collect the tariffs until after the panel ruled. However, the Commission argued that the tariffs, which would be backdated, would effectively prohibit (particularly small) companies from exporting. The USTR Charlene Barshefsky was so confident of the illegality of the EU regime that she effectively dared European companies to export.[19]

In April the WTO ruled that the EU banana regime was still inconsistent with multilateral rules and authorised $191m in sanctions. In addition to reducing the level of retaliatory tariffs, the Dispute Settlement Panel ruled that the US had acted too early in imposing sanctions. Decrying the use of 'unilateral sanctions', the EU filed a WTO dispute challenging US domestic trade legislation, Section 301.[21] A panel was convened on 2 March 1999, but later ruled in favour of the US.[22]

First come, first serve

The situation became more intense when the US Congress passed the Carousel Retaliation Act (2000) which was designed to maximise the impact of US sanctions on the EU in both the banana and the beef disputes.[23] Later that year EC agriculture ministers finally agreed to a fourth regime which would eliminate the tariff quota system and instead allow for a transitional period governed by three tariff quotas and a 'first come, first serve' allocation of licences (see Boxes 7.2; 7.4).

Historical reference licensing

The Commission was unable to gain approval of the first come, first serve licensing scheme. Thus, it was replaced in April 2001 (just three months before it was due to be implemented) with a historical reference licensing system, similar to that used in the third banana regime. The new regime essentially ended the banana dispute between the EU and the US. European Trade Commissioner Lamy and USTR Zoellick brokered the deal on 18 April 2001, which included provisions for the end to first come, first serve licensing and US retaliatory sanctions by 1 July 2001.

Under the deal, the plan to move to a tariff only system by 2006 remained, but the first come, first serve licensing scheme was scratched. The EU–US agreement established two phases of three-tiered tariff rate quotas for the transitional period (see Box 7.4) and accepted that a historical reference period (1994–96) would determine interim banana licences. The EU–US deal offered 'something for everyone' (see Table 7.1).[25] Non-traditional operators, such as Chiquita, gained access to tariff rate quotas, while traditional operators maintained the majority of category A and B licences. ACP producers were protected by tariff rate-quotas in the transitional phase, while Latin American producers were guaranteed the move to a tariff only regime, and the possibility of higher access to the EU market during the transition.

Box 7.2 The transitional first come, first serve licensing

- Licences allocated to the first boats to reach EU shores.
- Shippers would have to commit bananas to the vessel before submitting declaration of intent to import and to lodge a high security deposit to deter speculation.[24]
- After declaring their intention to import specified quantities, pre-allocation would be determined when vessels were within sailing distance from Europe to avoid discrimination against countries that were further away.

Box 7.3 Chronology of the banana dispute

1993

May	• GATT panel finds against EC member states. EC blocks panel report from being adopted by the GATT Council;
July	• The single market in bananas is launched with EC Regulation 404/93.

1994

January	• The GATT panel finds against Regulation 404/93;
February	• The EC blocks the GATT panel report on Regulation 404/93 from being adopted.

1995

January	• The new WTO dispute settlement provision prevents one member from blocking panel findings.

1996

September	• The US, Ecuador, Guatemala, Honduras and Mexico challenge banana ii under the WTO dispute-settlement mechanism.

1997

May	• The WTO panel rules against the EC regime;
July	• The EC appeals 19 findings in the WTO panel report;
September	• The WTO Appellate Body upholds panel findings of EC GATT/ GATS violations.

1998

January	• WTO arbitrator gives EC until 1 January 1999 to comply with WTO rulings;
June	• European Agriculture Council adopts modifications to banana regime;
July	• The EU adopts a revised banana import regime to be implemented January 1999;
November	• The US argues that the new EC regime is not compatible. USTR publishes its retaliatory sanction list in the Federal Register and seeks a WTO panel on the EU Banana Regime.

1999

January	• The third regime is implemented on 1 January 1999 and the United States seeks WTO authorisation to impose $500m in retaliatory tariffs on the EU under Article 22 of the DSU. The EU requests a WTO panel to rule on compliance under Article 21 of the DSU;
March	• The WTO panel announces it needs more time to rule on the EU banana regime. The US imposes sanctions and announces that customs duties will not be collected until the panel rules;
April	• The WTO panel rules that the EU banana regime is still inconsistent, and authorises US retaliatory tariffs amounting to $191.4 million a year;
May	• The Commission requests a Dispute Settlement Panel on US Section 301.

2000

May	• Carousel Retaliation is passed by the Senate as part of the Afro-

	Caribbean trade bill;
December	• The WTO rejects the EU request for a panel on Section 301. EU agriculture ministers agree to a new banana regime.
2001	
April	• A banana deal is struck between the EU and the US. EU agrees to drop first come, first serve licensing and implement historical references system by July 1, 2001. The US agrees to drop retaliatory sanctions on the same day.

Box 7.4 The EU banana regimes

Member state regimes	• Non-preferential duty free imports in Germany; • 20 per cent duty on imported bananas in Benelux countries, Ireland and Denmark; • Duty free imports in France, Italy, Portugal, Spain and the UK maintained duty free imports for ACP states.
Restrictive tariff rate quota	**Two-tiered tariffs** • ACP states: 857,000 tonnes of duty free imports from traditional ACP countries; • Latin America: 2 million tonne quota at 100 ecus per tonne, rising to 850 ecus. **Three-tiered licences** • Category A licences (66.5 per cent) of the 2m tonne quota allocated to traditional operators; • Category B licences (30 per cent) of the quota, awarded to operators with history in ACP trade; • Category C licences created for new producers.
Less restrictive tariff rate quota	**Two-tiered tariffs** • ACP: 857,000 tonnes of duty free imports (to be filled globally); • Latin American: 75 ecus for the first 2.553m tonnes. A new provision, however, was that this quota would be filled globally by ACP states. **Licensing** • Three-tiered system remained; • No distinction between ACP and Latin American producers for the allocation of import licences, but licence distribution based on historical reference (1994–96) for 1999 and 2000) for a period when levels of ACP bananas had been guaranteed by the EU regime.

Transition to tariff only system/FCFS licensing	**Tariff only system** • Move to tariff only system by 2006 after transitional period **First come, first serve licensing (transitional period)** • Three quotas would be managed fortnightly or weekly to control banana prices; • All categories of licences would be allocated on the first come, first serve basis. **Tariff only system** • Move to tariff only system by 2006 after transitional period.
Transition to tariff only system/ historical licensing	**Interim three-tiered licensing (two phases)** **Phase I (1 July 2001)** • Category A: 2.2m tonnes • Category B: 353,000 tonnes • Category C: 850,000 tonnes **Phase II (1 January 2002)** • Category A: 2.2m tonnes • Category B: 453,000 tonnes • Category C: 750,00 tonnes **Historical reference licensing** • Historical Reference licensing based on the distributions between 1994 and 1996. 83 per cent of A and B licences for traditional operators and 17 per cent for non-traditional.

The US negotiating position

This section questions the factors that influenced the US negotiating position during the banana dispute. Four key US policy decisions are examined, including the decision to file the GATT/WTO cases; to impose sanctions before the WTO ruling on the EU's less restrictive tariff quota; to target EU member states with sanctions using Section 301 and Carousel Retaliation; and finally, to accept the banana deal.

The WTO challenge

Many initially questioned why the Clinton Administration would involve itself in a trade dispute with Europe over a product that, unlike beef, has little domestic agricultural significance. Although US trade officials have tried to argue that they were defending Latin American banana producers and the multilateral trading system, the most common explanation for the US decision was the strong domestic lobbying position of Chiquita Corporation, the American based multinational banana producer operating in Latin America.

Chiquita applied for a Section 301 petition, requiring USTR to investigate the EU banana regime under the US 1974 Trade Act. Section 301 requires USTR to act if a trading practice is in violation of bilateral or multilateral trade agreements. Thus a USTR official argued that, 'There was little flexibility on this, USTR had to take the 301 Petition because GATT had found the EC in violation of rules'.[26]

Chiquita had a lot to gain in instigating the WTO case against the EU. It had reported over one billion dollars in lost revenue since the second banana regime was established in 1993, and in January 2001 it sued the European Commission for $519m in damages incurred as a result of the EU banana subsidies.[27] Despite the fact that American multinationals controlled three-quarters of the EU market, Chiquita's share dropped from roughly 40 to 20 per cent after the implementation of the single market regime. In addition, while Chiquita's market share dropped roughly 20 per cent, two other US banana multinationals, Del Monte and Dole, managed to diversify their markets and increase their market share over Chiquita.[28] Dole invested in ACP producing states such as Jamaica, Cameroon and the Ivory Coast, and bought up European importers that held the import licences, thus ensuring that Dole-Europe would benefit from EU quota-rents. Del Monte expanded European distribution, increasing its European business by 30 per cent, with half of its $2bn in revenues coming from the continent. Chiquita, who had sold its interests in the Irish based banana operator Fyffes, suddenly found itself in direct competition with companies who held European licences.[29] Dole and Del Monte not only opted to stay out of the banana dispute, they also publicly offered their support to the ACP states.[30]

While USTR is commissioned to protect US businesses, its avid interest in the banana dispute at the behest of one company against the rest of the industry drew heavy criticism. It was widely argued that Chiquita's privileged position was secured by its CEO, Carl Linder, who had made heavy campaign contributions to the Clinton Administration.[31] *Time* magazine reported that Chiquita's CEO 'got Washington to launch a trade war for him' (see Barlett and Steel 2000). Commissioner Brittan argued that US involvement in the dispute settlement process was 'driven by the fact that Chiquita is a company that gives money to political parties'.[32]

Chiquita also found strong allies in the US Congress. Twelve US Senators called for a formal inquiry into the EU banana regime, and USTR came under heavy pressure from Congress to exert maximum pressure on the EU to end the dispute. Congressional interest in bringing an end to banana subsidies was also tied to the larger goal of curbing unfair EU trading practices, a particular irritant of both American and European politicians' domestic agricultural lobbies.

Carousel Retaliation

The decision to sanction the regime prior to the WTO ruling raised the stakes in the dispute and increased tension between the transatlantic partners. In late 1998 USTR came under heavy pressure to retaliate, as Congress became increasingly frustrated with the EU's failure to implement a WTO consistent regime. USTR anticipated that the planned regime changes, which were set for implementation in January 1999, would not be WTO compatible. In November 1998 the House approved Resolution 213 calling for the Administration to actively pursue EU compliance in the banana and beef disputes. The Resolution, later approved by the Senate, states that, 'the President should develop a trade agenda which actively addresses agricultural trade barriers in multilateral and bilateral trade negotiations and steadfastly pursues full compliance with the dispute settlement decision of the World Trade Organisation' (US Congress 1998).

The decision to sanction the EU gained cross-party support from influential Democrats and Republicans in Congress, and featured lobbying by many heavyweights including the Speaker of the House Newt Gingrich, Senator Trent Lott and Senator Bob Dole as well as Minority Leader Richard Gephardt.[33] Congress exerted pressure on the Administration who in turn agreed to pursue 'all necessary action to ensure full and timely EU compliance in these cases'. In 1998, White House Chief of Staff Erskine Bowles outlined in a letter to several Congressmen in November 1999 the Administration's commitment to utilising (1) domestic, (2) bilateral and (3) multilateral channels to end the dispute.[34] First, bilateral discussion with the Commission would continue in accordance with commitments made under the NTA, but USTR would reserve the right to challenge the regime in the WTO. Finally, retaliation against the EU would be instigated under Section 301 of the 1974 Trade Act. Bowles also announced the Administration's intent to impose sanctions no later than 3 March 1999. The commitment to Congress locked USTR negotiators into a time frame for retaliation.

US decision makers appeared fairly united in their decision to sanction the EU.[35] However, the decision to pass the Carousel Retaliation Act, ironically as part of the Afro-Caribbean Trade Bill, highlighted differences between Congress and the US Administration. It also illustrated how Congress was able to directly impact US trade policy, and how Chiquita, as a strong supporter of Carousel, was able to exert additional pressure on USTR indirectly. Carousel Retaliation gained popular support in Congress because it was designed to maximise pressure in all trade disputes with the EU.[36]

Two factors helped maximise the lobbying efforts of Chiquita to pass Carousel Retaliation. Again, the hefty campaign contributions made by Carl Linder (around $5m) to both parties in Congress came under scrutiny. Moreover Chiquita's interests coincided with many in Congress who were interested in putting an end to other trade disputes where agriculture subsidies and tariff rate quotas formed non-tariff barriers to trade.[37] Chiquita gained wider political support by teaming up with the beef lobby, who had much more broad-based constituency support.[38] The US Beef Cattlemen Association and Chiquita Corporation ran an ad campaign drawing attention to domestic opposition to the EU's banana and beef regimes. The 'Message to Congress' was that US companies were paying the price for EU non-compliance with WTO rules.[39]

The idea that the European Commission was dodging the WTO decision was popular in Congress. One House staffer argued that, 'Once the banana case was won, Congress expected the Europeans to comply. That they don't is an affront.'[40] US Congressman John Thune argeed that, 'The EU–US beef and banana disputes were important tests for these new (WTO) procedures. The EU's refusal to live with the consequences of the decision is unacceptable. It defies the purpose of the WTO and breeds further scepticism among those who want free and fair trade.'[41] Carousel Retaliation was seen as a way of *forcing* the Commission to comply with the WTO ruling, thus putting an end to the dispute. However, it was highly controversial both in transatlantic relations, where it was unanimously condemned by European institutions, and domestically where the US Administration publicly voiced concerns over the new legislation. USTR Barshefsky testified before the Senate Finance Trade Sub-Committee that she opposed Carousel Retaliation.[42] Another USTR official noted that USTR already had the power to change the sanction list, adding, 'if we thought changing the list would do it, we would'.[43]

Carousel Retaliation highlights institutional rivalry between USTR and Congress on foreign trade policy. While USTR was more tuned to the external, bilateral and multilateral implications of using sanctions, Congress was acting solely in the interest of domestic businesses. One House Staff member noted with irritation that, 'Business argued that USTR should look at the products on the list to have full impact ... we were baffled that USTR refused to look at it ...'[44] One Senate staff member stated the view that officials in USTR simply 'oppose authority for Congress'.[45]

Sanctioning EU interests

The decision concerning which products to sanction, including a range of cheese, wine, clothing, appliances and beauty products increased the complexity of US policy towards the EU banana regime. Two factors were crucial to determining the sanctions list. First, officials asked where sanctions would most likely have an impact, and second, where minimum damage would be caused to US companies.[46] Ultimately, the decision lay with USTR, however the list of sanctions was available for public comment in the Federal Register. A comparison of the original and final lists sheds some light on which other influences shaped the US decision on 'who' to sanction. In addition it points to domestic casualties of the banana war.

The internal economic repercussions of US sanctions soon became apparent as specific US manufacturers, farmers and retailers reported lost exports and lost imports. For example, US farmers faced lost sales of raw ingredients to EU cookie producers, and Whirlpool halted shipments of certain coffeemakers.[47] US department stores such as Nieman Marcus[48] were forced to find alternative sources of cashmere and small retailers of bath products, for example, were unable to import products for distribution.

The damage to US companies had internal political repercussions. First, the viewpoint that US trade policy was dictated by large companies was reinforced by the fact that many large multinational companies, such as Gillette and Mattel, were able to lobby their European-made imports off the sanction list, while small companies without lobby facilities, which were often unaware of the dispute, were not.[49] Second, damage to US companies involved in foreign trade instigated backlash from companies who condemned the use of unilateral sanctions. A spokesperson for the American Association of Exporters and Importers in New York argued that, 'We would like to see rule of law rather than [the US] acting as jury and judge.'[50]

US policy decisions in the banana dispute also had external repercussions for bilateral US relations with other states. The decision to strategically target sanctions at the regime's strongest supporters threatened bilateral relations between the US and certain EU member states. In particular, the banana dispute soured the 'special relationship' between the US and the UK. While the UK had been spared from retaliation in the beef dispute, its strong support of the EU regime ensured it was one of the countries hardest hit by US banana sanctions.[51]

The US challenge to end the EU banana regime also threatened the US–Caribbean relationship. In March 1999 the Caribbean Community and Common Market (Caricom) suspended the Caribbean–US 'Partnership for Prosperity and Security in the Caribbean' or the Bridgetown Accord (1997) in protest at US sanctions. A Caricom spokesman confirmed that the suspension of the Accord was a means of communicating its disgust to the White House.[52]

Finally, the banana dispute put a strain on US–Latin American relations. In particular, the relationship with Columbia and Costa Rica was threatened when the two states signed a pact with the EU in which they withdrew their complaint against the banana regime. The deal was met harshly in the US Congress, where Senator Bob Dole (unsuccessfully) called for sanctions against these countries to be included in a budget bill (Greenwald *et al.* 1996). The tension between the US and Ecuador, who chose to accept the EU's first come, first serve proposal, was exemplified by the comments of Ecuador's Ambassador to the EU, Alfredo Pinoargote, who argued that 'Ecuador and the EU have been virtually taken hostage by the [US]'.[53]

Why this *deal?*

Three months into Bush's Presidency, the US government agreed to end the banana dispute with the EU. Why did the US government choose to accept *this* deal? From the start, the US had favoured the use of historical reference licensing over first come, first serve licensing, but a sticking point in previous negotiations had been the reference period used to determine banana licences. It was argued that a post-1993 reference period upheld the distortions of the EU banana regime because it issued licensing on the basis of volume distribution at a time when tariff-rate quotas existed for ACP bananas. The pressing question is why the US agreed to a deal that included a historical reference period of 1994–96 for licence distribution, the same period used in the third banana regime? Furthermore, how was USTR able to sell the deal at home?

A number of factors helped influence USTR's decision to accept the historical reference licensing scheme. First and foremost, noted one official, 'We wanted to end this dispute.' The close pre-existing relationship between Commissioner Lamy and USTR Zoellick arguably incited compromise.[54] Still, despite early meetings between the two, Zoellick testified in front of Congress in March 2001 that the EU would face sanctions unless it could show greater flexibility. It was widely believed that the Bush Administration – like its predecessor – was under pressure from Congress to implement Carousel Retaliation, which the Clinton Administration had shelved.[55] One USTR official argued that the perception of Congress was similar to the Administrations: 'they were sick of bananas'.[56]

USTR's mission was to find a compromise that could 'best' accommodate the interests of Latin America, the Caribbean and Chiquita.[57] Despite earlier objections from the Latin American producers and Chiquita, the historical reference system met a fundamental requirement of all three parties: it replaced the first come, first serve system. The threat of first come, first serve was particularly persuasive in convincing Chiquita to accept the historical references period of 1994–96. Although it stood to gain a few licences (overall the tariff quota for dollar bananas was increased by 100,000 tonnes), the numbers were not drastically different to those upheld by previous regimes. However, one USTR official noted that, 'Chiquita actually mortally feared [first come, first serve]. It fought until it became abundantly clear that it would be a reality.'[58] In addition, Chiquita was guaranteed a definitive date for the end of the tariff rate quota system.

The EU negotiating position

While US involvement in the banana dispute can be mainly attributed to domestic interests, at first glance the EU position seems to be the product of external factors, most obviously its relations with ACP states. US officials have argued, however, that the EU front as third-world protector is a cover for its real interest in protecting EU banana operators. This section considers the decision to maintain the tariff rate quota system, to change the regime, and finally to introduce first come, first serve licensing and a tariff only regime.

Pressure to maintain the regime

The main lobbies that fought to keep the EU regime were Caribbean farmers and EU banana operators.[59] EU operators favoured the historical reference period used in the regime's licensing scheme, because the time period used guaranteed more licences for EU companies who were already trading with ACP states.[60] The tariff quota maintained secure access for Caribbean and African bananas. Both lobby groups were able to maintain the support of the member states, particularly those with colonial ties, who in turn fought to keep the tariff rate quota regime.[61]

The reaction to US sanctions

The European Commission, the Council and the Parliament unanimously condemned US sanctions. Nonetheless, the WTO approval of sanctions acted as a catalyst of change. Carousel Retaliation increased pressure on decision makers to revise the regime. Although European leaders such as UK Prime Minister Blair argued that Carousel was totally unproductive, the threat of increased sanctions had the intended affect. First, some Commission officials admitted that Carousel Retaliation forced the EU to reconsider its plans for change more quickly. Second, sanctions not only instigated a backlash against the US, but also against the EU as European companies and member state governments became stuck in the crossfire of the transatlantic trade war.

Table 7.1 Licence preferences of banana players

Favoured first come, first serve licensing	*Favoured historical reference licensing*
US multinationals Dole Corporation	**US multinationals** Chiquita Corporation
ACP states None	**ACP states** All
Latin American producers Ecuador	**Latin American producers** All barring Ecuador
EU banana operators None	**EU banana operators** All

In September 2000, 16 months after the WTO ruled that the EU banana regime was inconsistent with WTO rules, a number of European companies announced that they were taking legal action against the Commission. Arran Aromatics, a Scottish manufacturer of bath products, reported that it was seeking legal consultation on reclaiming damages of £2m in lost export orders to the US (Eaglesham 2000). The Italian based Fiamm Spa, producers of batteries, announced it would be seeking 35bn lire compensation (*Il Sole 24 Ore* 2000) and Scottish cashmere producers threatened to sue the Commission for £5m (Chisholm 2000).[62] European companies argued they should not have to pay the consequences of 'the European principle of preference for our former Caribbean colonies'.[63] The companies backed the US argument that the Commission had failed to handle the dispute in a 'reasonable time span'.

In response to the threatened litigation, European Commission trade spokesman Anthony Gooch argued that these companies lacked 'a legal leg to stand on'.[64] It was argued that the blame was misplaced because the Commission had taken action to change the banana regime (including three major communications to the Council). The Commission argued that the re-negotiation of the banana regimes had been timely because the member states were unable to agree on a suitable replacement. While the UK and Germany pushed for a compromise, southern member states, including France and Spain, voted against the Commission's proposal for compromise.[65]

Negotiating first come, first serve

The negotiations on the fourth banana regime were held up by internal disagreement between the European Council and the Parliament.[66] Some ACP and Latin American states, EU banana operators and certain member states opposed the move to a tariff only system.[67] However, it was decided in July 2000 that the move was the only way to satisfy the US and end the WTO dispute. The Council asked the Commission to pursue more definitive plans for the transitional licensing scheme. However, internal conflict was publicised when agriculture ministers refused to grant the Commission a mandate to negotiate a direct move to the tariff only system should the transitional system fail to solve the dispute.[68]

The decision to move ahead with first come, first serve licensing met strong backlash from EU banana operators, ACP states and some Latin American countries. Banana operators from many member states and producers from the Caribbean and Latin America teamed up in an advertising campaign protesting against the first come, first serve system.[69] Atlanta (2000), the largest German fruit wholesaler and leading operator and distributor, argued that, 'first come, first served systems would force the operators to break up their shipping schedules which now are in line with the ripening cycles and the general requirements of the market'. Furthermore, it was argued that freelance traders would be able to block regular operators and that consumers would be hurt by the quality of the fruit, because companies would be unwilling to ship expensive high quality fruit given the risk of securing a licence. Caribbean banana producers also feared that the 'ship race' for licences would disadvantage small operators and rapidly push the Caribbean growers out of the market. American multinationals also had an advantage over Caribbean exports because their established markets in Eastern Europe provided the option of shipping on to other countries, should their bid for a licence be rejected near EU shores (Caribbean Bananas Exporters Association 2000a; 2000b).

American countries also opposed the first come, first serve system. Wilson (2001) reported that, 'They fear Ecuador, the biggest exporter, will further increase its market share at its neighbours' expense because of its low production costs.' US officials argued that the system was not compatible with WTO rules.[70] In short, as one US trade negotiator argued, 'First come, first serve will not end the dispute. Latin Americans oppose it. Caribbean producers oppose it. The Africans don't like it. Companies except for Dole don't like it.' Even the Commission admitted that 'The first come, first serve system has very limited support and constitutes a particular heavy administrative burden for the EC.' Morever, 'small time smaller operators which are not "primary importers" could be eliminated from the markets' (European Commission 1999b). Why, then, was this licensing scheme pursued?

The decision to implement such an unpopular regime was a strategic move by the Commission. Consistent WTO rulings and the threat of US sanctions meant that the regime needed to change, but negotiators had their hands tied at a political level by the member states and the lobbies behind them.[71] Commission officials argued that they had very little option in revising the banana regime; they believed that the tariff quota regime would have to be eliminated to end the dispute.

EU member states insisted on a transitional tariff rate quota system to protect ACP states. The tariff rate quotas required a licensing scheme, but finding a system which satisfied EU operators, Caribbean exporters and the WTO complainants was an impossible task. Member states were forced to choose the 'least worst' option when the Commission announced in July 2000 that without an agreement on a licensing system, a transitional shift to a tariff only regime would not be practical. Many were opposed to the first come, first serve licensing but most had much stronger objections to losing the transitional period.[72]

Why a deal now?

The Commission's decision to abandon the first come, first serve system was a compromise aimed at balancing multiple interests. By implementing the controversial licence system, the EU stood to alienate the banana operators and ACP farmers it had originally tried to protect. Even so, the reaction of these parties to first come, first serve licensing was well noted before the Council agreed to it. So why, in the end, did the Commission revert back to a historical reference system?

First, the Commission was unsure whether the first come, first serve system would be WTO compatible, but they were sure that its opponents would continue to challenge the regime. The US threat of Carousel Retaliation implementation increased the risk of damaging sanctions on EU companies. In addition the EU–US banana deal secured US support for the EU's WTO waivers for Most Favoured Nation (MFN) status under Article 1 of the Dispute Settlement Understanding (DSU), which the Commission feared it would not be able to secure.[73]

Second, the Commission played a crucial role in ending the dispute because it had wide discretion on the type of licensing system to be used during the transitional period. The threat of first come, first serve was originally designed to force the member states to agree to a historical licensing system. The Commission only accepted the first come, first serve system when the member states could not agree on a historical reference period.[74] Further, Commissioner Lamy argued that this unpopular regime was used to pressure the US to make a deal.[75] Many believe the Commission would have abandoned the controversial licensing system either way.

The Commission's final decision to relinquish the first come, first serve system also stems from the problematic implementation of the system. One Commission official noted that, 'when it came to actually putting it into practice, there were all sorts of technical problems – the whole system had to be created from scratch. There were serious doubts as to whether the system would be up and running by the deadline.'[76] Failure to implement the regime, noted one official, 'would create a real blot on the Commission's record.'[77]

To summarise, it can be argued that the EU's decision to revert back to the historical reference licence system was a means of 'best' accommodating interested parties. EU banana operators and ACP farmers accepted that they were losing the privileges of the previous regime, and favoured historical referencing for the interim period. The EU abandoned its ally in Latin America (Ecuador) in favour of more broad based support from other banana producing states and US agreement that the WTO challenge would not continue. The banana deal was a means of maintaining the EU's credibility.[78]

The wider implications of the banana dispute

The transatlantic banana dispute is such an important case study because it highlights the capacity of transatlantic disputes to undermine relations with third states. It demonstrates how conflict in the transatlantic relationship distracts from cooperation under the NTA. Finally, these combined factors illustrate the capacity of transatlantic disputes to threaten the stability and legitimacy of the multilateral trading system.

Caught in the crossfire

In the end, it can be argued that both the EU and the US acted like ‘bullies’. Strategically they used the position of smaller states to gain support throughout the dispute, and domestic decisions taken in the banana war carried greater implications for the smaller banana producing states.

First, the EU defended its position as ‘third-world champion’ by arguing that the US was bullying it into a policy that would undermine Caribbean economies. Ultimately it argued that the US challenge undermined efforts to prevent illicit activity in the region, because the lost market access for Caribbean bananas would result in employment loss, drug trafficking and high levels of illegal immigration to the US.[79] Thus, EU officials argued that the US challenge to the banana regime undermined their efforts to curb drug production in the Caribbean through, for example, the Caribbean Drugs Initiative (1997). A Council Secretariat official argued that, ‘The EU spent a lot of money fighting off drugs in Caribbean. The US is acting to destroy farmers.’[80]

Ironically, the most implicitly damaging outcome could have been the EU’s first come, first serve licensing scheme.[81] It too had the potential to undermine efforts to curb economic instability in Latin America. It was argued that lost employment in the banana industry could increase social tension, which in turn would fuel guerrilla movements and harm efforts to end civil conflict. Increased violence in Columbia, in turn would undermine EU and US efforts to end conflict through the hefty financial aid that has poured into the region.[82]

Bananas and the NTA

A significant test for NTA institutions is how effectively they manage trade disputes. The banana dispute had the capacity to undermine the NTA process both in real terms and by polluting the positive atmosphere that had been created by the new transatlantic dialogue.

EU–US trade disputes clearly have a negative impact on the transatlantic relationship. In general, one Commission official explained that disputes ‘take away from meetings where other issues could be discussed’.[83] The banana dispute was on the EU–US summit agenda for over three years, and it is blamed for overshadowing this event. However, while the dispute provided a diversion, it did block the NTA process from producing a number of deliverables, most notably the MRAs, the South-Eastern Europe Stability Pact, the AIDS initiatives in Africa and even the TEP. While the dispute may have interfered with increased cooperation, the whole NTA structure survived. As one Commission official argued, ‘conflict in one field does not break apart in other areas’.[84]

The most structural damage caused by the banana dispute was to the Transatlantic Economic Partnership. One Commission official observed that, 'TEP ran parallel to bananas, hormones, and Helms Burton. These disputes have had counter influence.'[85] A representative from the American Chamber of Commerce in Brussels agreed that these disputes damaged the TEP.[86] The argument follows that the period in which the TEP stalled (most of 1999) coincided with the most hostile year in the banana dispute.

Disputes, like that over bananas, interfere with transatlantic cooperation, because they occupy time and resources of the negotiators on both sides of the Atlantic, but the actual damage in terms of overall trade is overshadowed by the larger trading relationship. European officials often argue that bananas affect less than 1 per cent of trade but account for 95 per cent of media attention on transatlantic relations. One USTR official agreed, noting that, 'Disputes do not offset everything else. There is $300 million involved in disputes and $300 billion in trade. Journalists focus on news, that news is not that the US and the EU are trading swimmingly on $300 billion in trade.'[87]

Thus, despite talk of a transatlantic trade war, the EU and US remain partners within the NTA structure. A major shortcoming of this structure, however, was its failure to minimise 'surface' or superficial damage to the relationship that resulted from mishandling the dispute. The structure did not stop EU and US officials from having a public 'war of words' over bananas. Despite the established dialogue structure, EU and US officials took to what Prodi has characterised as 'megaphone' rather than 'telephone' diplomacy.[88]

Without underestimating the real damage to the EU–US partnership, it can be argued that the perception of damage did more to undermine the partnership. The EU's failure to design a WTO compatible regime led to harsh criticism in the US where, for example, USTR Barshefsky argued that the EU was forcing 'a major confrontation in transatlantic trade' (USTR 1999). The key factor was the US decision to impose sanctions in March 1999. Special trade negotiator Peter Scher maintained the time had come, 'for the EU to bear some of the consequences for its GATT and WTO obligations', while Commissioner Brittan argued that the US's 'politically unwise' decision to take unilateral sanctions was risking damage to the WTO and EU–US relations over 'a minor economic issue'.[90] A Council Secretariat official accused the US of 'taking hostages'.[91] And, the UK Minister for Trade and Industry stated that, 'I deplore the action which the United States has taken ... it is completely unauthorised by any WTO procedures.'[92]

The hostility of the banana dispute was most apparent among domestic actors who lacked direct access to transgovernmental networks. The dispute fuelled anti-American feelings in certain member state governments and anti-EU sentiment in Congress.[93] In particular, US sanctions alienated one of its greatest allies within the EU, leading one UK official to accuse the US of being 'irrational' and 'unacceptable'.[94]

The dispute had a disproportionate effect in Congress, where politicians have little knowledge and even less interest in the NTA or the TEP.[95] In Congress, the perceived 'stalling' of the EU in the WTO process generated perceptions that it was not 'playing fair'. Congress compared the US loss over Foreign Sales Corporations to the EU banana case. One House staff member argued that, 'In five months we were able to pass a major change to tax law, [to] respond quickly by law. Yet, the EU has failed to comply with WTO rulings in either the beef or the banana case in almost ten years.'[96]

To summarise, the banana dispute did increase tension in the relationship. It is hard to determine the exact impact of these negative perceptions, but a USTR official stated that, 'When you are throwing insults at each other – it is hard to kiss and make up.' Still, the dispute was not as detrimental to the NTA process as it was perceived to be. What is more damaging to the reputation of the NTA, is that it did not have a major impact on the banana dispute. The banana dispute highlights the inability of the NTA process to 'manage' diverging interests on either side of the Atlantic (see also Aaron *et al.* 2001).

Bananas and the WTO

Arguably the most important consequence of the banana dispute is the failure of the EU and the US to resolve the conflict through the WTO. Both sides have accused the other of breaking multilateral trading rules and of jeopardising the multilateral trading system. The unilateral nature of US sanctions and the EU failure to bring the regime in line with WTO rulings have called into question the effectiveness and legitimacy of international rules.

First, unilateral sanctions and the introduction of Carousel Retaliation led EU officials to question the compatibility of US domestic trade legislation with the WTO.[97] Sir Leon Brittan warned that: 'My message to the United States is a simple one: use the WTO.' The UK Trade Minister Brian Wilson argued, 'It is at this point that the Americans appear to have pulled the plug on the (WTO) procedures and acted unilaterally'.[98] Commissioner Lamy accused the US of making up its own rules.[99]

Arguably the US did 'break the rules' because the DSB concluded that it had acted too early in imposing sanctions. Nonetheless, it approved the sanctions and upheld the legality of Section 301 and Carousel Retaliation. The timing of the US request for retaliation exposed a 'loop' in WTO law. The US argued that the timing of the sanctions was dictated by Dispute Settlement Understanding (DSU) Article 22, which states that the complaining party must retaliate within twenty days after the 'reasonable time' deadline for implementation, in this case 1 January 1999. However, Article 22.6 requires the DSU to grant authorisation for retaliation within thirty days of the expiration period. This left a small window of opportunity – 21 January to 31 January – for the US to request retaliation. US officials argued (under Article 22.7) that if retaliation was not made within that time period, the 'negative consensus' rule would lapse, and the DSU would have to rule under 'positive consensus', which would allow any country, including the EU, to block retaliation.[100] The US requested a panel for DSB authorisation on 14 January 1999, and the panel was scheduled for the following day, within the 'window of opportunity' (see also Komuro 2000; Vallen and McGivern 2000; Ziedaliski 2000).

On the other hand, the EU requested the re-establishment of the DSB panel, which reconvened on 12 January 1999, under Article 21.5. The EU argued that the US could not retaliate until the Article 21.5 procedures had finished, or until the new EC banana regime was found to be inconsistent with WTO rules. Commission officials moved to suspend the US request for a panel decision on sanctions, claiming it was invalid until a Article 21.5 decision was made. The US in turn accused the EC of 'blocking tactics'. USTR Barshefsky argued, 'The EU today took the extraordinary step of shutting down the work of the WTO.'[101]

The dispute over Articles 21 and 22 highlighted a problem with the legal framework of the DSU. Article 21 makes no reference to the right to retaliation in Article 22 and Article 22 makes no reference to 21. The EU argued that Article 21 took precedence over Article 22. The US argued that the EU's reading of the relationship between Article 21 and Article 22 would render Article 22 inoperative because the thirty-day deadline for negative consensus (under Article 22) would expire before the ninety-day deadline for a DSB ruling (under Article 21.5). The US argued that the EU actions had invoked an 'endless loop of litigation'.

In this case, the timing conflict between Article 21 and 22 procedures[102] was reconciled by the DSB's request on 2 March for more time to gather information, which merged the deadlines for both Article 21 and 22 DSB decisions. The conflict over these articles, however, drew attention to deeper problems in the DSU framework. The 'contradictory' drafting of Articles 21 and 22 and the 'ambiguous' language of the DSU has subsequently arisen in other cases, including the Canadian–Australian salmon dispute (see also Vallen and McGivern 2000; Komuro 2000: 32).

Second, the EU failure to comply with the WTO ruling was heavily criticised, especially in Congress where the EU was seen to be undermining the credibility of the WTO. One USTR representative observed that the pressure coming from Congress was renewed after dispute settlement proceedings. He argued, 'After you battle and win, well you played the multilateral game the way the Europeans said you should and now they are not implementing!' He added that 'Europeans are thumbing their nose at [the WTO]'. For USTR this was a tough position because they had fought hard for Congressional support of the WTO on the grounds that the new system would be a serious medium for dispute resolution.[103] The message from Congress was clear: the EU needed to comply with the ruling. A Senate Finance Committee spokesperson argued that, 'We have lost many cases but we have always complied.'[104]

The WTO Dispute Settlement mechanism, however, does not require the EU to change its banana regime. Rather, it authorises sanctions to compensate the challenger. A Trade Committee staff member noted that, 'Europeans have made little effort to comply, but they are entitled to do this', adding ironically that, 'Congress made sure that Uruguay would allow us to accept retaliation the same!' Thus, the banana dispute exposed another loop in the WTO system. Gleason and Walther (2000: 716) argue that the WTO suffers from implementation problems including, 'inadequate safety checks, incentives, and/or sanctions to encourage the promptest-possible, good faith implementation'.

For many who supported the EU's banana subsidy regime the WTO ruling raised questions about the legitimacy of a trade policy which protects untamed liberalisation. The banana case fuelled the mobilisation against globalisation as NGOs, including TACD representatives, argued that the WTO should promote fair, if not always free trade.[105] As a direct result of this case, Congresswoman Maxine Waters argued that the WTO needed 'to begin listening to concerns of small farmers, labour union members, environmentalists, consumer advocates and human rights activists' (US Congress 1999).

The banana dispute is a test case for the WTO. While this was a classic dispute, many more up and coming disputes will be more difficult to manage given their predisposition to scientific (beef), cultural (GMOs) and legal (FSCs) differences between the EU and the US. What links these disputes is the fact that strong domestic political lobbies and internal pressure will continue to ensure that EU and US interests clash, and that trade negotiators will find themselves in direct conflict between domestic and WTO interests.

Conclusion

To summarise, this chapter sought to explain which factors could explain EU and US decision-making in the banana dispute. It was argued that ultimately the banana deal was a compromise of domestic and external interests.

What is also notable in the banana dispute is the way in which the dispute was handled. The banana case was negotiated in traditional diplomatic style by high-ranking, often intergovernmental, officials. Unlike the MRA or trafficking in women cases, transatlantic institutions were not instrumental in reaching an agreement on EU banana subsidies. Although the NTA institutions cushioned the impact of the dispute and kept officials talking, the dispute was not 'managed' through the NTA process. Institutionalisation did not, and some argue could not, prevent the banana dispute because the case demonstrated the classic clash of EU and US economic and political interests. In this respect the banana case study differs dramatically from both the trafficking information campaigns and the MRAs where transatlantic institutions facilitated cooperation on a technical level.

The case also highlighted the dilemma posed by conflicting international and domestic interests. Because these will always exist, the real test for transatlantic relations is in the capacity of the EU and the US to manage disputes in a way that minimises damage to bilateral and multilateral institutions. The negative atmosphere created by the banana dispute highlights the need to strengthen dialogue structures that can deal with conflict as well as cooperation. The way in which the dispute was handled also risked undermining the legitimacy of the WTO. In short the banana dispute exposed weaknesses of both the bilateral structure of the NTA and the multilateral trading system.

Notes

1 EU and US officials regularly quote this figure. A US Commission official argued that disputes in terms of the total economic relationship amounted to 'peanuts'. Another noted that disputes covered 1–2 per cent of trade but 95 per cent of media coverage.
2 For example, a search in the *Financial Times* Archive cite for 'EU banana' between 1996 and 2001 retrieves 750 mostly 'very strong' matches. A search using the same dates and the term 'MRA' retrieves only two relevant articles (see www.ft.com).
3 See for example the *Guardian*, 13, 16 April 1999; the *Independent*, 8 April 1999; *Financial Times*, 8 April 1999; *Irish Times*, 6 April 2001; BBC News Online, 5 December 1997, 17 December 1998, 1 January 1999, 4, 5 March 1999, 23 March 1999, 24 April 1999, 30 September 2000.
4 A search for 'EU banana' on the *Financial Times* 'global archive' which includes worldwide news sources returns 2993 hits between 1996 and 2001.
5 See also BBC News Online, 'UK Gets "Fair Trade" Bananas', 17 January 2000.
6 Interviews conducted in USTR, Washington DC, October 2000 and the House Subcommittee on Trade, Washington DC, October 2000.
7 Quoted in *European Union* Magazine (not dated).
8 Bananas were not covered by EC Common Agricultural Policy, nor by the Commercial policy (see Stevens 1996; 2000: 327).
9 See also Stevens (2000); Sutton (1997).
10 Latin American banana producers controlled virtually 100 per cent of the market in Germany, Denmark and Belgium and 90 per cent of the Irish and Dutch markets under the other two regimes, but European operated Geest and Fyffes controlled 65 per cent and 25 per cent in the UK of the market share (see Sutton 1997: 7).
11 Under the Lome Convention the EC agreed that 'no ACP state shall be placed, as regards access to its traditional markets and its advantages in those markets, in a less favourable position than in the past or at present'.
12 For a more detailed discussion of the history of the banana dispute see Stevens (1996; 2000) who argues that Latin American producers were angry first, that the single market for banana restricted access to Germany which had previously been duty free and second that access was restricted because the tariff quota for Latin American bananas

was too low.

13 This argument was made by a USTR official, interview, Washington DC, October 2000. The US argued that import licenses took away US business because of their allocation to French and British companies and EU ripening firms. USTR Press Release (1997).

14 90 per cent of category 'A' licences were given to Latin American countries (including Costa Rica, Columbia, Nicaragua and Venezuela) who had dropped their dispute with the EU, creating further disadvantage for Honduras, Guatemala, Mexico and Ecuador (see Sutton 1997).

15 The EC did exercise its right to appeal, but the decision was upheld in September 1997.

16 See 'The US/EU Banana Dispute: Modifications to the EC Banana Regime', DGI, External Relations, 10 November 1998, www. europa.org.

17 This regime change also brought criticism from ACP states who felt that the global allocation of licences would not guarantee individual states' traditional export levels.18

18 See US Administration Press Release (1998)

19 She is quoted in the *Guardian* (9 March 2000) as saying, 'If you believe the regime is WTO consistent – then ship'.

20 This was a significantly lower figure than that requested by the US.

21 See Commission Press Release, EC Request for establishment of a panel on Section 301 of the US Trade Act 1974, http://europa.eu.int, downloaded 29 November 2000.

22 See Agence Press (1999) 'Controversial US Legislation Does Not Violate WTO Rules', 22 December.

23 The Carousel Retaliation Act (2000), which is discussed in the second section of this chapter requires the USTR to rotate items on the sanction list thus creating constant fear for EU exporters.

24 This provision was introduced as a means of trying to maintain stable prices of the banana market, thus ensuring the protection of European consumers and domestic producers.

25 The only apparent losers were Ecuador and Dole Foods Corporation who had strongly supported the first come, first serve system. See 'US Calls on Ecuador to Support Banana Deal', *Financial Times*, 18 April 2000.

26 Still, it should be noted that the decision was unprecedented. Prior to USTR's decision to launch the 301 investigation, one USTR official argued it 'would break new ground, as this would be the first time that USTR had ever used Section 301 in connection with a product that was not exported from the US'. Quoted in Barlett and Steel (2000).

27 Sutton (1997) reports Chiquita's pre-1993 market share at 43 per cent and post-1993 at 18 per cent. See also Alden and Bowen (2001).

28 Chiquita claims its loses are a direct result of the EU banana regime, however, it has also been argued by the international consulting firm, Arthur D. Little International that Chiquita's losses are due to its earlier policy of oversupplying (see Sutton 1997: 25).

29 Interview, USTR official, Washington DC 2000; See also Alden and Bowen (2001).

30 Dole claimed that, 'precipitous change in current trading regime arrangement would cause disproportionate amount of harm to ACP and European banana producing regimes'. Del Monte reported that it activities in Cameroon, 'were part of a corporate strategy recognising the EU's need to provide some form of protection to EU growers and to honour the commitments made under Lome'. See Caribbean Banana Exporters Association, EU Banana Regime: Position of Del Monte and Dole Corporations, http://cbea.org (downloaded 22 November 2000).

31 See Laurance, B. (1999) 'The Big Banana', *Sunday Guardian*, 7 March.

32 Quoted in BBC News Online (1999d) 'Banana War Exposes Old Trade Divisions', 5 March. The argument over Chiquita's campaign contributions gave rise to speculation – mostly in the *European Voice* – that Dole's position would be more heavily protected under the Bush Administration because it had given more money to the Republican party (see European Voice 2000). However, this was disproved when the Bush Administration supported a deal opposed by Dole.

33 These politicians favoured the 'free trade' stance, while a movement of less influential Democrats has opposed the US challenge to subsidised Caribbean bananas in favour of 'fair trade'.

34 The letter stated, 'The Administration shares your view that the World Trade Organisation cases involving bananas and beef hormones are important tests of whether the European Union (EU) intends to implement WTO rulings issued against it'. The widely publicised letter is available from http://hill.beef.org/ft/wto8.htm.

35 Although it should be noted that some members of the House were opposed to sanctions and introduced House Resolution 1361 (sponsored by Democrat Representative Maxine Waters) to 'bar the imposition of increased tariffs or other retaliatory measures against the products of the European Union in response to the banana regime in the European Union', the resolution stated that US consumers and Caribbean farmers should not pay for losses to one US company. The resolution never re-surfaced from the House Subcommittee on Trade after it was logged there in April 1999.

36 Views expressed by interviews with House and Senate staff members, Washington DC, October 2000.

37 See European Union–Germany–France Report, June 1998, US Congress, Committee on Agriculture, Agriculture Trade Expansion Delegation.

38 The US Beef Cattlemen Association has the support of beef farmers, who are present in most US states, whereas Chiquita has no domestic agricultural base. Rather, its only direct constituency link is to its headquarters in Cincinnati, Ohio.

39 See also US Beef Cattlemen Association 1998.

40 Interview, Republican house staffer, Washington DC, October 2000.

41 See www.house.gov/thune.wto.htm.

42 See US Administration Press Release (2000), 'Carousel Revised Retaliation List in EU Disputes Delayed', 20 June.

43 Interview by telephone, USTR official, 2001.

44 Interview, House Staff, Subcommittee on Trade, Washington DC, 2000.

45 Interview, Senate Staff, Senate Finance Committee, Washington DC, 2000.

46 Interview, USTR official, Washington DC, 2000.

47 See Cox, J. (1999) 'Punitive Actions by US Felt World-wide', *US Today*, 11 March.

48 One USTR official notes that Neiman Marcus tried to lobby Scottish cashmere off the list by arguing that Chinese replacements were of lower quality.

49 See Barlett and Steel (2000). Members of Congress also lobbied to get some industries off the list. For example, Congressman Bill Delahunt, a strong supporter of US sanctions, actively lobbied USTR on behalf of New England candle makers and greeting card makers whose imports were on the original sanction list (USTR press release, 16 April 2001).

50 Quoted in CNN (1998a), 'US–EU Trade War Looms', 10 November.

51 The sanctions placed heavy pressure on the UK government because they threatened to shut down the Scottish cashmere industry. US industry and members of Congress strongly supported targeting cashmere because threatening an already fragile textile industry would maximise pressure and hopefully convince the UK government to use

its influence within the EU. Instead, the UK government turned and sharply criticised the US. In protest, the Department of Trade and Industry took the rare opportunity twice to summon the US Ambassador.

52 Wilkinson, B. (1999) 'Caricom Suspends Treaty with US Over Bananas', One World News, 9 March, www.oneworld.org.

53 Quoted in BBC News (2000a) 'Ecuador turns on US in trade war', 6 October. Ecuador's decision was said to be dictated by its dependence on EU imports, which kept it from imposing WTO approved sanctions.

54 One USTR interviewee argued that Commissioner Brittan and USTR Barshefsky had mismanaged the dispute. A *Financial Times* editorial stated that, 'Much of the deterioration in transatlantic trade relations since the mid-1990s was due to personal frictions between their predecessors, Sir Leon Brittan and Charlene Barshefsky. Messrs Lamy and Zoellick have had the maturity and good sense to rise above petty squabbling in the interests of bigger shared goals. That bodes well for the handling of future disputes.' Guy de Jonquieres, 'Lamy Feels the Sting of Cancun's Failure', *Financial Times*, 31 October 2003, 19:36.

55 A Senate Staff Member argued in October 2000, that 'Congress has put pressure on the Administration to get rid of these disputes.' Washington DC, October 2000.

56 Interview, USTR official, Washington DC, October 2000.

57 Interview, USTR official, Washington DC, October 2000.

58 Interview, USTR official, Washington DC, October 2000.

59 Through, for example, lobby groups such as the Caribbean Banana Export Association and the EU Banana Operators Association.

60 The *Financial Times* (1999a) reported that the regime 'largely benefit[ed] EU banana traders'.

61 It should be noted, however, that Germany opposed the new regime, because it previously had duty free imports for all bananas, be they Latin American, Caribbean or African. Germany challenged the single banana regime in the European Court of Justice, but the court upheld the EU wide tariff rate quota system.

62 This claim was made before cashmere was temporarily removed from the list.

63 Quote made by Ian Russell, managing director of Arran Aromatics, in Eaglesham (2000).

64 Quote found in *Wall Street Journal* (2000a), 'European Firms Seek EU Damages for Banana War', 30 August.

65 Germany and the UK were two of the member states hardest hit by US sanctions. While Germany had traditionally opposed the banana regime, the UK had been an avid supporter. Some argue the UK sold out to the US to protect the cashmere industry. After bilateral lobbying by Tony Blair US officials took cashmere off the list arguing that the UK had been less aggressive in its support for EU banana regime than other countries. See BBC News, 14 September 2000, 'Blair Wins Reprieve for Cashmere'.

66 The Commission (1999, 2000), the Council (1999) and the European Parliament (2000) argued against ending the tariff rate quota system.

67 Particularly Spain, France, Portugal; and Ireland and Greece: the former having strong colonial ties and the latter being small-scale banana producers.

68 See Smith, (2000b) (*Financial Times*) and *EU Business* (2000).

69 The ad campaign was run in *European Voice*, 23–29 November 2000; those countries included Austria, Belgium, Columbia, Denmark, Ecuador, Finland, France, Germany, Ireland, Italy, Jamaica, the Netherlands, Portugal, Spain, Sweden, the UK and the Windward Islands.

70 See *Financial Times* (1999a) 'US Rejects Brussels' Proposal on Bananas', 11 November; Alden, E. (2000) 'US and EU Still Split on Beef and Bananas', *Financial Times*, 19 December; *Independent* (1999b) 'US Rejects Banana Trade Deal', 11 November.
71 Viewpoint also expressed by Finnish Council Presidency officials, Interview, Brussels, September 1999.
72 See Smith (2000a).
73 Although consensus is not needed to secure a waiver, if a number of countries were willing to continue fighting, the dispute would continue.
74 See Commission Communication on FCFS, 4 October 2000, COM (2000) 621. Interviews by email, Commission official, April 2001; and by telephone, USTR official, April 2001.
75 See *European Voice*, 13 April 2001.
76 Interview by email, Commission official, April 2001.
77 Interview by telephone, USTR official, April 2001.
78 Argued by Commission official (via email), February 2000.
79 To highlight the scale of the problem Hallam and Preston (1997) note that in Dominica, for example, the banana industry is the only legal crop cultivated year round, and it supports 30 per cent of the workforce directly and 70 per cent indirectly (Hallam and Preston 1997).
80 This viewpoint was also expressed by officials in the European Commission (in the US) and in the UK Foreign Office.
81 See also *Daily Telegraph* 1999.
82 See also Wilson (2001).
83 Interview, Commission official, Brussels, September 1999.
84 Interview, Commission official, Brussels, September 1999.
85 Interview, Commision official, Brussels, September 1999.
86 Interview, US Chamber of Commerce Brussels, September 1999.
87 Interview, USTR official, Washington DC, October 2000.
88 Prodi commented after the June 2000 EU–US Summit, 'We decided that megaphone diplomacy would be replaced by telephone diplomacy', *Financial Times* (2000a), 'New Tact but EU–US Disputes Remain', 1 June.
89 Press release, USIS, 3 March 1999.
90 Commission Press Release (1998b) No. 96/98, 10 November.
91 Interview, Council Secretariat, Brussels, September 1999.
92 Quoted by Buerkle (1999).
93 Barnaby Mason argued in BBC News, for example, that the bitter dispute over bananas added to tension mounted by American exports of genetically modified crops, the acquittal of the American military pilot whose plane killed twenty people in Italy, and disagreement over Cuba, Iran, Iraq and Kosovo (Mason 1999).
94 BBC News Online, 3 May 1999.
95 Interview, Staff Member, Committee on Trade, Washington DC, September 2000.
96 Interview, Staff Member, Committee on Trade, Washington DC, September 2000.
97 Quoted in CNN (1998b), 'EU Agrees to Let Trade Body Referee Dispute if US Drops Sanctions Threat', 20 November.
98 Quoted in McSmith and Fraser (1999).
99 See Giles (2000).
100 See 'Summary of U.S. Legal Position on Dispute in WTO on EC Banana Regime', USTR press release, 12 January 1999, www.useu.be.
101 USTR Press Release (1999).
102 The Article 22 procedures required the DSB decision by 2 March 1999, but the Article

21 procedures were not due to be completed until 12 April 1999.

103 A USTR official argued, 'We promised them that the WTO would not be a General Agreement on Talk and Talk.' Interview, via telephone, June 2001.

104 Interview, Senate Finance Committee spokesperson, Washington DC, October 2000.

105 It should be noted that Ralph Ives has argued that, 'The WTO does not require free trade', because 'a WTO consistent regime doesn't mean no preferences' (USIS 1998).

8

Conclusions

This book raised a number of questions about the roles of institutions, actors, dialogue, and policy coordination in the process of EU–US relations. First and foremost it asked: do institutions matter and if so, why do they matter? It considered the capacity of the EU and the US not only to manage the relationship but also to exercise governance through transatlantic institutions. Second, it focused not only on institutions, but also on the actors who participate in them. It sought to gauge the extent to which the process of transatlantic institutionalisation allowed different categories of actors to engage in different types of decision-making. In short, it asked: who governs in the process and how?

The 'process' of transatlantic relations was dissected by specifying and analysing multiple types of decisions in EU–US policy-making and the roles of multiple types of actors. Three hypotheses were set out in Chapter 1 to help us analyse how the process works. First, it was argued that the TAD, the NTA and the TEP have created transatlantic institutions and that transatlantic actors perform functions of governance through these institutions. Second, it was argued that under that institutional framework, a decentralisation of decision-making powers had been allocated to transgovernmental actors who perform both 'setting' and 'shaping' functions in the policy process. Finally, we explored the role of transnational actors in transatlantic policy-making. It tested the idea that there has been a decentralisation of decision shaping to not only state, but also to non-state actors. Specifically, it explored the capacity of the TABD, the TACD and the TAED to influence transatlantic policies.

This final chapter summarises the evidence presented throughout this book. More generally, it asks what we have learned about EU and US relations from studying the relationship in the 1990s and how, if at all, major structural and institutional changes in the new millennium affect the conclusion that the new transatlantic institutions do matter. The first section examines the extent to which the relationship has been institutionalised under the TAD, the NTA and the TEP. It argues that the agreements have established a structure for transatlantic governance by creating a framework for policy-making and building institutions, which serve as decision-making structures.

The second section recaps how these governance structures have altered the scope for actor input into decision-making. It argues not only that transgovernmental networks have been institutionalised, but that their policy setting and policy shaping capacity points to a decentralisation of policy-making by state actors.

The third section summarises the role of non-state actors in the transatlantic policy process. It specifies the varied 'shaping' capacity of the formal transatlantic dialogues as well as the wider impact that corporations, interests groups and other non-state actors have in shaping transatlantic decisions at both a transnational and a national level.

Finally, the purpose of this research was not only to categorise the role of institutions and actors in transatlantic policy-making, but also to question the implications of the institutionalisation, decentralisation and privatisation of transatlantic decision-making. What do these developments tell us about EU–US relations and international relations more broadly? The final section recaps a number of themes that have been addressed throughout the book, particularly the dilemma facing policy makers seeking to strike a balance between effective governance and legitimate governance. It suggests the need for future research on the long-term affects of transatlantic institutionalisation and the implications of the de-politicisation of transatlantic foreign policy-making. Finally, it questions the effect that events such as 11 September, the war in Iraq, European enlargement and the Doha Round of the WTO have had on the new transatlantic agenda.

The institutionalisation of transatlantic relations

Three main analytical tasks were underlined in this book to gauge the extent to which transatlantic dialogue had been institutionalised into a structure of transatlantic governance.

- It sought to establish whether and how the relationship has been institutionalised.
- In the context of theoretical debates about the EU–US relationship and international relations in general, it questioned why the EU and the US chose to institutionalise the relationship.
- It asked whether and why the institutionalisation of the transatlantic dialogue matters?

Chapter 3 explored the creation, through the transatlantic agreements, of formal structures for decision-making and a policy framework for governance. The TAD and, particularly, the NTA and the TEP outlined policy areas where European and US leaders committed themselves to cooperation. The NTA Action Plan and TEP Action Plan specified the scope for policy coordination under the new transatlantic dialogue. The TAD institutionalised contact between heads of states via the biannual EU–US summit meeting. It also established a ministerial level dialogue as well as a political dialogue.

The density of different transatlantic institutions and dialogues is striking. EU–US decision-making structures developed through the NTA and the TEP with the creation of institutions such as the SLG, the NTA Task Force, the TEP Steering Group and the TEP Working Groups. The NTA and the TEP also encouraged the creation of the TABD, the TACD and the TAED. We are left, in this chapter, to try to come to a final judgement about whether these agreements and the dense layers of formal dialogue they created at many different levels, have complicated or simplified the process of EU–US cooperation, generally, and policy coordination, specifically. Is cooperation easier to achieve when more voices are heard in the policy process? Or does allowing new 'toddlers into the policy playpen' amount to expanding the number of actors wielding vetoes over cooperative agreements?

The TAD, the NTA and the TEP are products of intergovernmental 'history making decisions'. The motivation for these high level political decisions is best explained by rationalist rationale. In other words, it is argued throughout the book that the EU and the US chose to 'institutionalise' their relationship because it was in their interest to do so. As the Cold War period began to fade in 1989, both sides recognised that common ideas, values, culture and multilateral institutions could not hold the transatlantic partnership together as the common security threat of the Soviet Union had throughout the Cold War. However, the EU and the US identified mutual interest in maintaining the partnership, particularly in response to new soft security threats, such as the economically and politically unstable CEE and the Middle East, and in light of bilateral economic disputes over, for example bananas, beef and milk hormones. The EU was keen to demonstrate its capabilities as a foreign policy actor, and the US welcomed the prospects of burden sharing in light of its growing need to be a 'superpower on the cheap'.

The NTA arose out of fears that the TAD structure was not doing enough to narrow the gap between the partners. It sought more effective cooperation on policy areas where the EU had growing competence under the Maastricht Treaty. For example, Justice and Home Affairs issues, such as migration and international crime, made it onto the transatlantic agenda under the global challenges chapter of the NTA. The TEP also demonstrated mutual interest in getting more concrete economic results from the transatlantic partnership, including further market opening agreements and the containment of trade disputes.

Institutionalisation has had two broad implications for transatlantic relations. First, the creation of so many new and varied decision-making forums means that the decision-making process now has multiple tiers and multiple stages. The different institutions created by the transatlantic agreements point to the institutionalised role of intergovernmental actors (through the EU–US Summit), transgovernmental actors (through, for example the SLG, TEP

Steering Group) and transnational actors (through the TABD, TACD, TAED). Throughout this book, we have seen the capacity of intergovernmental actors to 'make' the high level political decisions which establish institutional change and policy expansion, but also of transgovernmental and transnational actors to 'set' and 'shape' policy.

Second, the institutionalisation of the dialogue exposes the different purposes served by the different transatlantic institutions. Intergovernmental decisions highlight the commitment of the EU and the US to fostering dialogue, and where possible policy coordination and conflict management. Specifically it can be noted that the intergovernmental decisions to include trafficking in women in the NTA global challenges chapter and the MRAs in the economic chapter (and later in TEP) are the decisions that established the scope for these transatlantic policies. Both decisions represented a broad commitment to policy coordination. Their inclusion in the transatlantic policy framework put transgovernmental actors in charge of producing substantive results. The agreements also committed the EU and the US to manage disputes through continued dialogue. In the case of the banana dispute, it can be argued that the institutional structure cushioned the impact of conflict between the partners. The institutions, at least, kept people talking.

The point is that the institutionalisation of the transatlantic relationship changed the way that actors operated within the system. While it is difficult to gauge just how the behaviour of social actors is shaped or altered by transatlantic institutions, institutions at least created the opportunity for actors with different interests to formally participate in the policy-making process. The second and third sections discuss, in more detail, how these actors operate with these decision-making structures.

Decentralised decision setting and shaping

The first hypothesis posited that the institutionalisation of the dialogue resulted in the creation of not only intergovernmental but also transgovernmental and transnational institutions. Chapter 3 explored the dense level of contacts that were forged between high and low level civil servants under the three transatlantic agreements. It questioned the extent to which intergovernmental actors had created room for transgovernmental actors to influence the process through the creation of economic, political and NTA institutions, and a specified early warning process. The book sought to make clear the functions of transgovernmental institutions in the process of transatlantic decision-making in order to establish that joint policies had been effectively decentralised from the intergovernmental level 'downwards'. It also uncovered evidence that transgovernmental actors had both 'set' and 'shaped' transatlantic policy.

The underlying question, for many scholars, is whether transgovernmental actors act independently of their political bosses or if they simply follow predetermined paths in transatlantic policy-making. In other words, does dialogue between transgovernmental actors result in preference convergence? It was argued that intergovernmental actors clearly maintain control of the policy process by 'making' the decisions, which establish the scope for policy coordination. To an extent transatlantic agreements, particularly the NTA and the TEP, created a mandate for transgovernmental actors to work within.

However, there is also evidence to suggest that transgovernmental actors exercise some control over the process, albeit within certain boundaries. For example, Chapter 3 established that a range of transgovernmental actors, at the ministerial level and at the agency level, had effectively acted as policy 'setters' by signing agreements, producing declarations or coordinating policies. Gauging the capacity of actors to 'shape' policy is more difficult. Unlike 'setting' decisions, written records of policy 'shaping' often do not exist. Furthermore, a wide variety of actors have the capacity to act as transatlantic policy shapers through, for example, the SLG, TEP Steering Group, NTA Task Force, TEP and Troika working group meetings. That interviewees went to great lengths to discuss the roles of these institutions suggests that they play a role in the process, but what role exactly? It was argued that these actors effectively helped decide not that the EU and the US would co-operate, but how they could co-operate.

Transgovernmental actors fulfilled a number of important shaping functions. First, transgovernmental actors helped shape the initial policy agendas of the NTA and the TEP by identifying areas where cooperation might be feasible. Once intergovernmental actors decide that cooperation should be pursued, transgovernmental actors continue to *shape* the policy agenda by outlining specific issue areas, within policy sectors, where the EU and the US could reach consensus. In short they identify 'policy options'.

Transgovernmental actors also establish 'policy details' once the intergovernmental actors 'make' the decision to pursue a policy, in a variety of ways. Institutions like the SLG provide political oversight and establish time frames for cooperation in the early stages of policy formation. They also establish potential language for 'setting' decisions. In the case of trafficking in women for example, the concept of an information campaign and the details of the transatlantic project were derived at the working group level. Effectively the dialogue was set by foreign ministers at a ministerial level dialogue, where ultimately the decision to coordinate that policy rested. However, a dialogue between US Mission, US State Department, DG Justice and Home Affairs and DG External Relations officials determined key details of the transatlantic anti-trafficking policy including:

- where to target transatlantic efforts;
- how to technically coordinate the anti-trafficking plans;
- who should implement the transatlantic campaigns.

The transatlantic anti-trafficking campaigns were also shaped by the NTA Task Force and the Senior Level Group who were charged with overseeing policy development, keeping it on the NTA agenda and acting as a problem solving forum, for example over funding problems.

The role of transgovernmental actors in the MRA case was somewhat easier to document and more significant given the higher profile and domestic implications of the agreements. The USTR and Commissioner for Trade publicly 'set' the transatlantic regulatory policy by signing the MRA agreement. Many more actors played a role in shaping the policies. While trade officials exercised control over the overarching framework agreement, domestic regulators shaped the policy details in each of the individual annexes. Transatlantic institutions played a key role in pushing negotiations ahead and striking a balance between trade and regulatory authorities. The Joint Committee and Joint Sectoral Committee tried to strike a bargain between regulators and trade officials. The SLG and the TEP Steering Group monitored the process, helped identify achievable goals on a sector by sector basis and kept the negotiations to a time schedule by establishing and monitoring deadlines.

In some ways, at least, the wide range of policy shapers in the process of transatlantic decision-making complicates the policy process because it makes the task of reaching consensus laborious. The NTA institutions seek to reach a consensus among policy shapers before decisions can be set. At the same time the MRA case, in particular, demonstrates the capacity of the NTA institutions to facilitate cooperation by forging compromise among a wide range of actors with different interests and with different levels of access to the policy process. In particular transatlantic institutions were credited with managing, but not overcoming, the differences between the trade camp and the regulatory camps. The banana dispute also highlighted the capacity for domestic actors to shape transatlantic policy decisions. In that case, however, the NTA institutions did not serve as decision-making forums. Rather, actors sought to shape policy by lobbying domestic institutions.

In both the trafficking in women and MRA case studies, intergovernmental actors indicated an interest in joint cooperation. Overall, the 'shaping' capacity of transgovernmental actors demonstrates that decentralised transatlantic institutions also serve as policy-making mechanisms, in addition to acting as forums for the exchange of dialogue, information and ideas. The capacity of transgovernmental actors to act as policy shapers sheds some light on the rationalist–constructivist debate outlined in Chapter 1. Although ultimately the scope for policy coordination is determined by self-interest, the policy details are derived from the transgovernmental dialogue. Arguably the institutions are more than just talking shops.

However, there is less evidence to suggest that these institutions are effective where the EU and US political leaders' interests do not coincide. As one Council Presidency official argued, 'where there are disputes, our hands are usually tied at a political level'.[1] This argument is consistent with Slaughter's argument on transgovernmentalism: mainly that transgovernmental networks can gradually achieve politicial convergence, but they are less likely to contain serious political or economic conflict (Slaughter 1997: 196). In the banana case, for example, the NTA process kept up dialogue between the leaders and sheltered the rest of the policy agenda from the dispute, but transgovernmental institutions did little to manage or resolve the dispute.

The broader argument is that decision-making powers are less decentralised where high political interest is involved. Nonetheless, decentralised dialogue has been deemed an important part of the conflict management process. The creation of the Early Warning System and the Biotechnology Forum demonstrates an interest in fostering dialogue at lower levels to prevent conflict, where possible. The idea that disputes can be managed from the bottom up is illustrated by one Commission official's comment that, 'closer contact and more consultation slowly breeds more broad understanding'.[2] While the potential for transgovernmental conflict management exists, the institutions are still at an early stage of developing the capacity to manage disputes.

Policy shaping by non-state sectors

The institutionalisation of the transatlantic relationship extends to the private, as well as the public sector. The development of transnational dialogues such as the TABD, the TAED, the TACD and the TALD, was also documented throughout the book. It questioned why these dialogues were created by the EU and US governments under the NTA, how they became institutionalised, and the extent to which they have fostered communication across the Atlantic. Subsequently, we looked for evidence to support the idea that decision shaping powers had been delegated to non-state actors under the NTA. The emphasis, thus, was not only on the existence of transnational networks or of transnational dialogue, but also on the capacity of these dialogues to 'shape' transatlantic decisions.

Chapter 4 outlined evidence to support the idea that an institutionalisation of the TABD, the TACD, the TAED (before its suspension) had occurred. Each of these dialogues established some type of organisational structures to facilitate consensus between European and American counterparts. Dialogue between these groups has resulted in a process of policy learning as American and European businesses and NGOs exchange information, share strategies and seek consensus. In particular American consumer and environmental NGOs have learned from European groups, who have more experience operating in policy networks and influencing the European Commission. The TALD was the only case examined that cannot be considered to be a serious dialogue structure. As such, the failure of the TALD means that labour actors have no institutionalised access to the transatlantic policy process.

The other dialogues established regular high level and working level dialogues with the US Administration and the Commission. It is clear that groups involved in these dialogues communicate with (especially transgovernmental) networks of officials. But how effectively do they shape transatlantic policy?

The business, consumer, environmental (and even labour) dialogues were encouraged by EU and US officials to develop into policy shapers. The US administration was convinced that the TABD would support the US negotiating position. Generally, the EU and the US both had an interest in encouraging civil society participation to balance the power of the TABD. The Commission also believed that the TACD and TAED would become an ally in negotiations with the US over food safety and privacy. The TEP congratulated the TABD for its role in securing transatlantic agreements and encouraged consumers and environmentalists to make a constructive contribution to policy-making. The dialogues' members, business and NGOs alike, have argued that the dialogues could not continue without concrete policy results.

It was noted throughout the book, however, that the transatlantic dialogues have had a varied shaping capacity. The TABD is the only dialogue to have had a visible impact on the policy process. It is widely praised by EU and US officials for helping find consensus on a range of policies. A high percentage of TABD recommendations have been addressed. It is credited with helping to facilitate the MRAs. On the other hand the social dialogues have not achieved similar results. Neither the TACD nor TAED claims to have had any impact on the process and the future of all of the civil society dialogues depends on their willingness and capacity to secure private funding. One NGO observed that, 'they are telling us what they are doing, rather than taking our advice. We have access but we don't learn specifics. TAED participants argue that US officials seem to be just going through the motions.'[3]

The argument made in Chapter 4 was that while the TABD case strongly supports the hypothesis that a decentralisation of decision shaping has been delegated to private actors, the TACD, TAED and TALD do not. The TACD, as the most organised civil society dialogue, has the potential to be a future policy shaper. However, time will tell if the Commission's sponsorship of the society dialogues will prove useful in future debates on food safety, data protection and waste management.

Chapter 6 also demonstrated the shaping capacity of the TABD, but not the TACD or TAED, in the MRA negotiations. Many officials argued that both TABD recommendations and the lobbying action of TABD members had a major influence on the process. A major advantage of the TABD is that it has managed to concentrate on a number of policy sectors where common goals are held by the EU and US, most notably the facilitation of trade liberalisation as a major component of the New Transatlantic Marketplace. On the other hand the TACD and TAED have an interest in and have focused on areas where the EU and US disagree.

The banana case also demonstrated the capacity of private actors to shape transatlantic policy. However, the influence of private actors centred around national rather than 'transatlantic' policy makers. Chiquita corporation invoked US domestic legislation and lobbied Congress to influence US policy. Transnational consumer and development groups and banana operators were able to influence the EU's policy on bananas. Unlike the MRA case, however, the existence of transatlantic business consensus was blocked by the lack of common economic interest. The power of 'business' interests over 'fair trade' supporters was also demonstrated in the banana case. However, it was WTO, rather than transatlantic rules that created the bias.

In areas where EU and US business consensus exists, the TABD has started to play a role in transatlantic conflict management. By identifying early warning issues, the transnational business group has tried to resolve and prevent transatlantic disputes that would have negative effects for industry. For example, the Commission demurred from creating a new trade dispute on metric labelling on the recommendation of the TABD.

Chapter 5 also examined the role that non-state actors play in political sectors examined by the NTA. First, the rise of transnational criminals created the need for transatlantic cooperation on trafficking in women. It was noted that a wide range of NGOs have worked with governments at the international and national levels to combat the problem of trafficking in women. This case demonstrates the capacity of the private sector to perform functions of governance because NGOs have the capacity to provide administrators with practical policy solutions, particularly at the local level. Yet, the trend in the anti-trafficking policy sector is one of moving away from directly utilising NGOs for the information campaigns, and turning instead to international organisations. That said, NGOs play an important role as they are subcontracted out by the International Organisation on Migration. It was also argued that further decentralisation of the trafficking dialogue and better private–public cooperation, through something like a transatlantic or indeed global anti-trafficking dialogue, could be a way to achieve, in effect, 'privatised' governance in this sector.

Effective and legitimate transatlantic governance?

The transatlantic institutions that have been the focus of this book could plausibly be viewed as fulfilling their basic purpose: to inject new focus into transatlantic relations and keep both sides committed to the pursuit of a true partnership. As one Commission official argued, 'the NTA became the new "glue" in transatlantic relations'.[4]

However, the interest more specifically was not only with the impact that the transatlantic agreements had on transatlantic relations but on the process of transatlantic governance. It was argued that the institutionalisation of the new transatlantic dialogue created a formal structure for collective transatlantic governance.

The institutionalisation of different levels of transatlantic dialogue arguably facilitated cooperation and increased the capacity for consensus reaching among transatlantic actors. The institutions created by the transatlantic agreements have increased the opportunity for dialogue, deliverables and debate. The decentralisation of the transgovernmental dialogue has fostered a more sustainable habit of cooperation between the EU and the US. For example, the anti-trafficking information campaigns, while certainly rather modest policy actions, are the first step in forging cooperation on migration issues and other global challenges. The MRAs have helped build confidence between regulators that will effect EU–US regulatory cooperation more broadly.[5] Transatlantic mechanisms may also prove useful in both the prevention and management of conflict. If the Early Warning System works, in practice, it could prevent some future trade disputes. While transatlantic mechanisms have been less successful at 'managing' system friction in highly political disputes, such as the banana case, the decentralisation of transatlantic policy coordination has, nonetheless, ensured that cooperation in other areas continues.

Most notably, the dense levels of contact established by the transatlantic agreements have been utilised to facilitate 'governance' between two systems where decision-making competency is shared between many different actors. The mechanisms created by the transatlantic agreements endeavour to compensate for the institutional rivalry among domestic actors, which is ever-present in multi-level systems of governance. This book has portrayed both the EU and the US as multi-level systems and argued that one effect of the sharing of power across multiple levels of governance is to place stark limits on EU–US cooperation. Witness, for example, the proposal of Gordon Brown, the UK Chancellor, for the EU–US equivalent of the study that preceded the launch of the EU's single market programme in the 1980s. On the US side, the Administration of George W. Bush gave no official response, as it struggled to win trade negotiating authority from Congress for a new WTO round. US manufacturers of products with high duties, such as textiles, clothing and footwear lobbied both the White House and Congress to reject Brown's proposal. Meanwhile, Brown's proposal received a cool reception at the WTO in Geneva, particularly among developing country delegates who naturally feared that the transatlantic partners were looking for alternatives to a new trade round. And, in Brussels, a senior Commission official dismissed Brown's idea as 'one of a number of balloons' being floated, and stressed that it could only proceed if backed by the Commission and other EU member states.[6]

Thus, barriers to entry into new realms of EU–US cooperation are high.

However, transatlantic institutions created in the 1990s act to protect existing realms of cooperation from atrophy or backsliding. The sub-summit decision-making procedures essentially put lower level civil servants in charge of 'managing' the dialogue and increasing the international awareness of domestic actors. As Frellesen (2001) argues, the process gives experts a dose of 'transatlanticism'.

The institutionalisation of transgovernmental as well as intergovernmental contacts is one way to compensate for the capabilities–expectations gaps incurred in both the EU and US systems, because transgovernmental actors have a joint mission to establish precisely how cooperation can be pursued. For example, transgovernmental contact between JHA, DG I and US officials enabled actors to establish how the EU and US could cooperate in a policy sector where the EU is widely perceived to be incapable of strategic action. In the MRA case, transatlantic institutions helped overcome the capabilities–expectations gap which arises from the sharing of competency between US trade officials and domestic regulators. Thus, the transatlantic dialogue is designed not only to facilitate consensus between the EU and US, but among domestic actors as well.

Above all, the transatlantic governance process is pragmatic. It is designed to facilitate policy 'deliverables' where the EU and the US have common interests. The transatlantic system of governance is 'efficient' not only because it brings possibly contentious actors into the dialogue process, but because it avoids them where possible. As bureaucratic agreements, not treaties, the NTA and the TEP de-politicise the process of governance. The decentralisation of decision-making to the expert, or working level, is a way to take many issues out of the political debate and into the technocratic arena. Private decision shaping, in the case of the TABD, is also a way for the government and the business community to reach consensus on a range of liberalisation policies.

Yet, it is impossible to avoid wondering whether this effective mode of transatlantic governance comes at a price. Again, the question of how transatlantic decision-making fares in the debate on technocratic governance needs to be addressed. The debate is significant given the role of the EU–US decision-making process as a case study for transnational governance more generally.

While the de-politicisation of policy-making increases the threshold for cooperation, it also raises questions about the legitimacy of transatlantic governance. A number of concerns were raised throughout this book about governance through bureaucratic networks. First, the bureaucratic control over the NTA process has been criticised, for example by civil society groups, who argue that legislators should have a more important role in the process. The weak nature of the TLD compounds the problem, and it was argued in Chapters 3 and 4 that more parliamentary dialogue could increase domestic acceptance of the NTA process.

Second, the decentralised and de-politicised policy-making process may undermine the transparency of transatlantic governance. NGOs, in particular, have argued against the incorporation of regulatory policy in the TEP generally and against the MRAs specifically. The transatlantic partners, led in particular by the US administration, have continually argued the need for more open decision-making proceedings and have attempted to make the process more transparent by introducing Joint Guidelines for Regulatory Co-operation. They have also invited wider public participation through the civil society dialogues. The TACD and TAED were brought into the NTA process to legitimise the TEP. Furthermore, the guidelines on dialogue participation were established to ensure equal access for the dialogues. However, the unequal capacity of private and NGO actors to engage in effective decision shaping highlights another problem with transatlantic decision-making.

However, the relative shaping capacity of business groups over other civil society groups is not specifically a transatlantic problem. The statement made by one MEP, that 'they [consumer and environmental groups] will never have the same influence. They do not have the same money or clout',[7] could just as easily describe domestic and EU politics. The problem for transatlantic policy makers however, is that the impact of the TABD has become a focus of anti-globalisation groups who are part of larger international social movements aimed at controlling the transfer of 'governance' away from the nation state. As the civil society dialogue, particularly the TACD, continues to develop, policy makers face the task of practically balancing the interests of different actors. Decision-makers will have to weigh the effectiveness and legitimacy of the transatlantic dialogue in the context of wider debates about the access and impact of environmental, consumer and labour movements at the WTO, the G8, and the EU.

In conclusion, the NTA process has been criticised for being only a limited process of governance that fails really to deliver in terms of policy output. The limitations of the new transatlantic dialogue were highlighted throughout the book. However, it was argued that many deliverables have been first rather than final steps, and that the transatlantic institutions fulfil necessary functions in the process of governance. If Leon Brittan (1998: 2) is to be believed, 'the results may sometimes be relatively unglamorous, but they are certainly not insignificant'. In particular it is argued that, 'the NTA has fostered a habit of contact and dialogue across broad areas of our administration, which might otherwise not have been brought to talk to each other'.

Interviewees agreed that the NTA managed the daily relationship and got bureaucrats talking about ways to cooperate in a range of areas where EU and US civil servants would not necessarily have had contact. That dialogue is, arguably, the most important deliverable of the process. As one Commission official argued, 'the logic of the NTA is similar to the thinking behind the EU. If we are constantly talking, it is less likely that we will be fighting'.[8]

The New Transatlantic Agenda in the new millennium

This book was mainly a discussion of EU–US relations in the 1990s when a new wave of transatlantic institutionalisation commenced, but how are these conclusions affected by major structural and institutional changes in the new millennium? The impact of three major events are discussed below: 11th September and the subsequent war on terrorism and tyrants; the deepening and widening of the European Union and the failure to conclude the Doha Round of WTO talks.

New security threats

This discussion of transatlantic relations mainly focused on the economic and non-security political relationship, but events this decade only reiterate how interconnected trade, politics and security really are. The terrorist attacks against the World Trade Center (WTC) in New York on 11 September 2001 highlight the most significant global challenge faced by the EU and the US in the new millennium. Transnational terrorism has become the new common security threat.

EU member states took immediate action in reaction to this worldchanging event. They offered their complete support for the US, and set out determining how they could increase counter-terrorism cooperation both within the EU and with the US. However, the US war on terrorism that was sparked by the WTC attacks would ultimately prove damaging to the relationship. Although there were some smaller rifts over military action in Afghanistan, these were nothing compared to those that would emerge over the US decision to enter Iraq.

Several member states were strongly against the war in Iraq. France and Germany, traditionally one of the strongest US allies, teamed up with the Russia in opposition to the US. The UK, Italy and Spain did send troops to Iraq, but each of these governments suffered as domestic public opinion against the war increased at home. In the UK, popular support for Prime Minister Tony Blair decreased dramatically throughout the Iraqi crisis, and two ministers resigned from the Labour Government over this issue (see Serfaty 2003). Massive anti-war demonstrations were held in Italy and the Spanish Government, which had sent troops to Iraq despite majority public opposition to the war, lost out on re-election days after terrorist attacks on its capital city.

The Iraqi war has caused one of the biggest crises between Europe and the US in the history of the Atlantic Alliance (see Hamilton 2003). A number of important conclusions can be drawn from this crisis. First, it is clear that neither the EU, nor NATO for that matter, is close to being in a position to exercise a single foreign policy. In this instance the US was able to form alliances with individual member states, causing divisions not only in the transatlantic relationship but also within the EU. Foreign policy divides are likely to re-surface over how to manage other hotspots such as North Korea and the Middle East. On the other hand, the 11 March 2004 terrorist attacks in Spain should re-emphasise the point that transnational terrorism is a common threat that requires increased cooperation. The global challenges chapter of the NTA is one policy forum that can be used to increase joint EU–US anti-terrorism efforts.

An enlarged European Union

In May 2004 the European Union accepted ten new member states enlarging its total to twenty-five countries. The EU's enlargement could have several implications for both its economic and political relationship with the US. First, it will be interesting to see to what extent the larger membership of the Union affects its capacity to act as a unitary foreign policy actor. There are fears that EU enlargement will increase the capabilities–expectations gap it already experiences in external negotiations. Some feel that the capacity of the EU to exercise foreign policy will widen, but that the US will likely find new security allies in many of the Eastern European member states (see Serfaty 2003). On the other hand some argue that an enlarged EU will be a bigger actor in international affairs, perhaps shifting the balance of power between the EU and the US. Others still argue the EU could become inward looking as it becomes increasingly engaged in both further enlargement and constitutional reform (see Braun 2004).

European enlargement is likely to alter economic negotiations and raise the threshold, in particular, for regulatory agreements. We noted in Chapter 6 that US regulators already strongly oppose the idea that all European standards are equal. They are even less likely to accept standard levels that have yet to be tested in the European market. In addition, enlargement nearly doubles the number of conformity assessment systems that will need to be tested in order to make even one MRA annexe operational.

Disputes, Doha and the Positive Economic Agenda

Although a deal was struck on bananas, a number of ongoing trade disputes over steel, citrus fruit and poultry have continued to overshadow the EU–US economic relationship. Perhaps most damaging, was the failure to strike a deal on agriculture, which led to the breakdown of WTO talks in Cancun in September 2003. Although USTR Zoellick and Trade Commisioner Lamy have vowed to pick up the lost momentum and get the Doha Round of talks back on track, there are many fears that it is exactly this type of discord which overshadows and undermines both the transatlantic relationship and the multilateral trading system.

The EU–US Positive Economic Agenda attempts to counterbalance disputes and discord in the transatlantic relationship. It was agreed in December 2002 (a year before the WTO talks collapsed in Mexico), and represents a renewed commitment to 'goodwill' in transatlantic economic relations. It is a roadmap for increased cooperation which includes new commitments to bilateral trade and regulatory agreements and which has created new institutional links such as the Financial Markets Dialogue between the European Commission and the US Treasury.

Final thoughts

Despite differences over Iraq and Doha, the US preoccupation with homeland security and EU pre-occupation with enlargement, the NTA process continues to operate in the background. The EU–US summit goes on, new deliverables are being produced and the dialogue between transatlantic actors continues.

While the 'staying' power of transatlantic institutions is not guaranteed, the commitment of both sides to the process of institutionalisation in the 1990s has proved to be more than symbolic. We have seen that institutions – intergovernmental, transgovernmental and transnational – were continually developed in the years after the Transatlantic Declaration was unveiled in 1990 and that current discussions are under way to make transatlantic institutions more effective. The potential for further decentralisation over decision-making to institutions such as the SLG and the NTA Task Force is under consideration (Commission 2001). US and European governments have also encouraged future participation from non-state actors, most notably the TABD and the TACD (see EU–US Summit 2001; Warnath 1998). In the end, the institutionalisation of the transatlantic dialogue is best viewed as an ongoing process. Further research will be needed to assess the long-term development of transatlantic institutions and the process of transatlantic governance more widely.

Notes

1 Interview, Finnish Council Presidency, Brussels, October 1999.
2 Interview, Commission official, Brussels, September 1999.
3 Interview, American NGO, Washington DC, October 2000.
4 Interview, Commission Official, DG External Relations, Brussels, September 1999.
5 It is perhaps revealing that after the dramatic blocking of the merger between General Electric and Honeywell (both US-headquartered firms) by the EU Commission in 2001, after the merger had been cleared by US anti-trust authorities, both the Commission and the George W. Bush Administration agreed to explore an upgrade in cooperation on competition matters to avoid such outcomes in future.
6 Quoted in *Financial Times*, 26 July 2001, www.ft.com.
7 Interview, European Parliament, Brussels, September 1999.
8 Interview, Commission official, Brussels, May 2000.

Research notes

This research was primarily interview driven. In total sixty-four elite interviews were conducted (between July 1998 and June 2001) with a wide range of members of the following institutions in Brussels, Washington DC, London and Budapest: the US Mission, the European Commission, the Council Secretariat, the European Parliament and Parliament Secretariat, the US State Department, USTR, US Commerce Department, US Federal Drug Administration, Congressional staff, European Environmental Agency, members of the TABD, the TACD, TAED and TALD and their secretariats, Anti-Slavery NGOs, UK Foreign Office, US Embassy London, European Commission Delegation DC and the International Organization of Migration.

The idea was to obtain both public and 'behind the scenes' information about the input of different types of actors in the decision-making process in a range of policy sectors. Intergovernmental actors' input in the process was determined mainly from EU–US summit reports, press releases and speeches, as access to these officials was not feasible. Policy output at the intergovernmental level is well documented, because the NTA process is driven by the desire for 'deliverables'. However, assessing information about meetings where disputes were discussed was more problematic, as EU and US press releases tend to re-enforce their individual positions rather than the content of joint dialogue. Many official documents were obtained from the US Mission, EU Delegation to the US, State Department, USTR, and Transatlantic Information Exchange Services (TIES) websites.

Interviews were needed to determine 'who does what' at the transgovernmental level, where meetings are conducted with less transparency. It proved difficult to piece together formal, let alone informal meetings, from public records, but elite interviews proved indispensable for these purposes. A vast range of people work on the topics covered in this book. A number of factors influenced the selection of interviewees. Mostly civil servants working on specifically 'transatlantic' issues were approached, except in the policy sectors covered by the case studies, where the opinions of people working in domestic, transatlantic and international forums was sought. In most cases the number of people working on specific topics, for example on the summits or on the TLD or the TABD or TACD and on specific policy sectors, such as trafficking, MRAs and bananas, was limited. The project was based on the input of both high level officials and specified policy 'experts', often lower level civil servants. The selection of high level interviews was determined in most cases by access to officials, which proved more problematic. The strategy in most cases was to aim high and settle for who was willing and available to discuss the project. Many officials failed to answer letters, faxes, emails or telephone messages. Scheduling also proved problematic as many high level officials were unavailable or had to cancel appointments. The cost of travelling to Washington DC and Brussels meant that interviews, conducted in person, had to fall within limited windows of opportunity. A number of unavailable high level officials instructed members of their staff to meet with me in their place. A number of key people in the US Mission, EU Delegation to the US, DG External Relations North America Unit, to remain anonymous here, provided invaluable assistance in bridging contact to other officials and generally offered advice. Many other interviewees also suggested people I should contact for subsequent interviews.

Members of the TABD, TACD, TALD and TAED were generally willing to meet and were more available for scheduled appointments. The TABD, TACD, TAED secretariat websites proved useful in identifying people and secretariat staff often directly contacted members on my behalf. I also acted as an observer at a number of meetings. I attended the May 2000 TAED meeting as well as a number of informal meetings that were attended by TABD members. I was invited to observe the 2001 TACD meeting in Brussels, however was unable to attend given prior commitments to the US ECSA conference. I made two attempts to attend the annual TABD meeting in Berlin in 1999 and Cincinnati in 2000. However, I was told that I would have limited (press core) access to press conferences but not working group meetings, in which case I determined that the cost of attending the meeting would outweigh the benefits. A relatively small sample of active TABD, TACD, TAED and TALD members was interviewed. The possibility of conducting a wider questionnaire was discussed with the dialogue secretariats. However, I was warned against doing so. It was argued that member responses would be more sincere in person or by telephone or email, and that many businesspeople and NGOs would consider themselves too busy to take the time to answer a questionnaire.

While the main focus on transnational actors was with these structured dialogues, a number of other private actors showed shaping capacity. In particular, US Mission, Commission and IOM officials suggested I contact NGOs working on the problem of trafficking in women. A number of NGO websites were also regularly consulted. In addition, regarding the banana dispute, contact was made with European Banana operators, for whom Atlanta corporation offered a spokesperson. Dole, Del Monte and Chiquita Corporations refused to comment but their websites and those of Fyffes, the

US Beef Cattlemen Association and the Caribbean Banana Exporters Association provided useful information.

The reluctance of interviewees to go 'on the record' was determined very early on in the interviewee process. State Department and Commission officials were particularly concerned about anonymity. In order to allow interviewees to speak freely, all interviews for the project were conducted on a strictly non-attributable basis, without a dictaphone. Most interviewees were offered, and many insisted on, obtaining a list of questions in advance of our meeting. Many interviews were followed up with email and telephone contact, and in some cases second interviews.

Interviews were conducted using a semi-structured method. Interviewees were divided by policy sector and where possible by 'rank', and asked a number of identical questions. Each interviewee was also asked specific questions relating to their role in the policy process, as well as questions sparked by interviews with other officials.

The methodology employed in this book was strictly qualitative. The introduction to this book noted that other studies on the NTA have attempted to measure policy output in quantitative terms. This books did not try to present a quantitative measure of what has been achieved under the NTA, for a number of reasons: it was difficult to establish a causal relationship between institutions and policy output, because institutions cannot be eliminated from the equation. In addition, official documents provide only part of the picture, particularly as transatlantic policy-makers have a tendency to 'recycle' and 'repackage' their announcement of policy successes. The interest of this book was not only in substantive policy output but also on the perceptions of actors who participate in the policy process. Measuring 'perceptions' quantitatively proved impossible given the wide range of answers returned by interviewees and in most sectors the very small sample of interviewees, as dictated by access to officials and also the often small number of people involved in individual policy sectors.

References

Books and journals

Aaron D., J. Macomber and P. Smith (2001) 'Changing Terms of Trade: Managing the New Transatlantic Economy Atlantic', Council of the US, www.acus.org.

Allen, D. (1998) 'Who Speaks for Europe? The Search for an Effective and Coherent External Policy', in J. Peterson and S. Sjursen (eds) *A Common Foreign Policy for Europe? Competing Visions of the CFSP*, London: Routledge.

Anderson, J. (1999) *Regional Integration and Democracy Expanding on the European Experience*, Oxford: Rowman and Littlefield.

Aron, R. (1977) 'Europe and the United States: The Relations Between European and Americans', in D. Landes (ed.) *Western Europe: The Trials of Partnership*, Toronto: Lexington Books: 25–54.

Bail, C., W. H. Reinicke, and R. Rummel (1997) 'The New Transatlantic Agenda and the EU–US Joint Action Plan: an Assessment', in C. Bail, W. H. Reinicke and R. Rummel (eds) *EU–US Relations: Balancing the Partnership*, Baden-Baden: Nomos Verlagsgellschaft.

Baldwin, D. (ed.) (1993) *Neorealism and Neoliberalism: The Contemporary Debate*, New York: Columbia University Press.

Bignami, F. and S. Charnovitz (2001) 'Transnational Civil Society Dialogues', in M. Pollack and G. Shaffer (eds) *The New Transatlantic Dialogue: Intergovernmental, Transgovernmental and Transnational Approaches*, Oxford: Rowman and Littlefield.

Blank, K., L. Hooghe and G. Marks (1994) 'European Integration and the State', paper presented at *American Political Science Association* conference, 1–4 September, New York.

Boekle, H., V. Rittberger and W. Wagner (1999) 'Norms and Foreign Policy: Constructivist Foreign Policy Theory', University of Tubingen Working Paper, www.uni-tuebingen.de/uni/.

Braun, M. (2004) 'EU Enlargement and Transatlantic Relations after September 11', American Institute for Contemporary German Studies, www.aicgs.org/research/eu/baun.shtml.

Brooks, S. (1997) 'Dueling Realisms', *International Organization*, 51 (3): 445–77.

Bronstone, A. (1998) *European Union: United States Security Relations*, Basingstoke: Palgrave.

Brown, C. (1997) *Understanding International Relations*, London: Macmillan.

Buck, M. (2000) 'The Role of the NTA Dialogue', paper presented to the New Transatlantic Agenda Dialogues on EU–US Co-operation for Sustainable Development Conference, 6–8 June, Lisbon.

Cable, V. (1999) *Globalisation and Global Governance*, London: Royal Institute of International Affairs.

Calleo, J. (1982) 'The Atlantic Alliance: A View from America', in A. Alting von Geusau (ed.) *Allies in a Turbulent World*, Toronto: Lexington Books: 3–20.

Calvocoressi, P. (1991) *The World Since 1945*, 6th edition, London: Longman.

Carroll, J. and G. Herring (eds) (1996) Modern American Diplomacy, Wilmington, DE: Scholarly Resources.

Checkel, J. (1999) 'Why Comply? Constructivism, Social Norms and the Study of International Institutions', ARENA Working Paper, WP 99/24, Oslo.

Checkel, J. (1998) 'The Constructivist Turn in International Relations Theory', *World Politics*, 50: 324–48.

Cowles, M. Green (forthcoming) 'Transatlantic Co-operation and Discord in the New Economy', paper presented at the ECSA Seventh Biennial Conference, 31 May–2 June, Madison, WI.

Cowles, M. Green (2001a) 'Private Firms and US–EU Policymaking: The Transatlantic Business Dialogue', in E. Philippart and P. Winand (eds) *Ever Closer Partnership, Policy-making in US–EU Relations*, Presses Interuniversitaires Europeennes: Brussels: 283–312.

Cowles, M. Green (2001b) 'The Transatlantic Business Dialogue (TABD): Transforming the New Transatlantic Agenda', in M. Pollack and G. Shaffer (eds) *The New Transatlantic Dialogue: Intergovernmental, Transgovernmental and Transnational Approaches*, Oxford: Rowman and Littlefield.

Cowles, M. Green (1997) 'The Limits of Liberalization: Regulatory Co-operation and the New Transatlantic Agenda', conference report, American Institute for Contemporary German Studies, 16 January, The Johns Hopkins University, Washington DC.

Cowles, M. Green (1996) 'The Collective Action of Transatlantic Business: The Transatlantic Business Dialogue', paper presented at the 1996 Annual Meeting of the American Political Science Association, San Francisco, CA.

Curtis, T. and Vastine, J. (1971) *The Kennedy Round and the Future of American Trade*, New York and London: Praeger.

Dahrendorf, R. (1974) 'Europe and the United States: The Uneasy Partner', in G. Mally (ed.), *The New Europe and the United States*: Toronto: Lexington Books: 67–72.

Danna, D. (2000) 'Organisations Active in the Field of Prostitution in a Comparative Western European Perspective', paper presented for workshop, ECPR Joint Session 2000 'Prostitution and International Trafficking as Political Issues', Copenhagen.

Demarat, P. (1986) 'The Extraterritoriality Issue in the Transatlantic Context: A Question of Law or Diplomacy', in L. Tsoukalis (ed.) *Europe, America and the World Economy*, Oxford: Basil Blackwell for College of Europe.

Den Boer, M. and H. Wallace (2000) 'Justice and Home Affairs', in H. Wallace and W. Wallace (eds) *Policy-making in the European Union*, 4th edition, Oxford: Oxford University Press: 401–26.

Devuyst, Y. (2001) 'European Union in Transatlantic Commercial Diplomacy', in E. Philippart and P. Winand (eds) *Ever Closer Partnership, Policy-making in US–EU Relations*, Brussels: Presses Interuniversitaires Europeennes: 283–312.

Devuyst, Y. (1995) 'Transatlantic Trade Policy: US Market Opening Strategies', Center for West European Studies, Pittsburgh, PA: University of Pittsburgh.

Devusyt, Y. (1990) 'European Community Integration and the United States: Towards a New Transatlantic Relationship?' *Journal of European Integration*, xiv (1).

Donfried, K. (1996) 'The New Transatlantic Agenda of December 1995: An American Perspective', *European Access*, 2 (April): 7–9.

Duigan, P. and L. H. Gann (1994) *The USA and the New Europe* 1945–1993, Oxford: Blackwell.

Egan, M. (2001a) 'Creating a Transatlantic Marketplace: Government Strategies and Business

Strategies', conference report, The American Institute for Contemporary German Studies, Washington DC.

Egan, M. (2001b) 'Mutual Recognition and Standard-Setting: Public and Private Strategies for Governing Markets', in M. Pollack and G. Shaffer (eds) *The New Transatlantic Dialogue: Intergovernmental, Transgovernmental and Transnational Approaches*, Oxford: Rowman and Littlefield.

Eichengreen, B. (ed.) (1995) *Europe's Post-war Recovery*, Cambridge: Cambridge University Press.

Eising, R. and B. Kohler-Koch (1999) Introduction, in R. Eising and B. Kohler-Koch (eds) *The Transformation of Governance in the European Union*, London: Routledge: 1–23.

Featherstone, K. and R. Ginsberg (1996) *The United States and the European Community in the 1990s*, 2nd edition, London: Macmillan.

Finklestein, L. (1995) 'What is Global Governance?', *Global Governance*, 1 (3): 367–72.

Frellell, R. (1996) 'The Truman Era and European Integration', in F. Heller and J. Gillingham *The United States and the Integration of Europe: Legacies of the Postwar Era*, London: Macmillan.

Frellesen, T. (2001) 'Processes and Procedures in EU–US Foreign Policy Co-operation: From the Transatlantic Declaration to the New Transatlantic Agenda', in E. Philippart and P. Winand (eds) *Ever Closer Partnership, Policy-making in US–EU Relations*, Brussels: Presses Interuniversitaires Europeennes: 313–50.

Frost, E. (1998) 'The Transatlantic Economic Partnership', *International Economics Policy Brief*, 98–6, Washington DC: Institute of International Economics.

Frost, E. (1997) *Transatlantic Trade: A Strategic Agenda*, Washington DC: Institute of International Economics.

Funkt, A. (1999) 'The Third Pillar of the EU and the Limits of Transatlantic Co-operation', unpublished paper, Transatlantic Governance Conference, June.

Gardner, A. (1997) *A New Era in US–EU Relations? The Clinton Administration and the New Transatlantic Agenda*, Aldershot: Ashgate Publishing.

Geipel, G. and R. Manning (1996) *Rethinking the Transatlantic Partnership: Security and Economics in a New Era*, Washington DC: Hudson Institute.

Giplin, R. (1991) 'Three Ideologies of Political Economy', in K. Stiles and T. Akaha (eds) *International Political Economy: A Reader*, New York: Harper Collins.

Gleason, C. and P. Walther (2000) 'The WTO Dispute Settlement Implementation Procedures: A System in Need of Reform', *Law and Policy in International Business*, 31 (3): 709–36.

Grieco, J. (1990) *Co-operation Among Nations: European, America and Non-Tariff Barriers to Trade*, London: Cornell University Press.

Grossman, L. (1998) *The Political Ecology of Bananas: Contract Farming, Peasants and Agrarian Change in the Eastern Caribbean*, Chapel Hill, NC: University of North Carolina Press.

Guzzini, S. (1998) *Realism in International Relations and International Political Economy: The Continuing Story of a Death Foretold*, London: Routledge.

Haas, P. M. (1992) 'Epistemic Communities and International Policy Coordination', *International Organization*, 46 (1): 1–35.

Haass, R. (1999) *Transatlantic Tensions: The United States, Europe, and Problem Countries*, Washington DC: Brooking Institute Press.

Hallam, D. and Lord Preston (1997) *The Political Economy of Europe's Banana Trade*, Reading: Reading University Press.

Hamilton, D. (2003) 'Renewing Transatlantic Partnership: Why and How', Testimony to the House Committee on International Relations European Subcommittee, 11 June, Washington DC.

Hasenclever, A., P. Mayer and V. Rittberger (1996) 'Interests, Power, Knowledge: The Study of International Regimes', *Mershon International Studies Review*, 40: 177–228.
Henderson, C. (1998) *International Relations: Conflict and Co-operation at the Turn of the 21st Century*, London: McGraw Hill.
Heuser, B. (1996) *Transatlantic Relations, Sharing Costs and Ideas*, London: Chatham House Papers, Royal Institute of International Affairs.
Hill, C. and W. Wallace (1996) 'Introduction, Actors and Actions', in C. Hill (ed.) *The Actors in Europe's Foreign Policy*, London: Routledge.
Hill, C. (1996) *The Actors in Europe's Foreign Policy*, London: Routledge.
Hill, C. (1993) 'The Capability-Expectations Gap, or Conceptualising Europe's International Role', *Journal of Common Market Studies*, 31 (3): 305–28.
Hindley, B. (1999) 'New Institutions for Transatlantic Trade', *International Affairs* (75): 145–60.
Hix, S. (1994) 'The Study of the European Community: The Challenge to Comparative Politics' *West European Politics* , 17 (1): 1–30.
Hoffman, S. (1977) 'Uneven Allies: An Overview', in D. Landes (ed.) *Western Europe: The Trials of Partnership*, Toronto: Lexington Books: 55–110.
Hoffman, S. and C. Maier (eds) (1984) *The Marshall Plan: A Retrospective*, London: Westview Press.
Hogan, M. (1984) 'European Integration and the Marshall Plan', in S. Hoffman and C. Maier (eds) *The Marshall Plan: A Retrospective*, London: Westview Press: 1–6.
Hooghe, L. (1999a) 'Supranational Activists or Intergovernmental Agents. Explaining the Orientation of Senior Commission Officials Towards European Integration', *Comparative Political Studies*, 32: 435–63.
Hooghe, L. (1999b) 'Images of Europe: Orientations to European Integration Among Senior Officials of the Commission', *British Journal of Political Science*, 29: 345–67.
Horton, L. (1998) 'Mutual Recognition Agreements and Harmonisation', *Seton Hall Law Review*, 29 (2): 692–732.
Hughes, D. (2000) 'The Natasha Trade: Transnational Sex Trafficking', *National Institute of Justice Journal*, 246, www.uri.edu/artsci/wms/hughes/natasha.htm.
Huntington, S. (1991) 'The U.S. – Decline or Renewal', in K. Stiles and T. Akaha *International Political Economy: A Reader*, New York: Harper Collins.
Ives, R. (1997) 'The ABC's of MRAs', statement, Limits of Liberalization Conference, 16 January, Washington DC.
Jachtenfuchs, M. (2001) 'The Governance Approach to European Integration', *Journal of Common Market Studies*, 39 (2): 245–64.
Jachtenfuchs, M. and B. Kohler-Koch (1995) 'The Transformation of Governance in the European Union', conference paper, Fourth Biennial International Conference of the European Community Studies Association, 11–14 May, Charleston.
James, H. (1987) 'The IMF and the Creation of the Bretton Woods System 1944–58', in B. Eichengreen (ed.) *Europe's Post-War Recovery*, Cambridge: Cambridge University Press: 93–126.
Johnson, D. (1999) 'Trafficking of Women into the European Union', *New England International and Comparative Law Annual Online*, 5, www.nesl.edu/annual/vol5index.htm.
Karol, D. (2000) 'Divided Government and US Trade Policy: Much Ado About Nothing?', *International Organization*, 54 (4): 825–44.
Katzenstein, P. (1993) 'Regions in Competition', in H. Haftendorn and C. Tuschhoff (eds) *America and Europe in an Era of Change*, Boulder, CO: Westview Press.
Kennedy, C. (1989) *The Rise and Fall of Great Powers: Economic Change and Military Conflict from 1500–2000*, New York: Random House Vintage.

Keohane, R. (1993a) 'The Diplomacy of Structural Change: Multilateral Institutions and State Strategies', in H. Haftendorn and C. Tuschhoff (eds) *America and Europe in an Era of Change*, Boulder, CO: Westview Press.

Keohane, R. (1993b) 'Institutional Theory and the Realist Challenge After the Cold War', in D. Baldwin (ed.) *Neorealism and Neoliberalism: The Contemporary Debate*, New York: Columbia University Press.

Keohane, R. (1989) 'Neoliberal Institutionalism: A Perspective on World Politics', in R. Keohane (ed.) *International Institutions and State Power: Essays in International Relations Theory*, Boulder, CO: Westview Press.

Keohane, R. (ed.) (1986) *Neorealism and its Critics*, New York: Columbia University Press.

Keohane, R. (1984) *After Hegemony: Cooperation and Discord in the World Political Economy*, Princeton, NJ: Princeton University Press.

Keohane, R. *et al.* (1977) *Power and Interdependence: World Politics in Transition*, Boston, MA: Little Brown.

Keohane, R., P. Haas and M. Levy (1993) *Institutions for the Earth*, London: MIT Press.

Keohane, R. and J. Nye (1993) Introduction, in R. Keohane, J. Nye, and S. Hoffman (eds) *After the Cold War, International Institutions and State Strategies in Europe, 1989–1991*, London: Harvard University Press.

Keohane, R. and J. Nye (1989) *Power and Interdependence: World Politics in Transition*, 2nd edition, New York: Harper Collins.

Kissinger, H. (1994) *Diplomacy*, London: Touchstone.

Knauss, J. and D. Trubek (2001) 'The Transatlantic Labor Dialogue: Nothing Signifying Something', in M. Pollack and G. Shaffer (eds) *The New Transatlantic Dialogue: Intergovernmental, Transgovernmental and Transnational Approaches*, Oxford: Rowman and Littlefield.

Komuro, N. (2000) 'The EC Banana Regime and Judicial Control', *Journal of World Trade*, 34 (5): 1–87.

Krasner, S. (1993) 'Power Polarity, and the Challenge of Disintegration', in H. Haftendorn and C. Tischhoff (eds) *America and Europe in an Era of Change*, Boulder, CO: Westview Press.

Krenzler, H. and A. Schomaker (1996) 'A New Transatlantic Agenda', *European Foreign Affairs Review*, 1 (1).

Krenzler, H. and E. Wiegand (1999) 'EU–US Relations: More than Trade Disputes?', *European Foreign Affairs Review* (4): 1–27.

Laffan, B. (1997) 'The European Union: A Distinct Model of Internationalisation?', paper presented at workshop 'Europeanisation in International Perspective', University of Pittsburgh, September.

Landes, D. (1977) *Western Europe: The Trials of Partnership*, Lexington, MA: Lexington Books.

Legro, J. and A. Moravscik (2000) part of correspondence 'Brother Can You Spare a Paradigm? (Or was anybody ever a realist)', *International Security*, 25 (1): 165–93.

Lergo, J. and A. Moravscik (1999) 'Is Anybody Still and Realist?' *International Security*, 24 (2): 5–55.

Lohman, S. and S. O'Halloran (1994) 'Divide Government and US Trade Policy: Theory and Evidence', *International Organization*, 48: 595–632.

Lumsdaine, D. H. (1998) *Moral Vision in International Politics: The Foreign Aid Regime, 1949–1989*, Trenton, NJ: Princeton University Press.

Lundestad, G. (1998) *'Empire' by Integration: The United States and European Integration, 1945–1997*, Oxford: Oxford University Press.

Mally, G. (1974) *The New Europe and the United States*, Toronto: Lexington Books.

March, J. and J. Olsen (1998) 'Institutional Dynamics of International Political Orders', *International Organization*, 52 (4): 943–69.

March, J. and J. Olsen (1989) *Rediscovering Institutions*, New York: Free Press.

Marks, G., L. Hooghe and K. Blank (1996) 'European Integration from the 1980s State-Centric v Multi-level Governance', *Journal of Common Market Studies*, 34 (3): 341–77.

Marsh, D. and R. A. W. Rhodes (1992) *Policy Networks in British Government*, Oxford: Clarendon Press.

Martin, P. and M. Miller (2000) 'Smuggling and Trafficking: A Conference Report', *International Migration Review*, 34 (3): 969–75.

Mattli, W. (1999) *The Logic of Regional Integration Europe and Beyond*, Cambridge: Cambridge University Press.

McBride Stetson, D. (2000) 'The Invisible Issue: Prostitution and Trafficking of Women and Girls in the United States', paper prepared for workshop 'Prostitution and Trafficking as Political Issues', European Consortium for Political Research Joint Sessions Workshops, April, Copenhagen.

Mearsheimer, J. J. (1990a) 'Back to the Future: Instability in Europe After the Cold War', *International Security*, 15 (1): 5–56.

Mearsheimer, J. J. (1990b) 'Why We Will Soon Miss the Cold War', *Atlantic Monthly*, August: 35–50.

Merrill, R. (1998) 'The Importance and Challenges of "Mutual Recognition"', *Seton Hall Law Review*, 29 (2).

Meunier, S. (2000) 'What Single Voice? European Institutions and EU–US Trade Negotiations', *International Organization*, 54 (1): 103–35.

Meunier, S. and K. Nicolaïdis (1999) 'Who Speaks for Europe? The Delegation of Trade Authority in the EU', *Journal of Common Market Studies*, 37 (3): 477–501.

Miko, F. (2000) 'Trafficking in Women and Children: The US and International Response', *Congressional Research Service Report*, 98–649 C.

Milner, H. (1997) *Interests, Institutions, and Information*, Princeton, NJ: Princeton University Press.

Milward, A. (1984) *The Reconstruction of Western Europe 1945–51*, London: Methuen.

Monar, J. (1998) *The New Transatlantic Agenda and the Future of EU–US Relations*, London: Kluwer Law International.

Moravcsik, A. (1998) *The Choice for Europe: Social Purpose and State Power from Messina to Maastricht*, New York: Cornell University Press.

Moravcsik, A. (1993a) 'Integrating International and Domestic Theories of International Bargaining', in B. Evans, H. Jacobson and R. Putnam (eds) *Double-Edged Diplomacy*, London: University of California Press.

Moravcsik, A. (1993b)'Preferences and Power in the European Community: A Liberal Intergovernmentalist Approach', *Journal of Common Market Studies*, 31 (4): 473–519.

Morgenthau, H. (1985) *Politics among Nations*, 5th edition, New York: Knopf.

Murphy, C. (2000) 'Global Governance: Poorly Done and Poorly Understood', *International Affairs*, 76 (4): 789–803.

Nicolaïdis, K. (1997a) 'Mutual Recognition of Regulatory Regimes: Some Lessons and Prospects', Jean Monnet Working Papers, Harvard University, www. Harvard.edu/programs/JeanMonnet/papers/97/97–07–1.htm.

Nicolaïdis, K. (1997b) 'Negotiating Mutual Recognition Agreements: A Comparative Analysis', paper presented at Annual Meeting of the American Political Science Association, 28–31 August, Washington DC.

Nicolaïdis, K. and R. Howse (2001) *The Federal Vision: Legitimacy and Levels of Governance in the*

United States and the European Union, Oxford: Oxford University Press.

Nixon, R. (1974) 'Europe and the Atlantic Alliance', in G. Mally (ed.) *The New Europe and the United States*, Toronto: Lexington Books: 3–10.

Nye, J. (1993) 'Patrons and Clients: New Roles in the Post-Cold War Order', in H. Haftendorn and C. Tischhoff (eds) *America and Europe in an Era of Change*, Boulder, CO: Westview Press.

O'Neill, A. (1999) 'International Trafficking in Women to the United States: A contemporary manifestation of slavery and organised crime,' CIA Intelligence Report, www.state.gov/www/global/women/index.html.

O'Toole, L. (1997) 'Treating Networks Seriously Practical and Research Based Agendas in Public Administration', *Public Administration Review*, 57 (1): 45–52.

Pelkmans, J. (1998) 'Atlantic Economic Co-operation: The Limits of Plurilateralism', Working Document (122), Brussels: Centre for Policy Studies.

Pelkmans, J. (1986) 'The Bickering Bigemony: GATT as an instrument in Atlantic trade policy', in L. Tsoukalis *Europe, America and the World Economy*, Oxford: Briar Blackwell.

Peters, B. G. (1999) *Institutional Theory in Political Science. The 'New Institutionalism'*, London: Continuum.

Peterson, J. (2001a) 'Shaping, Not Making: the US Congress and US–EU Relations', in E. Philippart and P. Winand (eds) *Policy-Making in the European Union*, Brussels: Peter Lang.

Peterson, J. (2001b) 'Get Away from Me Closer, You're Near Me Too Far: Europe And America after the Uruguay Round', in M. Pollack and G. Shaffer (eds) *The New Transatlantic Dialogue: Intergovernmental, Transgovernmental and Transnational Approaches.* Oxford: Rowman and Littlefield.

Peterson, J. (1996) *Europe and America, The Prospects for Partnership*, 2nd edition, London: Routledge.

Peterson, J. (1995) 'Understanding Decision-making in the European Union: Towards a framework or analysis', *Journal of Common Market Studies*, 2 (1) 9–93.

Peterson, J. (1994) 'Europe and America in the Clinton Era', *Journal of Common Market Studies*, 32 (3): 411–26.

Peterson, J. and E. Bomberg (1999) *Decision-making in the European Union*, London and New York: Macmillan and St Martin's Press.

Peterson, J. and L. O'Toole, Jr. (2001) 'Federal Governance in the United States and the European Union: A Policy Network Perspective', in K. Nicolaïdis and R. Howse (2001) *The Federal Vision: Legitimacy and Levels of Governance in the United States and the European Union*, Oxford: Oxford University Press.

Peterson, J. and H. Sjursen (eds) (1998) *A Common Foreign Policy for Europe? Competing Visions of the CFSP*, London: Routledge.

Peterson, J. and H. Ward (1995) 'Coalitional Instability and the New Multidimensional Politics of Security: a Rational Choice Argument for EU US Co-operation', *European Journal of International Relations*, 1 (2): 131–56.

Philippart, E. and P. Winand (2001) 'Ever Closer Partnership? Taking Stock of US–EU Relations', in E. Philippart and P. Winand (eds) *Ever Closer Partnership, Policy-making in US EU Relations*, Brussels: Presses Interuniversitaires Europeennes.

Piening, C. (1997) *Global Europe: The European Union in World Affairs*, London: Lynne Rienner Publishers.

Pollack, M. (2001) 'International Relations Theory and European Integration', *Journal of Common Market Studies*, 39 (2): 221–4.

Pollack, M. and G. Shaffer (2001) 'Transatlantic Governance in a Global Economy: Introduction', in M. Pollack and G. Shaffer (eds) *The New Transatlantic Dialogue:*

Intergovernmental, Transgovernmental and Transnational Approaches. Oxford: Rowman and Littlefield.

Prakash, A. and J. Hart (1999) *Globalisation and Governance*, London: Routledge.

Puchala, D. and R. Hopkins (1983) 'International Regimes: Lessons from Inductive Analysis in D. Krasner', in D. Puchala and R. Hopkins (eds) *International Regimes*, Ithaca, NY: Cornell University Press.

Putnam, R. (1998) Diplomacy and Domestic Politics: The Logic of Two Level Games, *International Organization* 42: 427–60.

Putnam, R. (1993) 'Two-Level Games: The Impact of Domestic Politics on Transatlantic Bargaining', in H. Haftendorn and C. Tischhoff (eds) *America and Europe in an Era of Change*, Boulder, CO: Westview Press.

Reinicke, W. (1996) *Deepening the Atlantic: Towards a New Transatlantic Marketplace?* London: British Foreign Policy Resource Centre.

Rhodes, R. A. W. (1997) *Understanding Governance: Policy Networks, Governance, Reflexivity and Accountability*, Buckingham: Open University Press.

Risse, T. (2000) 'Let's Argue! Communicative Action World Politics', *International Organization*, 54 (1): 1–39.

Risse, T. (1995a) *Bringing Transnational Relations Back In: Non-state Actors, Domestic Structures and International Institutions*, Cambridge: Cambridge University Press.

Risse, T. (1995b) *Cooperation Among Democracies: The European Influence on U.S. Foreign Policy*, Princeton, NJ: Princeton University Press.

Ronit K. and V. Schneider (1999) 'Global Governance through Private Organisations', *Governances: An International Journal of Policy and Administration*, 12 (3): 243–66.

Rosenau, J. (1992) 'Governance, Order and Change in World Politics', in J. Rosenau and E. O. Czempiel *Governance with Government Order and Change in World Politics*, New York: Cambridge University Press: 1–29.

Ruggerio, V. (2000) 'Transnational Crime: Official and Alternative Fears International', *Journal of Sociology of Law*, 28: 187–99.

Ruggerio, V. (1997) 'Trafficking in Human Beings: Slaves in contemporary Europe', *International Journal of Sociology of Law*, 25: 231–44.

Ruggie, J. (1998) *Constructing the World Polity: Essays on International Institutionalization*, London: Routledge.

Sbragia, A. (2000) 'Governance, the State, and the Market: What is Going on?', *Governance: An International Journal of Policy and Administration*, 12 (3): 243–50.

Schloenhardt, A. (1999) 'Organised Crime and the Business of Migrant Trafficking: An economic analysis', *Crime Law and Social Change*, 32 (3): 203–33.

Serfaty, S. (2003) 'EU–US Relations Beyond Iraq – Setting the Terms of Complimentarity, *Euro-focus*, 9 (3).

Skogstad, G. (2002) 'The WTO, the European Union, and Food Safety Regulatory Policy Harmonization', *Journal of Common Market Studies*, 29 (3).

Slaughter, A. M. (1997) 'The Real New World Order', *Foreign Affairs*, 76 (5): 183–97.

Smith, M. (2001) 'The United States, The European Union and the New Transatlantic Marketplace: Public strategy and private interests', in E. Philippart and P. Winand *Ever Closer Partnership, Policy-making in US–EU Relations*, Brussels: Presses Interuniversitaires Europeennes: 267–82.

Smith, M. (1998) 'Does the Flag Follow Trade? "Politicisation" and the Emergence of a European Foreign Policy', in J. Peterson and S. Sjursen (eds) *A Common Foreign Policy for Europe? Competing visions of the CFSP*, London: Routledge: 77–94.

Smith, M. (1997) 'Competitive Co-operation and EU/US Relations: Can the EU be a strategic partner for the US in the world political economy?', paper presented at ECSA Fifth Biennial Conference, 29 May–1 June, Seattle, WA.

Smith, M. (1990) 'The Devil you Know: The United States and a changing European Community', *International Affairs*, 68 (1): 103–20.

Smith, M. (1984) *Western Europe and the United States: The uncertain alliance*, London: George Allen and Unwin.

Smith, M. and S. Woolcock (1993) *The United States and the European Community in a Transformed World*, London: Royal Institute of International Affairs.

Smith, P. (1993) *The Challenge of Integration Europe and the Americas*, London: Transaction Publishers.

Steffenson, R. (2005) 'Competing Trade and Regulatory Strategies for the Mutual Recognition of Conformity Assessment in the Transatlantic Marketplace', in M. Egan (ed.) *Creating a Transatlantic Marketplace: Government policies and business strategy*, Manchester: Manchester University Press.

Steffenson, R. (2004) 'Global Strategies and Local Best Practices: Policy responses to trafficking in persons', British Council Globalization Series.

Steffenson, R. (2002) 'The EU's Exportation of Mutual Recognition: A case of transatlantic policy transfer', European University Institute Working Paper, Transatlantic Series.

Stehmann, O. (2000) 'Foreign Sales Corporations under the WTO: The panel ruling on US export subsidies', *Journal of World Trade*, 34 (3): 127–56.

Stevens, C. (2000) 'Trade With Developing Countries', in H. Wallace and W. Wallace, *Policy-making in the European Union*, 4th edition, Oxford: Oxford University Press: 401–26.

Stevens, C. (1996) 'EU Policy for the Banana Market', in H. Wallace and W. Wallace, *Policy-making in the European Union*, 3rd edition, Oxford: Oxford University Press: 325–52.

Stoecker, S. (1999) 'Transnational Crime Institute Sex Trade: Trafficking of women and children in Europe and the United States', hearing before the Commission on Security and Co-operation in Europe, 28 June (Helsinki Commission).

Stoecker, S. (1998) 'Crime and Corruption in the Digital Age', *Journal of International Affairs*, 51 (2): 605–20.

Stokes, B. (1999) 'Transatlantic Trade Frictions', *Internationale Politik*, September, www.cfr.org/p/pubs/StokesTradeOp-ed.html.

Stone, D. (2000) 'Non-Governmental Policy Transfers: The strategies of independent policy institutions', *Governance*, 13 (1): 45–62.

Strange, S. (1996) *The Retreat of the State: The Diffusion of Power in the World Economy*, Cambridge: Cambridge University Press.

Strange, S. (1982) 'The Money Tangle', in F. Alting von Geusau (ed.) *Allies in a Turbulent World*, Toronto: Lexington Books.

Sutton, P. (1997) 'The Banana Regime of the European Union, the Caribbean, and Latin America', *Journal of Interamerican Studies and World Affairs*, 39 (2): 5–36.

Taylor, I. and R. Jamieson (1999) 'Sex Trafficking and the Mainstream Market Culture: Challenges to Organised Crime Analysis', *Crime, Law and Social Change*, 32 (3): 257–78.

Tsoukalis, L. (1986) 'Euro-American Relations and Global Economic Interdependence', in L. Tsoukalis (ed.) *Europe, America and the World Economy*, Oxford: Briar and Blackwell.

Vadney, T. (1999) *The World Since 1945*, New York: Puffin.

Vallern, C. and B. McGivern (2000) 'The Right to Retaliate Under the WTO Agreement: the "Sequencing" Problem', *Journal of World Trade*, August, 34 (2): 63–84.

van den Broek (1993) *Transatlantic Relations in the 1990s: The Emergence of New Security Architectures*, Medford, MA: Institute for Foreign Policy Analysis.

Vogel, D. (1998) *Barriers or Benefits? Regulation in Transatlantic Trade*, London: Brookings.

Wallace, H. and A. Young (1996) 'The Single Market', in H. Wallace and W. Wallace (eds) *Policy-making in the European Union*, Oxford: Oxford University Press: 125–56.

Waltz, K. (1986) 'Response to my Critics', in R.O. Keohane (ed.) *Neorealism and its Critics*, New York: Columbia University Press.

Waltz, K. (1979) *Theory of International Politics*, Reading: Addison-Wesley.

Young, A. (2001) 'Domestic Politics of Transatlantic Governance: Hormones, Genes, and Risk', EUI Working Paper.

Ziedaliski, B. (2000) 'The World Trade Organisation and the Transatlantic Banana Split', *New England International and Comparative Law Annual*, www.nesl.edu/annual/vol5indx.htm.

Official documents and speeches

Atlanta Atkiengesellschaft (2000) letter to European Community Banana Trade Association, 4 August.

Background Brief 4 (1998) realised in correlation with May Summit, London, www.useu.be/SUMMIT/summit0598.html.

Baker, J. (1991) Berlin speeches, addresses to Berlin Press Club, 12 December 1989 and the Aspen Institute, 18 June 1991, London: Embassy of the United States of America.

Barshevsky, C. (1997) USTR press release, 13 June, Washington DC.

Berry, W. (2001) 'Statement of European American Business Council to the Senate Banking Committee Hearing on Reauthorization of the Iran–Libya Sanctions Act', 28 June.

Botti, A. (1998) 'Trafficking in Women and Girls', statement made to the ODCE Implementation Meeting on Human Dimension Issues.

Brittan, L. (1998) 'Europe: The New Tiger? The Shape of Tomorrow Global Economy', speech given at the Kennedy School, Harvard University, 18 March, Boston, MA.

Brittan, L. (1995) 'The EU–US Relationship: Will it Last?', speech given to the American Club of Brussels, 27 April, Brussels.

Brown, R. (1994) speech to American Chamber of Commerce, 15 December, Brussels.

Caribbean Banana Exporters Association (2000a) 'EU Banana Regime: Position of Del Monte and Dole Corporations', http://cbea.org.

Caribbean Banana Exporters Association (2000b) 'Reform of the Banana Regime: A Dire Threat to the Caribbean', October, www.cbea.org.

Clinton (1997) New Briefing, 16 December, Washington DC.

Clinton, W., J. Delors and K. Kohl (1994) 'Statement to EU–US Summit', 11 January, Berlin.

Daley, W. (1997) 'The US Administration's Priorities and Prospects for Economic and Business Relations with Europe', speech given to the *European Institute*, 14 March, Washington DC.

Dehaunt, William (2001) press release, 16 April.

Early Warning System Statement (1999) announced at EU–US Summit, June, Bonn, www.useu.be/DOCS/Index.html#3.

Eizenstat, S. (1997) speech given to the European Committee of the American Chamber of Commerce, 11 September, Brussels.

Escaler, N. (1998) statement on United States–European Union Transatlantic Seminar to Prevent Trafficking in Women, IOM Deputy Director General, 9–10 July, L'viv.

European American Business Council (2001) press release, 'States Enjoy Trillion Dollar Benefit From EU–US Trade and Investment Relationship', www.eabc.

European Commission (2001) 'Reinforcing the Transatlantic Relationship: Focusing on

Strategy and Delivering Results', COM(2001) 154, 20 March, www.eurunion.org/partner/backgrounddoc.htm.

European Commission (2000a) 'Commission Gives New Impetus to Resolve Banana Dispute', press release, 5 July 2000, www.europa.eu.int/comm/trade.\ 4.

European Commission (2000b) Communication from the Commission to the Council on the First Come, First Served Method for the Banana Regime and the Implications of a 'Tariff Only' System, 4 October.

European Commission (2000c) 'Commission Proposes Solution to End Banana Dispute', press release, 4 October, www.europa.eu.int/comm/trade.\ 4.

European Commission (1999a) 'Commission Proposes to Modify the EU's Banana Regime', press release, 10 November, www.europea.eu.int/comm/trade.

European Commission (1999b) 'The Commission Reports to the Council on Consultation With a View to Settlement of the Banana Dispute', press release, 26 May, www.europea.eu.int/comm/trade.

European Commission (1998a) 'Communiqué to the Council on the New Transatlantic Marketplace Agreement', March.

European Commission (1998b) 'US/EU Banana Dispute: Modifications to the EC Banana Regime', DG I, External Relations, 10 November 1998, www.europa.org.

European Commission (1995) 'Europe and the US: The Way Forward', Commission communication on EU–US relations, 26 July, www.europa.eu.int/comm/dg01/commind.htm.

European Council of Ministers (1999) Council Regulation amending EEC No. 404/93 on the Common Organisation of the Market on Bananas.

European Parliament (2000) Agriculture and Rural Development Committee draft response to the EU Commission's proposals for an amended banana regime.

EU–US Guidelines/Principles on Co-operation and Transparency in Establishing Technical Regulations (2000), released EU–US Washington Summit, www.eurunion.org.

Friends of the Earth (1999) 'The New Transatlantic Agenda (NTA) as a Challenge for Sustainable Societies on a Global Scale', 1–2 May 1999, statements from first meeting of TAED, www.foeurope.org/press/new_transatlantic.htm.

Gramegna, M. (1996) Statement made to EU Conference on Trafficking in Women for Sexual Exploitation, International Organization of Migration, representative, Vienna.

Grossman, M. (1998) 'The United States and the European Union: State of Relations as Austria Assumes Presidency', speech given at Princeton University Conference, 'The European Union, Austria and the Future of Central Europe', 1 May, New Jersey.

Holston, S. (1998) 'Testimony to the House Committee on Commerce', Subcommittee on Oversight and Investigations on EU Mutual Recognition Agreements, 2 October.

International Organization for Migration (2003a) Report on International Dialogue on Migration, Seminar on Trade and Migration, 12–14 November.

International Organization for Migration (2003b) Report on International Dialogue on Migration, Seminar on Trade and Migration, 12–14 November.

International Organization for Migration (2001) 'Victims of Trafficking in the Balkans: A study of trafficking in women and children for sexual exploitation to through and from the Balkan region', IOM: Geneva.

International Organization for Migration (1999) Fifth Quarterly Progress Report, 'Trafficking Prevention in Ukraine', Winrock International and NIS–US Women's Consortium.

International Organization for Migration (1998) Information Campaign Against Trafficking in Women in the Ukraine, Project Report, IOM: Geneva.

Lamy, P. (1999) speech at TPN Meeting, 22 May, Brussels, http://tabd.org/resources/content/

mylamy.html.
Larson, A. (1997) 'The Transatlantic Marketplace', speech given at The European Institute forum, 11 March, Washington DC.
Loy, F. (1999) Testimony to the Senate Foreign Relations Committee, http://secretary.state.gov/www.picw/trafficking/loy.htm.
Mutual Recognition Agreements (1997) signed by USTR, European Commission and European Council Presidency, 1 December 1998, http://useu.be/DOCS/mra.98.pdf.
New Transatlantic Agenda (1995) signed by the European Commission, President of the European Council and President of the United State, 3 December, Madrid, www.useu.be/ISSUES/nta1295.html.
New Transatlantic Agenda Joint Action Plan (1995) 12 December 1995, Washington DC, www.useu.be/DOCS/nta2.html.
OSCE (1999) 'Trafficking in Human Beings: Implications for the OSCE', Review Conference, September, ODIHR Background Paper 1999/3.
OSHA (2000) Federal Register Nationally Recognized Testing Laboratories Fees; Public Comment Period on Recognition Notices – 65:46797–46819.
People to People Conference Report (1997) 'Building Bridges Across the Atlantic' conference, May, Washington DC.
Petriccione, M. (2000) 'Mutual Recognition Agreements', speech given to TACD Meeting, 10–12 February, Washington DC.
Pickering, T. (1998) Remarks made at Europe Magazine Forum, 22 May, Washington DC.
Senior Level Group Reports (2001–1998) Reports to the EU–US Summits, www.useu.be/us-eusummits.html.
Sheil, S. (1998) 'EU/US Free Trade Area' Internal Briefing Document: Institute of European Affairs.
Stern, P. (1996) 'Transatlantic Business Dialogue: A New Paradigm for Standards and Regulatory Reform Sector by Sector', www.tabd.com/resources/content.stern.html.
Stern, P. (1997) 'The Success of the MRAs', www.tabd.comhttp://www.tabd.com/index1.html.
TABD (2000) Mid Year Report, May, Brussels, www.tabd.com.
TABD (1999) Mid Year Report, 10 May, Washington DC, www.tabd.com.
TABD (1998) Mid Year Scorecard, www.tabd.com.
TACD (2000a) 'US & EU Consumer Groups Call For Swift Action To Balance Trade Dialogue', press release, 30 March.
TACD (2000b) 'Principles of Harmonisation', TACD Trade Document Trade –8–00, February, www.tacd.org.
TACD (1999) 'TACD Recommendations, Fair Trade', Document 4–99, www.tacd.org.
TACD–TAED (1999) 'EU–US Summit Rejects Environment and Consumer Groups Participation, Invites Business Representatives', joint press release, 18 June.
TACD–TAED (1998) 'Comments by the TACD on the TEP Action Plan', December, www.tacd.org.
TAED (2000a) 'Transatlantic Environment Dialogue Suspends its Activities Due to the Failure of US Government to Stick to its Commitments', press release, 21 November.
TAED (2000b) 'Mutual Recognition Agreements Draft Policy Statement of the Transatlantic Environmental Dialogue', presented at the Third Meeting of the TAED, 10–13 May, 2000.
TAED (2000c) 'A Draft Political Assessment of the First Year', unpublished paper distributed to TAED members.
TAED (1999) press release, 'European and U.S. Environmental Organisations Launch the

Transatlantic Environment Dialogue (TAED)', 3 May.
TAED (1998) 'Discussion Paper on the Opportunities for Environmental Advocacy in Trade Policy Created by NGO Participation in the New Transatlantic Agenda', September, www.nwf.org/ internationaltrade/taedrpt.html.
TALD (2001) 'Statement by AFL-CIO President John Sweeney on the ETUC Trade Union to the US–European Union Summit', December.
Transatlantic Declaration (1990) signed by President of US, President of Commission and President of the European Presidency in Paris.
Transatlantic Economic Partnership (1998) signed by the EU and the US, 18 May, London, http://europa.eu.int/comm/dg01/decl.htm.
Transatlantic Economic Partnership Action Plan (1998) press release EU–US Summit, Washington, www.useu.be/DOCS/nta2.html.
Transatlantic Economic Partnership Steering Group (2000) 'Report to Meeting of Trade and Economic Ministers at EU–US Summit', 31 May, Lisbon.
Transatlantic Economic Partnership Steering Group (1997) 'Report to Meeting of Trade and Economic Ministers at EU–US Summit', 17 December, Washington DC.
Transatlantic Partnership on Political Co-operation (TPPC) (1998) signed in conjunction with EU–US Summit, London.
Transatlantic Policy Network (1999) Towards Transatlantic Partnership, Co-operation Project, Brussels.
Transatlantic Policy Network (1998) Towards Transatlantic Partnership Co-operation Project Report, Brussels.
Transatlantic Policy Network (1995) Towards Transatlantic Partnership, The Partnership Project, Brussels.
US Administration (2000) press release, 'Carousel Revised Retaliation List in EU Disputes Delayed', 20 June.
US Administration (1998) press release, 'US Officials Stress Interest in Resolving EU Banana Dispute', 12 September.
US Administration (1998) press release, 'USTR Barshefsky Reacts to EC Banana Decision', November.
US Beef Cattlemen (2000) 'A Message to Congress, Advertising Campaign', www.hill.beef.org.
US Beef Cattlemen Association (1998) press release, 'Europe's "Solution" to the Beef and Banana Cases: An "Endless Loop" Designed to Evade the Law', 30 November, www.hill.beef.org.
US Congress (1999) House Resolution 1361, 'To Bar the Imposition of Increased Tariffs or other Retaliatory Measures Against the Products of the European Union in Response to the Banana Regime of the European Union', introduced by Representative Maxine Waters, 25 March.
US Congress (1998) House Resolution 213, 'Calling for the Administration to Make the Beef and Banana Disputes a Top Priority', 30 November.
US Embassy Kyiv Ukraine (1999) Crime Digest, January, www.usemb.kiev.ua/rso/CrimeDigest9901.html.
USIS (1999) 'Statement by Ambassador Peter Scher on EU Banana Regime', 3 March.
USIS (1998) 'Barshefsky says No US–EU Free Trade Agreement Envisioned', 3 February, United States Information Agency.
USIS (1998) 'US Officials Stress Interest in Resolving EU Banana Dispute', 12 September.
US Mission (1998) 'Fact Sheet: The Transatlantic Economic Partnership', 18 May, Brussels.
US Mission (1997) 'EU–US Reach Agreement on Mutual Recognition of Product Testing and Approval Requirements', 13 June, Brussels.

US State Department (2003) Trafficking in Persons Report, www.state.gov/g/tip/.
US State Department (1999) 'Highlights from NGO Public Briefing Meeting', archive, 'STOP Trafficking', Bureau of Population, Migration and Refugees.
US State Department (1998) 'President's Policy Statement on Trafficking in Women', archive, 'STOP Trafficking', Bureau of Population, Migration and Refugees.
USTR (2000) press release, 'US Legal Position on Dispute in WTO on Banana Regime', 12 January.
USTR (1999) press release, 'Ambassador Barshevsky Expresses Dismay at European Union Blocking Tactis in WTO', 25 January.
USTR (1997) press release, 'WTO Banana Report Confirms US Win', 22 May.
Warnath, S. (1998) 'Trafficking of Women and Children: The Future Direction of United States Policy, Remarks made by the Senior Advisor on President's Interagency Council on Women', presented at the US–EU Transatlantic Seminar to Prevent Trafficking in Women, 10 July, L'viv, Ukraine.
White House (1996a), Office of Press Secretary, 'Fact Sheet: Mutual Recognition Agreements', 16 December, Washington DC.
White House (1996b) press briefing, 'Good Manufacturing Practices', 16 December, Washington DC.

News sources

AFX Europe (2000) 'EU Commission Says Will Contest Banana War Damages Claims From 2 EU Companies, 30 August.
Agence Press (1999) 'Controversial US Legislation Does Not Violate WTO Rules', 22 December.
Alden, E. (2001) 'Mismatch on Product Safety Puts Accord on Danger List, *Financial Times*, 9 November.
Alden, E. (2000) 'US and EU Still Split on Beef and Bananas', *Financial Times*, 19 December.
Alden, E. and C. Bowen (2001) 'US Banana Producers Find Different Ways of Living With EU Restrictions: Chiquita has gone head on and is close to bankruptcy, Dole and Del Monte have learned to live with the curbs', *Financial Times*, 16 February.
Barlett, D. and J. Steel (2000) 'How to Become a Top Banana', *Time Magazine*, 155 (5), 7 February.
BBC News Online (2000a) 'Ecuador Turns on US in Trade War', 6 October, http://news.bbc.co.uk/.
BBC News Online (2000b) 'Firm to Sue Over Banana War "loss"', 31 August, http://news.bbc.co.uk/.
BBC News Online (2000c) 'EU and US Avert Trade War', 30 September, http://news.bbc.co.uk/.
BBC News Online (1999a) 'New Trade War Looms', 25 April, http://news.bbc.co.uk/.
BBC News Online (1999b) 'Beefing Up the Trade War', 23 March, http://news.bbc.co.uk/.
BBC News (1999c) 'Clinton: It's about Rules not Bananas', 6 March, http://news.bbc.co.uk/.
BBC News Online (1999d) 'Banana War Exposes Old Trade Divisions, 5 March, http://news.bbc.co.uk/.
BBC News Online (1999e) 'US Retaliates in Banana War', 4 March, http://news.bbc.co.uk/.
BBC News Online (1999f) 'Banana Trade War Looms', 12 January, http://news.bbc.co.uk/.
BBC News Online (1998) 'Banana Trade War', 17 December, http://news.bbc.co.uk/.
BBC News Online (1997) 'No Trade War Blair', 5 December, http://news.bbc.co.uk/.
Buckley, N. (1998) 'France Blocks Bid for EU–US "Marketplace"', *Financial Times* Archives, 28 April, www.ft.com.

Buerkle, T. (1999) 'EU Warns US it Risks "Major" Trade Battle in Banana Feud', *International Herald Tribune*, 5 March.
CEO (1998a) 'TABD: Who's Keeping Score?', *Corporate European Observer*, October, www.xs4all.nl/~ceo/observer2/tabd.html.
CEO (1998b) 'The TEP of the Iceberg: How the New Transatlantic Marketplace Became the New Transatlantic Economic Partnership', *Corporate European Observer*, 2, October, www.xs4all.nl-ceo/observer2/tep.htm.
Cox, J. (1999) 'Punitive Actions by US Felt World-wide', *US Today*, 11 March.
Chisholm, W. (2000) 'Cashmere Industry Threatens EC Over US Sanctions Fears', *The Scotsman*, 1 September.
CNN (1998a) 'US–EU Trade War Looms', 10 November.
CNN (1998b) 'EU Agrees to Let Trade Body Referee Dispute if US Drops Sanctions Threat', 20 November.
Daily Telegraph (1999) 'American Warned of Drugs Danger over Banana War', 9 March.
de Brie, C. (1999) 'Watch Out for MAI Mark II', *Le Monde*, 21 May.
de Jonquires, G. (2003) 'Lamy Feels the Sting of Cancun's Failure', *Financial Times*, 31 October.
de Jonquires, G. (1998) 'Regionalism', *Financial Times*, 18 May.
Eaglesham, J. (2000) 'Scots may Seek Recompense', *Financial Times*, 1 September.
Economist Archive (1998) 'That Awkward Relationship', 16 May, http://economist.com.
The Economist (1999) 'Fruitless but Not Harmless', 10 April.
EU Business (2000) 'EU Foreign Minister Divided on Banana Policy', 11 July.
Euracom (1995) 'Commission Strategy for Deeper EU–US Ties', May.
European Union Magazine, 'An Interview with Charlene Barshefsky', www.euruion.org/magazine/9905/interviews_barshefsky.htm.
European Voice (2000a) 'Trade', 6 (46), 14 December.
European Voice (2000b) 'New Conflicts Set to Strain Relations', 6 (43), 23 November.
European Voice (2000c) 'Deals on Beef and Bananas in Sight as US Averts "Mother of all Trade Wars"', 6 (43), 23 November.
European Voice (2000d)'MEPs' Stand-off Threatens Deal Over Bananas', 6 (42), 16 November.
European Voice (2000e) 'Trade', 6 (29), 20 July.
European Voice (2000f) 'Washington Delays New Sanctions List', 6 (25), 22 June.
European Voice (2000g) 'Firms Face Long Wait for End to US Sanctions', 6 (24), 15 June.
European Voice (2000h) 'Trade', 6 (23), 8 June.
European Voice (2000i) 'Union "Closer" to Deal With US on Bananas', 6 (11), 16 March.
European Voice (2000j) 'Trade', 6 (4), 27 January.
European Voice (2000k) 'Governments Strive for Early End to Banana War', 6 (4), 27 January.
Financial Times (2000a) 'New Tact but US–EU Disputes Remain', 1 June.
Financial Times (2000b) 'US Calls on Ecuador to Support Banana Deal', 18 April.
Financial Times (1999a) 'US rejects Brussels' proposal on bananas', 11 November.
Financial Times (1999b) 'The Bad Blood Behind the Bananas', 5 March.
Financial Times (1998)'France Blocks Bid for EU–US "Marketplace"', 28 April.
Financial Times (1997) 'Inspection Pact "Will Save Millions"', 19 June.
Giles, W. (2000) 'Carousel Deepens Row over Banana Trade', *Financial Times*, 9 July.
Greenwald, J., V. Novak and A. Zagorin (1996) 'Ever Wonder What Businessmen Get for Campaign Contributions? Take a Look at Carl Linder', *Time Magazine*, 146 (4), 22 January.
Guardian (2000) 'Bananas: The View From America', 9 March.
Guardian (1999a) 'EU Ready to Accept Banana War Defeat', 16 April.
Guardian (1999b) 'Why Are We Being Force-fed? American's victory in the banana war

shows free trade has lost US legal control over our food and health', 13 April.
Il Sole 24 Ore (2000) 'Fiamm Asks EU for Damages', 31 August.
The Independent (1999a) 'Time to Admit Defeat in Banana War', 8 April.
The Independent (1999b) 'US Rejects Banana Trade Deal', 11 November.
Irish Times (2001) 'Banana War Must be Brought to an End', 6 April.
Financial Times Online (1999) 'Jaw-Jaw', 23 June 1999, www.ft.com.
Journal of Commerce (1998) 5 February 1998, quote available from TABD, 'What They Have Said About the TABD', www.tabd.org.
Laurance, B. (1999) 'The Big Banana', *Sunday Guardian*, 7 March.
Mason, B. (1999) 'Transatlantic Tensions Deepen', BBC News Online, 5 March, http://news.bbc.co.uk.
McSmith, A. and D. Fraser (1999) 'Banana Peace Talks Fail to Heal Split', 7 March.
Peter, C. (1998) 'Business is the Buzzword: Environmentalists Gear up for Transatlantic Talks', Transatlantic Information Exchange Service, Environment Section, http://www.ties.org.
Smith, M. (2000a) 'EU Slip Up Over Import of Bananas', *Financial Times*, 18 July.
Smith, M. (2000b) 'Banana Deal Stalled by EU Foreign Ministers', *Financial Times*, 11 July.
Taylor, S. (1999) 'Banana War to Drag on into Autumn', *European Voice*, 22 July.
Transatlantic Information Exchange Web (TIES) (1999) Interview with Jake Caldwell on the TAED, April, http://www.tiesweb.org.
Wall Street Journal (2000a) 'European Firms Seek EU Damages for Banana War', 30 August.
Wall Street Journal (2000b) 'The Clintons' Shrug at Sex Trafficking', 10 January.
Wilkinson, B. (1999) 'Caricom Suspends Treaty with US Over Bananas', One World News, 9 March, www.oneworld.org.
Williams, F. and de Jonquieres, G. 'Europeans Block Biotech Move', *Financial Times* Online, 3 December.
Wilson, J. (2001) 'Columbia Fears Banana Ruling, *Financial Times*, 2 January.
Winneker, C. (2000) 'EU Banana Boost', *European Voice*, 12 December.

Websites

US Government

US Mission: www.useu.be
US State Department: www.state.gov
USTR : www.ustr.gov
Commerce: www.commerce.gov
FDA: www.fda.gov

European Union

DG Trade and External Relations: www.europa.eu.int
US Commission Delegation: www.eurunion.org

Dialogues

TABD: www.tabd.org
TAED: www.tacd.org
TACD: www.taed.org

Index